More praise for MissionNext:

Next generation ministry has become a global force. Men and women from a variety of traditions have come to see the value of the church's mission to the young. With this, global church leaders are also recognizing that ministry to the rising generation is at its core missional. This is why Eric Larsen's *MissionNext: How the Church Can Reach a Global Generation* is a vital new resource to provide theological and contextual training for anyone anywhere serving the young in the name of Christ. This will be a foundational tool for years to come.

Chap Clark, PhD
Author, *Hurt 2.0, Sticky Faith,* and *Adoptive Youth Ministry*
Professor of Youth, Family and Culture, Fuller Theological Seminary

For more than 20 years, I have witnessed Eric Larsen's honest grappling with the questions that one would hope all in ministry would ask. But he doesn't stop there. Thankfully, Eric's grit and tenacious passion for answers has resulted in *MissionNext*. In one volume, we now have an incredibly well-researched written guide that integrates biblical principles, solid experience and cultural context—all with a heart and optimism for practitioners. Let Eric come alongside you like a wise sherpa.

Benjamin K. Homan
President, Langham Partnership USA (formerly John Stott Ministries); former President, Food for the Hungry

MissionNext is an excellent resource for all who have a heart for next generation ministry. Theologically solid, inspirational, and accessible. Larsen has produced a magnum opus for those engaged in making disciples among the global youth.

Lloyd Kim, PhD
Coordinator, Mission to the World

This is THE book the church needs for next-generation ministry!

Rev. Len Teague
Professor, Youth Ministry, Covenant College
Pastor of Youth and Families, Lookout Mt. Presbyterian Church

Nearly half the world's population is under 25 years old. Reaching and training the next generations will not only advance the global mission of the Church, it will ensure the very future of a healthy, Gospel-grounded church. My brother and friend Eric Larsen has given his life toward that end. His life and teaching ring with truth and grace.

Michael Oh, PhD
Executive Director/CEO, Lausanne Movement

The world's population continues to get younger and younger. Therefore, if you want to be involved in God's kingdom work young people must be a major part of your focus. Into this world *MissionNext: How the Church Can Reach a Global Generation* by Eric Larsen, is a must read.

Paul Kooistra, PhD
President, Erskine College and Theological Seminary

Eric Larsen's book, *MissionNext: How the Church Can Reach a Global Generation*, is a much needed book. First, because it is about God's work in His world through His workers. Second, because it points to the church as the means. Thirdly, because it is about reaching the next-generation not only across the street but around the world in a practical way.

Rev. Dr. Elias Medeiros, PhD
Harriet Barbour Professor of Missions, Reformed Theological Seminary

Eric Larsen insight-fully guides the reader to appreciate that new methodologies and approaches are necessary to reach the next generation. He demonstrates how contextualization, used for generations by international missionaries with great benefit, is a crucial component of successful ministries to the next generation—and not just on the global scale across the ocean but across the street and across the breakfast table as well. This book will serve as a helpful resource for anyone seeking to minister to current and coming generations.

M. David Sills, D.Miss., Ph.D.
A.P. and Faye Stone Professor of Christian Missions and Cultural Anthropology, The Southern Baptist Theological Seminary
Founder and President, Reaching & Teaching International Ministries

Dr. Larsen has given the global church a precious gift: a very practical biblical theology of next gen ministry that will enable and equip us to meet the missional challenges of the global youth culture of the 21st century in our local context. Anyone who is seriously committed with the generational mission of God must read MissionNext and encourage others to read it.

Rev. Dr. David Correa
Director, Youth Ministry Institute, San Pablo Theological Seminary, Mérida, México
Pastor, Iglesia Jesus Presbyteriana

MissionNext is an essential companion for any church, ministry leader, or parent as they journey toward understanding and reaching the next generation. Don't start charting your course without it!

Wes Vander Lugt, PhD
Lead Pastor, Warehouse 242, Charlotte, NC
Author, *Living Theodrama*, *Theatrical Theology*, and *Pocket Dictionary of the Reformed Tradition*

For many, ministry to adolescents and emerging adults is mysterious and frightening. Eric Larsen, in *MissionNext*, analyzes young people and their culture on the basis of sound biblical exegesis in a way that clears up the mystery and alleviates our fears.

Allen Curry, EdD
Former Vice President for Academic Affairs, Reformed Theological Seminary
Author, *The God We Love and Serve*

With more than 50% of the world's total population living in cities and more than 50% of that population being made up of youth, the church faces a strategic mission calling: to reach the ever-globalizing emerging generation. Eric Larsen presents this compelling call, unpacking this opportunity with theologically sound reasoning, cross-cultural sensitivity, and practical ministry wisdom. Whether you are a missionary, pastor, ministry leader, or parent, you must read this book!

Gary Watanabe
Church Planter Catalyst and Coach, Redeemer City to City, Asia Pacific

With an invitation to go beyond pragmatics, polemics and just plain old panic, Eric Larsen invites us to think about next-gen ministry deeply and holistically. With a professor's gift for clarity and a practitioner's heart for everyday ministry, *MissionNext: How the Church Can Reach a Global Generation* challenges all of us who love young people to embrace an approach to ministry that is grounded enough to be genuinely faithful, intentional enough to be truly missional, and strategic enough to be authentically fruitful. I really appreciate the way this book connects the dots offered by some of ministry's best thinkers so that pastors, parents, and leaders can get a big picture sense of how the church can reach a global generation.

Dr. Duffy Robbins
Professor of Youth Ministry, Eastern University
Author, *The Ministry of Nurture* and *This Way to Youth Ministry*

An amazing book! Rather than offering another method for weary ministry leaders to try, *MissionNext* calls us back to the basics—how and why timeless, God-centered truth is still the foundation for reaching the hearts and minds of rising generations, no matter how different their external worlds are from those in the past. Larsen describes the stages of adolescence and emerging adulthood in a way that will benefit parents as well. A "must read"!

Ruth E. Van Reken
Co-author, *Third Culture Kids: Growing Up Among Worlds*
Co-founder, Families in Global Transition

MissionNext makes a significant and unique new contribution to God's people who desire to fulfill God's call to reach the nations, generations, and all of life. Larsen draws on his deep study and unusual combination of local and international experiences to give us a rare combination in next generation literature of a solid biblical-theological foundation, gospel ethos, kingdom missional passion, case studies, practical tools, and wise contextual understanding that makes this a must have resource for those want to reach "tweens, teens, and twentysomethings" today.

Dr. Mark Dalbey
President, Covenant Theological Seminary

For those engaged with or concerned about next generation ministry *Mission-Next* should be placed at the top of your reading list. Culturally, it is a must-read because it deals with the often-neglected topic of cross cultural youth ministry. Theologically, this book should not be ignored as it clearly demonstrates how our ministry methodology should flow from our theology. Missiologically, it is an important read because Dr. Larsen does an excellent job helping the reader understand that the Great Commission is both geographic and generational. And for those seeking to better understand adolescents, this book gives us plenty to think about from their developmental stages to their spiritual formation. Dr. Larsen has given us a book with the research and depth necessary to work well in academic environments, practicality and wisdom that comes from decades as a next generation ministry practitioner, and the readability that makes the book accessible to anyone. That is a rare combination and one of the many reasons that I will use this book not only in the classroom but will keep it on my bookshelf to serve as a valuable resource for years to come.

Rev. Danny Mitchell
Coordinator of Youth Ministries, Committee on Discipleship Ministries, Presbyterian Church in America.
Adjunct Youth Ministry Professor, Covenant College
Visiting Instructor of Next Generation Ministry, Covenant Seminary

A "must read" for anyone involved in ministering to tweens, teens and twentysomethings. Eric not only makes sense out of what is happening in the "glocal" world of adolescents and emerging adults, he also provides a framework for effective next-gen ministry in any culture and any time.

Marc Kyle
Director of Operations, Serge

MissionNext is an extremely helpful resource for ministry to young people today. Eric shows how churches anywhere in the world are facing so many of the same issues. Combining wise theological insight and great personal stories, he provides much needed tools to chart a course for next gen ministry.

Dr. David Rock
Director, Irish Methodist Youth and Children's Department

This easy-to-read resource is a treasure that will contribute to the health of any church. In *MissionNext*, Eric Larsen diagnoses why churches struggle with next-gen ministries, but also shows a path that brings hope. This resource is valuable for anyone who has a heart for the future of the church, those engaged in ministry to the next generation (novice or veteran): pastors, lay leaders, parents… anyone. In reading it, I was inspired to engage more intentionally with "generation next."

Stephen Estock, PhD
Coordinator, Committee on Discipleship Ministries, Presbyterian Church in America

Eric Larsen's prophetic call for the Church is both refreshing and bold. *MissionNext* urges us to engage young people, and to flat-out love them as never before!

Paul Suzuki
Japan Director, SEND International

In *MissionNext* Eric Larsen equips leaders, believers and churches to take the faith that changes and powers their lives into the hearts of rising generations. Larsen gives clear direction for leaders and churches to renew their commitment to reach young people together. He brings a clear read of culture matched with wise organizational insight. And he applies these gifts to help us make our love practical: equipping us to engage the young people in our communities despite cultural difference and organizational tangles.

Best of all, Larsen understands that plans and programs have no power unless people who know Christ and his grace take his love across cultures into the world where our youth live. He sends us with the grace and hope that can be found in Christ. Larsen wants to see our churches make real relationships in living communities to engage adolescents and emerging adults with the love of Christ. Larsen sees this generationally cross-cultural work—the 'Mission-Next'—as foundational to our missional calling and future of the church. And I agree. I recommend the book for all concerned with reaching the next generation personally or organizationally.

Josiah Bancroft
Director of Mission, Serge

Eric Larsen's book, *MissionNext: How the Church Can Reach a Global Generation*, is a treasure. In the messy and often biblically compromised world of next-gen ministry philosophy, Larsen offers a sane and sensible approach. His careful examination of how Scripture relates to current cultural mores in the area of ministry to rising generations is masterful. Church leaders should be encouraged to both read and discuss the book's contents immediately. I highly recommend it!

Derek W H Thomas, PhD
Senior Minister, First Presbyterian Church, Columbia SC
Robert Strong Professor of Systematic and Pastoral Theology, RTS Atlanta

Writing from a biblically sound and experienced perspective, Eric Larsen has crafted a powerful book that challenges the church with foundational and timeless principles in a timely and highly practical way. Every leader concerned with reaching rising generations is sure to be energized and equipped as they read this thought provoking book.

Rev. Matt Brinkley
PACT Ministry

MissionNext is not only informative but also transformative! Larsen provides rich insights and even passion for the mission to our next generation. This book should be widely read among university ministry workers.

Jongho Kim
President, InterVarsity Christian Fellowship, Korea

Eric Larsen is one fearless man, scaling that rugged mountain known as next-gen ministry. To the task he brings the relentless energy and zeal of a youth himself, plus the experience of a seasoned climber. *MissionNext* lays solid theological groundwork for churches, pastors, and parents to engage in all stages of adolescent and emerging adult ministry, setting a vibrant context for local ministry among a truly global generation. It's a great read, and a much-needed book!

Mindy Belz
Senior Editor, World Magazine
Author, *They Say We Are Infidels: On the Run from ISIS With Persecuted Christians in the Middle East*

The exploding number of youth in the midst of a globalizing, post-modern world is shifting the very meaning of adolescence and creating unprecedented challenges for the church in the 21st century. Drawing on sound theology, the latest research, and Dr. Larsen's vast experience, *MissionNext* meets these challenges head-on, providing a valuable resource to equip both professionals and parents for the task ahead.

Brian Fikkert, PhD
Co-author, *When Helping Hurts*
President, the Chalmers Center, Covenant College

MissionNext offers biblical, theological and practical guidance for reaching the next generation. Excellently put together! Written by one seasoned in ministry and leadership. Dr. Larsen's research provides several significant principles and directions in global and intercultural ministries for today's churches around the world.

Eunsoo Kim, PhD
President, Global Reformed Seminary

Eric combines theological rigour and commitment to the Great Commission with years of experience in reaching the next generation with the Gospel. The result is a book that is profoundly challenging and practically helpful for anyone who cares about God's mission through His people—not just for those involved in youth ministry. This book will be required reading for all of my colleagues!

Mark Stirling, PhD
President, Chalmers Institute, St. Andrew's, Scotland
Lead Pastor, Cornerstone Church, St. Andrew's

MissionNext deals with a very central issue facing the global church: The global new generation's reticence to commit to the church and its mission, lost in a rapidly changing world. Dr. Larsen offers pastors, missionaries, ministry leaders, and parents a deep theological and practical guide for the "glocal" church's next mission. Every church planter should read *MissionNext* before starting a church.

Rev. Andres Garza
Latin America Regional Director, Redeemer City to City

MissionNext does not try to offer another fad for ministry to the young. Instead, it moves to build a foundation for reaching out and raising up the next generation. *MissionNext*'s solid theology and missional mindset makes it a must-read for every church leader who wants to engage the next generation.

> **Rev. John Chung**
> Pastor of Spiritual Formation, The Journey (Acts 29 Network)

Here is a wonderfully practical book that brings together an understanding of changes in adolescence, global shifts, the importance of the local community, and the mission that grows out of the Gospel. I especially encourage all who lead the church in reaching tweens, teens, and twentysomethings to read Eric Larsen's sensible guidebook.

> **Kelly M. Kapic, PhD**
> Professor of Theology, Covenant College
> Author, *For God so Loved the World He Gave*

There are many ministry books offering "how to's," but very few ask "why." Dr. Larsen examines the "why" questions as well as the "how to's," delivering helpful insights mined from the past and offering brilliant hope for the future of the church. This book reignited my heart to reach the next generation and gave me a new vision for knowing how.

> **Rev. Mark Davis**
> Senior Pastor, Park Cities Presbyterian Church

Many years ago a pastor to young people shared with me that he felt much of the time as if he was living out the title to Bruce Springsteen's 1980s hit song, "Dancing in the Dark." Eric Larsen has contributed a great deal of light to the next-gen ministry "dance" with his book, *MissionNext*. It's a thoroughly researched, biblically rich, comprehensive contribution to the exceptionally important and often underserved topic of ministry to global youth. It's also immensely practical without being overly prescriptive. I highly recommend Eric's book to anyone interested or involved in ministry to tweens, teens, and twentysomethings—your "dancing" will greatly improve!

> **Bruce Terrell**
> Executive Director, Redeemer Church, New York City

Most of us are near-sighted—we are only thinking about the church today. Eric Larsen in *MissionNext* helps us to think biblically, theologically, and practically about how to deal with the next group of global church leaders, today's adolescents and emerging adults. If you are interested in the health of the church in the last half of the 21st century you will want to read and study this book.

John Leonard, PhD
Pastor, Cresheim Valley Church
Former Professor of Practical Theology, Westminster Theological Seminary

With the cultural context of youth ministry changing at break-neck speed, ministry practitioners must constantly be on their toes as they look for ways to reach young people and lead them into a deep, life-changing, and fully integrated faith. First and foremost, Eric Larsen's *MissionNext* is tethered to the Gospel. It provides a theologically vibrant and biblically-faithful approach to reaching the rising generation. He tells us why we need to seriously consider the 10/30 ministry window, who our ministry efforts target, and how to effectively remodel and re-envision our ministries to tweens, teens, and twentysomethings. Anyone who ministers to adolescents and emerging adults will benefit from pausing to read and digest *MissionNext*, then rebooting their ministries in ways that are faithful to the scriptures while addressing unfolding cultural realities.

Dr. Walt Mueller
Founder and President, Center for Parent/Youth Understanding

MISSION NEXT

MISSION NEXT

How the Church Can Reach a Global Generation

Dr. Eric Larsen

MissionNext: How the Church Can Reach a Global Generation

Published by:

Doulos Resources. PHONE: (901) 201-4612 WEBSITE: www.doulosresources.org.

© Copyright 2017 Eric Larsen. Some rights reserved. This work is licensed under the Creative Commons Attribution-NonCommercial-NoDerivs License. To view a copy of this license, (a) visit www.creativecommons.org; or, (b) send a letter to Creative Commons, 171 2nd Street, Suite 300, San Francisco, California, 94105, USA.

Please address all questions about rights and reproduction to Doulos Resources:

PHONE: (901) 201-4612; E-MAIL: info@doulosresources.org.

Unless otherwise noted, Scripture quotations are from THE HOLY BIBLE, NEW INTERNA-TIONAL VERSION®, NIV® Copyright © 1973, 1978, 1984, 2011 by Biblica, Inc.® Used by permission. All rights reserved worldwide.

Published 2017

Printed in the United States of America by Ingram/Lightning Source

Colophon:

Cover design by Josh Kenfield; interior design by J.E. Eubanks, Jr.

Copyediting by J.E. Eubanks, Jr.; proofreading help provided by: David Stewart.

Typefaces include Adobe Garamond Pro (body text set in 10.5pt.); Pretender Regular; League Gothic.

This book is printed using 50lb. 444 ppi archival paper that is produced according to Sustainable Forestry Initiative® (SFI®) Certified Sourcing.

Larsen, Eric, 1970–

MissionNext: How the Church Can Reach a Global Generation.

ISBNs: 978-1-937063-51-1 (print); 978-1-937063-50-4 (digital)

2017940057

13 14 15 16 17 18 19 20   10 9 8 7 6 5 4 3 2 1

To...

Rebecca—My very heart.

Abby, Meghan, Natalie, and Emma—My greatest treasures.

And above all, to Jesus—My all-in-all.

*"For from him and through him and to him
are all things. To him be the glory!"*

Contents

Introduction

"RIGHT ON TIME."

Friends told me you could set your watch to the trains in Tokyo. They were right. The precision and efficiency of the *Shinkansen* (or bullet train) was matched by its speed. We shot across the landscape at 300 kilometers per hour. Land that at one time took hours to cross, technology had reduced to a journey of mere minutes. Technology, speed, and progress.

As the train quickly made its way across the city, this picture of human progress took my thoughts to another level: Where were we going so fast? Where *are* we going so fast? Where are we as a people heading? Are we really making "progress"? Or are we in some ways regressing from the way things are meant to be—from *who we're meant to be*?

Tokyo is one of the most crowded cities I've ever been to in my life: collectivistic, yet lacking in community… high population density, but little intimacy. Every teenager and young adult seemed to be making their way in silence and often alone, with headphones and cell phone screens for companions.

I looked up from my seat on the train to see a young woman listening to her iPod while texting simultaneously on two cell phones—one in each hand! "I've just witnessed the next evolution in human development," I thought. "How can she do that!?" For all the isolation and lack of connection, I consoled myself with the fact that at least the young people I observed were texting.

I turned to my friend, a university campus minister in Tokyo: "At least they are communicating with someone—that's worth something, right?"

Introduction

At this, my friend replied with resignation, "That's just it," he said. "It's not that they are texting with someone else. Most of them are simply updating their status or posting to their blog."

The gravity of that reality struck, immediately conjuring in my mind the image of a castaway tossing his message in a bottle out to sea, hoping someone might find it. *Somebody out there **know** me.* As the train raced along, I wondered again, Where are we going so fast?

Today's world is rapidly changing. High mobility, technology, media, and the global economy are shrinking our planet. At the same time, we are experiencing explosive growth in the global youth population unlike any other time in history: over 52 percent of the world's population is now under the age of 30.[1] In turn, more and more cultures and communities across the globe are reporting an extension of adolescence in their populations: it starts earlier and finishes later. Adolescence begins with puberty and ends with membership in the adult community. The global average seems to begin around 10 years of age and end around 30. On top of this, young people around the globe are increasingly marginalized and isolated from the adults in their world. These unique and pervasive factors have led to the rise of a global youth culture. In many ways, young people around the world today have more in common with each other than they do with adults in their own communities. In essence, global youth are the largest under-reached people-group in the world today: the *"10/30 Window."*

How can this be true when adolescent and emerging adult ministry as a field has more practitioners than ever? The reality is that most are recasting the same tired models and methods inherited from North American parachurch ministries of seventy years ago. Ministry to tweens, teens, and twentysomethings has become a profession and programmatic enterprise of the church. Churches, ministry leaders, and parents have neglected to engage in theological reflection that takes seriously a changing world. As a result, the global church is struggling to effectively pass the baton of faith to the next generation.

How should the local church respond to these global realities?

Think Theologically, Act "Glocally"

God's world mission is both geographic and generational. That is, he pursues his people throughout time and around the globe. The church, God's chosen agent of redemption in this broken world, is called to join him in reaching the nations and the next generation with the gospel. We must engage the *global* youth culture as expressed in the unique and *local* places where God has us: the *global* church, expressed in *local* congregations, investing deeply and intentionally in the lives of the young people in their context. The church is called to move toward the 10/30 Window—that is our "**MissionNext.**"

MissionNext must be grounded in God's redemptive story and guided by his kingdom trajectory. To move toward the "10/30 window," adults must engage the global and local realities of adolescents and emerging adults. The changing landscape within MissionNext means the church must not get stuck in one model or method, but continually seek renewal.

Let's pursue a biblical theology of next-generation ministry, and develop a *glocal* approach to reaching "tweens," teens, and twenty-somethings with the gospel.

Introduction

Notes

1   "Special Report: The World's Youngest Populations," *Euromonitor International.* 13 February 2012; retrieved 8 February 2013.

PART I.
STARTING OUT

"He used often to say there was only one Road; that it was like a great river: its springs were at every doorstep, and every path was its tributary. 'It's a dangerous business, Frodo, going out of your door,' he used to say. 'You step onto the Road, and if you don't keep your feet, there is no knowing where you might be swept off to.'"[1]

NEXT-GENERATION MINISTRY IS A JOURNEY. Perhaps you are venturing out into the field for the first time, stepping across the threshold with anxiety and uncertainty over the task ahead? Or maybe you come to this book tired—even disillusioned—from trekking in the world of adolescents and emerging adults for many years. Wherever you are from, and whether you are a youth minister, parent, pastor, missionary, or simply a concerned adult—all of us around the world share this in common: engaging the emerging generation is hard. The call to next-generation ministry is an invitation to walk a hard but rewarding path—to follow Christ in the journey of faith as we throw our arms around younger brothers and sisters along the way.

As with any adventure, some accept the challenge, though many shrink from the quest. Throughout the world we see a growing disconnection between adults and kids. The global church is struggling to reach and raise the next generation with gospel impact. Many, if not most, churches pour their resources, training, and more mature leadership into serving the adult population. Is it any wonder the church is struggling to see young people emerge from her ranks with transformed hearts, intimate connection within the community of faith, and lives lived in radical abandon to Christ's kingdom mission?

At the same time, "youth ministry" as a particular field and focus seems to be expanding with more resources, greater professional and academic recognition in the church and academy, and more vocational practitioners. But it is still relatively young in its formation as a discipline.[2] It does not yet have the same rich history of development to look to and draw upon that other roles in the church have. We do not yet have a long legacy of youth ministry proponents that stretches beyond a few decades, let alone emerging from around the world.[3] In fact, I have heard youth workers referred to as "veterans" who have had as little as five years of experience in ministry. Many of the most significant contributors to the field are alive today, belying its limited heritage. Books are being churned out by the bucketful on youth ministry topics, but the majority are recasting the same recent ideas as opposed to drawing from a rich heritage of theological tradition—let alone doing the hard work of biblical exposition and application. And the bulk of these books are practical in nature: offering ideas, resources, and curriculum for the programmatic enterprise that makes up much of the global church's approach to next-gen ministry.

It seems youth ministry itself is but a youth. As such, it is poised for growth and development—yet still in its formative years as a discipline. It is also poised precariously: should the global church fail to invest deeply in thinking and acting theologically about the task, youth ministry will spiral away from God and into an ineffective, unproductive, nominal exercise, full of bells and whistles, models and methods, but free from its moorings, adrift with the tide.[4]

Now is the time for significant work to be done and contributions made that will shape the future of youth ministry by providing sure footing for the journey as we venture out in ministry to the emerging generation.[5] Without a compass to point us in the right direction, we'll find ourselves lost.

Notes

1   J.R.R. Tolkien, *Lord of the Rings* (Harper Collins UK, London, 2004), p. 74.
2   Jon Pahl, *Youth Ministry in Modern America: 1930 to the Present* (Peabody, MA: Hendrickson Publishers, 2000); see also Mark H. Senter, *When God Shows Up: A History of Protestant Youth Ministry in America,* (Grand Rapids, MI: Baker Academic, 2010).
3   Merton Strommen, Karen E. Jones, and Dave Rahn, "A Recent Invention: The Profession of Youth Ministry," in *Youth Ministry that Transforms*, 1st ed. (El Cajon, CA: Youth Specialties Books and Zondervan Publishing House for Youth Specialties Academic, 2001), pp. 31–33.
4   David F. Wells, "Christianity for Sale" in *The Courage to Be Protestant: Truth-lovers, Marketers, and Emergents in the Postmodern World,* (Grand Rapids, MI: Eerdmams, 2008) p. 28.
5   Dean Borgman, "Overview of the Theological Task," in *When Kumbaya Is Not Enough: A Practical Theology for Youth Ministry*, 4th ed. (Peabody, MA: Hendrickson Publishers, 2002), p. x.

CHAPTER 1
LOST: Misguided Pathways

FROM 2004 TO 2010, AUDIENCES worldwide found themselves "lost" along with the passengers of Oceanic flight 815—vicariously crash-landing on a mysterious island in the South Pacific. The television series, *Lost*, captivated and frustrated viewers with the plight of its characters as they struggled to survive. The scene opened in the aftermath of the crash, with nobody knowing where they were or how they got there. We found them stumbling around, trying to make sense of their surroundings with little to direct them. Over time it became increasingly hard to determine what was even real. And as the story unfolded, more questions were raised than answered, more confusion introduced rather than clarity of understanding and direction.

Such a story line may make for entertaining television, but not for effective next generation ministry. Like the passengers of Oceanic flight 815, we too often find ourselves lost, stumbling along unwittingly in our attempts to engage adolescents and emerging adults. Without good theology to ground and guide us along the way, we are left to our own devices and rely on our own instincts. In turn, most of us take one or more of the following well-worn pathways in the journey of youth ministry:

- *Whatever Works*: The path of pragmatics
- *Bring It On*: The path of polemics
- *The Sky Is Falling*: The path of panic

Typical forms of modern youth ministry have been developed largely from a pragmatic approach, as opposed to building from a biblical foundation.[1] Adults often adopt a "whatever works" mentality, employing models and methods with little prayer or theological discernment. In turn, much of the theological work that has been done has been done in a polarizing, polemical fashion—flowing from debate between models, camps, and over particular issues in ministry to adolescents and emerging adults. In recent years, we've seen an increase in what seems to be a "panic" mode of ministry in churches around the world. This happens when parents, youth workers, and organizations seize upon an issue, elevate it as the critical issue of the day (the "crisis" over which the battle for the next generation will be won or lost), and marshal all resources to combat this "epidemic."

Each of these approaches launches ministry from a weak foundation and skews its trajectory. It is time to step back and take a look at our theological presuppositions and their implications for the task of ministry to the rising generation.

Whatever Works: The Path of Pragmatics

The story is told of a young boy who received a bow and arrow set as a gift. Anxious to try his hand at archery, he excitedly asked his father, "Dad, can I run out to the backyard and try it right now?!"

"Of course," his father replied, delighted with his son's enthusiasm over the gift. The boy was out the door in a flash. In next to no time he came running back inside, barely able to contain his excitement. "Daddy, come quick! You've got to see what I've done!"

As the father rounded the corner into the backyard he couldn't believe his eyes. There, across the side of the old family barn, were a series of targets. Amazingly enough, each had an arrow lodged perfectly in its center. Dumbfounded, the father exclaimed, "Son! I can't believe my eyes! You've barely had time to practice! How did you manage to hit the bull's eye every single time?"

Beaming with pride, the son replied, "Oh, that was easy. I just shot the arrows first and then drew the targets around them."

Time and again, the church is guilty of a "Ready, FIRE, aim" approach to next generation ministry: acting from instinct and intuition, rather than first adjusting our aim through careful theological reflection. As in archery, we must paint the target, plant our feet, and align our sites before launching into ministry to the next generation.

10

The most well-worn path within the field of next-gen ministry is a pragmatic one. Many, particularly in the West, have successfully turned the task of ministering to young people into a market research-driven exercise, as opposed to a Spirit-driven one—leaning on utilitarianism, as opposed to the unchanging Word of God.[2] This is often fueled by faulty motives: to impress people with the glitz of programs and numbers of students, or to sell products. Even good intentions (i.e., reaching more students, recruiting more volunteers, acquiring more resources to do the work, and so on) aren't enough, if not born of theological convictions, and executed as theological activity.[3]

John Stott calls next generation ministry leaders to think theologically about their task when he writes, "To use our minds enriches our discipleship, no part of which is possible if we don't use them, every part of which is enriched if we do. Failure to use our minds in the Christian life condemns us to spiritual stagnation and perpetual immaturity."[4] Indeed, if we are to "prepare God's people for works of service, so that the body of Christ may be built up until we all reach unity in the faith and in the knowledge of the Son of God and become mature, attaining to the whole measure of the fullness of Christ" (Eph. 4:12–13), then we need to be mature (and ever maturing) in our theology. Otherwise, we are guilty of the very charge so often leveled against those who invest in youth: that we are as immature as those we are trying to reach and raise up.

The pathway of pragmatics, on the other hand, begins with intuition or experience and finds Scripture to "back it up." We often do what we want to do, or what "works" in youth ministry, tacking on a verse to support our preconceived premise and plan, as opposed to beginning with the Word and letting it form our presuppositions, trajectory, and modality. It is an "ends justify the means" approach to ministry, which denies the fact that God is concerned with every facet of ministry to young people: the grounds, the goals, and the way we get from "A" to "B."[5]

By approaching next generation ministry pragmatically, we fail to see God as the author and hero of the story. Instead we, however subtly, set ourselves up as the brokers of transformation. In this way, ministry is based on human effort: relying on techniques and tools, as opposed to God's power and plan. We may "baptize" our pragmatism in the language of spirituality, but forms without foundation will always fail.[6] They will not only fail to see lives genuinely changed, but also fail to see God glorified.[7] A pragmatic approach makes ministry to adolescents and emerging adults shortsighted, producing impact that is short-lived.

Certainly God can overrule, and indeed uses even the broken attempts of man to bring about his perfect plan. This is evident in Joseph's response to his brothers at the end of Genesis: "What you intended for evil, God intended for good, for the saving of many lives" (Gen. 50:20). The Apostle Paul demonstrates this perspective writing from prison:

> It is true that some preach Christ out of envy and rivalry, but others out of goodwill. The latter do so in love, knowing that I am put here for the defense of the gospel. The former preach Christ out of selfish ambition, not sincerely, supposing that they can stir up trouble for me while I am in chains. But what does it matter? The important thing is that in every way, whether from false motives or true, Christ is preached. And because of this I rejoice. (Phil. 1:18)

While God in his grace overrides our misguided attempts, we are not given license to do ministry in an ignorant, renegade, reckless fashion (let alone, from selfish intent). Instead we are enjoined throughout Scripture to minister in reliance on God's Word and in the power of the Spirit of Christ. Paul writes to Timothy, reminding him of the centrality, authority, and sufficiency of God's Word: "All Scripture is God-breathed and is useful for teaching, rebuking, correcting and training in righteousness, that the man of God may be thoroughly equipped for every good work" (I Tim. 3:16). In his second letter to the church in Corinth, Paul acknowledges the true source of power for ministry when he writes, "But we have this treasure in jars of clay to show that this all-surpassing power is from God and not from us" (II Cor. 4:7). In Ephesians 2 we are reminded that God has prepared good works in advance for us to do—the implication being that ministry is not of our own design, but ordained by him to be done his way. Jesus assures his disciples that he will send them the Comforter—the Counselor—the Holy Spirit to lead them "into all truth" (John 16:13). And Paul warns Timothy of those "having a form of godliness but denying its power" (II Tim. 3:5).

I recently attended a national conference for next generation ministry professionals. Seminars included titles like: "Recruiting volunteers," "Ideas for games and contests," "How to organize small groups," "Creative teaching techniques," and "Leveraging social networks," to name a few. The vast majority focused on programs and techniques. Wandering into the exhibition hall I was overwhelmed by the number of booths vying for the participants' attention and business: camping and retreat venues, short-term mission trip planning, media resources for creating slideshows and videos, curriculum kits promising to captivate adolescents and emerging adults and reduce the leader's prep time, custom T-shirt ordering, and more.

Something else caught my attention, which at first encouraged me, but then left me wondering. I noticed that the convention offered opportunities for tired and burned-out next-gen pastors and ministry leaders to meet with spiritual guides, as well as provided a quiet room for rest and reflection. In turn, the emcee invited participants who were exhausted and run-down from ministry to skip any or all sessions to rest and recover before returning to their churches and organizations. "What irony," I thought to myself. "The pragmatic path leads to burnout."

The temptation in the world of "next-gen" ministry today is to place more trust in methods and means than the Spirit and Word. We often opt for style over substance. Too often we buy the lie that the church is by nature irrelevant and lacking in creativity—it doesn't have to be. But the answer isn't in departing from our moorings and adopting wholesale the world's techniques. While we may indeed redeem them and implement, adopt, or adapt them (for all truth is God's), this only happens as we "take captive every thought to make it obedient to Christ" (II Cor. 10:5). Only as we turn and return to the ministry of Christ and the Word of God, ensuring all that we do in ministry is saturated, supported, and surrounded by biblical theology, will we experience true, Spirit-led creativity and relevance.[8]

Dorothy Sayers writes, "It is the neglect of dogma that makes for dullness. The Christian faith is the most exciting drama that ever staggered the imagination of man—and dogma *is* the drama."[9] The message and modality of our ministry doesn't need to depart from theology in order to be exciting or attractive. In fact, few ministers and ministries have the ability to keep up and compete with the entertainment industry on its turf. Moreover, pop culture is caving in on itself—a culture of consumers with every resource and amusement available, that nevertheless is bored and dissatisfied, and emptier than ever.[10]

By contrast, ministry in the biblical story leads us to deeply engage the culture, while living a radically counter-cultural lifestyle—embodying and effecting God's restoration of the world, inviting the next generation to join us in the journey with Him.

Bring It On: The Path of Polemics

Through the years I have participated in a number of local networks of next-gen ministers. These grassroots cohorts come together for mutual support, prayer, ministry sharpening, and collaboration as we all strive to reach the young people in our cities. As we become aware of new pastors and youth ministers in our area, we make an effort to build a relationship and invite them to join us. For various reasons, some choose to participate; some do not.

Occasionally we encounter a pastor like Sean. Sean was a young husband and father, fresh out of seminary, with little experience under his belt. But Sean had some strong opinions about how to do (and not do) youth ministry. I called Sean soon after he arrived in town and invited him to coffee. As we spoke it became clear that Sean was not interested in building a relationship; he was more interested in proving himself and making sure I understood his strong views on emerging generation ministry. There seemed to be little charity and humility in his demeanor and tone. I invited him to our local network, but it was pretty obvious he wasn't interested. And why would he be? He had it all figured out—he was right and everyone else was wrong, or at least terribly misguided.

As we parted I couldn't deny the nagging sense that he wouldn't make it in ministry, and may take a lot of people down with him. Invitations to fellowship and collaboration were declined, suggestions went ignored, and any criticism was met with defensiveness—and even sharp rebuke. Unfortunately, that instinct was right: Sean's rigid interpretation and application of his theology, coupled with his arrogant and attacking posture, led to an exodus of young people from the congregation and rapid decline of the church. Within a year of his arrival, Sean was fired.

There are many such examples where a polemic approach rears its ugly head in the church today. For instance, division over models of next-gen ministry: should they be staff-driven or volunteer-driven or parent-driven? Should they emphasize student leadership or a therapeutic approach? Should they be seeker-sensitive or traditional?

Arguments also arise over methods used in ministry to young people. Should they employ social media and multimedia technology? Should they engage, emulate, or escape the culture? Should they include catechism instruction, confirmation/communicants' classes, or evangelism training programs? Should they consist of small groups or be a campus ministry?

Some ministries emphasize or specialize in one particular facet of ministry, such as teaching, outreach, worship, or service, which becomes divisive when that facet is lifted up as the standard-bearer for every youth ministry. Fundamental philosophies vary and can become alienating when proponents develop one polemic over and against other positions. Examples of such positions are whether to nurture "covenant children" or reach unbelievers, or whether the ministry should be family-based, church-based, or based in a parachurch organization.

This polemical tone stands in stark contrast to Jesus' prayer for his disciples:

> My prayer is not for them alone. I pray also for those who will believe in me through their message, that all of them may be one, Father, just as you are in me and I am in you. May they also be in us so that the world may believe that you have sent me. I have given them the glory that you gave me, that they may be one as we are one: I in them and you in me. May they be brought to complete unity to let the world know that you sent me and have loved them even as you have loved me. (John 17:20–23)

The call to reach and raise the rising generation is too important to be caught up in heated argument and animosity. Such distractions are a waste of time and resources. Worse, they sully the name of Jesus. If it is true that "all men will know [we] are [Jesus'] disciples if [we] love one another" (John 13:35), then shouldn't we want to take care not to send the watching world the kind of message that results when we fight, mock, avoid, or stand aloof from one another in a polemical approach to next-gen ministry? Instead, those involved in ministry to young people must be careful to examine their motives and humbly invite others to point out their blind spots. Jesus issues this indictment in his Sermon on the Mount:

Why do you look at the speck of sawdust in your brother's eye and pay no attention to the plank in your own eye? How can you say to your brother, "Let me take the speck out of your eye," when all the time there is a plank in your own eye? You hypocrite, first take the plank out of your own eye, then you will see clearly to remove the speck from your brother's eye. (Matt. 7:3)

We are talking about priorities here, not denials of secondary things (as Paul writes about in I Cor. 15:1–4 and II Cor. 2:2). In this light, those of us in "next-gen" ministry learn to lay our own agendas at the feet of Christ and give ourselves first and foremost to his leading. Ego and personality give way to camaraderie. A spirit of competition no longer precludes cooperation. Denominational allegiance and regional territorialism no longer trump commitment to the Kingdom. Personal style and pet traditions aren't allowed to take precedence over Christ and his Word, taking care not to confuse personal convictions and doctrinal commitments with the core beliefs of orthodox Christianity.

Just as ministry that flows from a pragmatic approach is skewed in trajectory based on its faulty foundation, so too is ministry that is driven by polemics. A polemical approach to ministry fuels conflict and division, rather than demonstrating a humble heart for truth and unity in mutual submission. It is more often than not an intellectualizing and spiritualizing of envy. From a posture of polemics, we are less likely to see and celebrate what God is doing in and through other brothers and sisters in the body of Christ, let alone allow their perspectives and practice to challenge and stimulate our own.

By using theology to reinforce our own private ends, we are in danger of making God's Word say what we want to hear and support our personal interests. What would it look like to to lay our personal preferences, fears, traditions, and convictions at the feet of the Lord, allowing his Word to form our theological foundation and the shape of our ministry to youth and their families.

The Sky Is Falling: The Path of Panic

Oak Hill Church had a reputation for community engagement, local church planting, and commitment to world mission. Each time the church grew in numbers, they would commission a group to go and plant a daughter church. As members of the congregation encountered needs in the community, they were encouraged to engage in opportunities to serve and were celebrated and supported by the congregation and leadership in doing so. This missional environment saw many members developed and sent as missionaries to every corner of the globe.

However, over time Oak Hill Church stopped planting daughter churches. The church became more and more ingrown. More and more staff were hired and programs developed to serve members, while less and less was done in the community. As members got more involved in church programs, they became less engaged with those outside the church. Commitment to world mission was soon reduced to a budget and relegated to a few members of the congregation to manage. Not only did the church begin to insulate the "insiders" from the "outsiders," but they failed to engage the young people in the community. Rather than reaching out to tweens, teens, and twenty-somethings in the area, Oak Hill's approach to next-gen ministry became all about the youth in the church.

Then along came Sam and Susan. This young, vibrant married couple was passionate and gifted in working with youth, and had all the credentials. Oak Hill Church called them to come and minister to their teens and college students. Sam and Susan embodied the original ethos on which Oak Hill was founded. They began getting into the community and building relationships with young people in the neighborhood. They helped equip and encourage a team of like-minded adults equally committed to engaging the next generation in the community. In time the youth ministry was brimming with new faces.

But things were getting messy. Some parents in the church began complaining that Sam and Susan were not guarding the integrity of the church. They feared that the kids from the community would exert a bad influence on their children. A lot of the young people who were coming did not fit the culture of the church, and some members were uncomfortable with their clothing and behavior. The Christian school that shared the facilities feared that these kids would steal from classrooms or vandalize the buildings. One set of parents even formed their own "alternative" Sunday school class. The pastor avoided conflict and the church board was divided. As much as they loved the kids, Sam and Susan were suffocating under the anxiety in the system and losing hope for renewal.

It was apparent the church was careening down a pathway of panic. Unable to effect a change of course, Sam and Susan decided to leave and pursue another call. Tragically, a few years later they received word that the pastor and another staff member were both having affairs. To make matters worse, it came out that the new youth minister (brought in to focus on the church kids) was inappropriately involved with several students. He was later convicted and sentenced, but the young people and the congregation were deeply wounded and took years to recover.

A church that turns inward will cave in on itself. A fear-based culture leads to unhealthy ministry and only results in hurting the very youth it purports to protect. In recent years I have noticed an increasing sense of panic in the world of next-gen ministry. Parents, churches, and others in the adult community become anxious as they see their young people facing cultural challenges they never experienced. This anxiety peaks as they face their own inability to help their tweens, teens and twentysomethings navigate the changing landscape of adolescence and emerging adulthood.

Pastors and ministry leaders in the trenches begin to despair, seeing the pain and brokenness of the adolescent world. In fear and desperation, some adults in their concern about the next generation grasp for a key issue to help them make sense of what is going on and give them a focus for their efforts. Unfortunately, a panic approach to youth ministry results in a posture of attack, retreat, or defeat, none of which is an effective platform for ministry.

Attack

Something in each of us longs for what is definitive, contained, and controllable, especially when it comes to raising our children. We want to protect them and remedy any problems that come up. Deeply embedded in our psyche is the idea that if we can diagnose the problem, we can cure it.

This can lead to panic, and even pro-active attack—therefore over-simplifying and hyper-elevating an issue, marshaling resources and focusing efforts. For instance, concern about teen sexual behavior may lead a panic-stricken youth ministry to make this issue its central focus, resulting in programs, pledge cards, and an overarching emphasis on sexual "purity" or abstinence.

However, fear-based ministry does not result in lasting transformation, nor is it built upon good theology. Recent studies have shown that teens who participated in the True Love Waits program and signed commitment cards promising not to have sex until married merely delayed their sexual activity by a year or two.[11] Even then, those who signed such cards were much less likely to use protection against pregnancy and sexually transmitted diseases; often, they also engaged in oral or anal sex, seeing these as acceptable alternatives to vaginal intercourse.

A panic approach to ministry can result in retreat or defeat, neither engaging the culture with the redemptive work of God nor resting in his sovereign hand. Parents and leaders affected by this approach need to reflect on God's priorities and rely on his power. The Psalmist writes: "When the foundations are being destroyed, what can the righteous do? The Lord is in his holy temple; the Lord is on his heavenly throne" (Psa. 11:3–4a). God's grace and sovereignty must undergird and guide our response to adolescent issues and our approach to ministry among the emerging generation.

A Pre-Modern Map for a Postmodern World

We need a pre-modern map for a postmodern world. Pre-modern maps were created with a central *locus*—a "you are here" point of reference—around which the surrounding landscape was oriented. In an increasingly postmodern world, we need a pre-modern map to orient us from a central theological *locus* as we navigate the changing landscape of adolescence. We need our ministry grounds and goals defined by theological reflection—looking to God's timeless truths to guide us in engaging our times.

LOST: Misguided Pathways

Questions for Reflection & Discussion

1. What are some reasons we see next generation ministry using highly programmatic materials?

2. Which pathways (pragmatic, polemic or panic) have you recently experienced in next generation ministry? What things might have influenced the move down each of the three pathways?

3. What pitfalls occurred when the ministry went down a particular pathway? To what degree did the leadership team seem to trust in methods more than trusting in the Spirit and in God's Word?

4. Think of a recent time the ministry leadership seemed to make planning decisions out of fear. What were the results?

5. What are some practical ways the ministry team could build in more time for theological reflection in planning? What are some challenges to designating this time?

Notes

1   Doug Fields, "The Power of God," *Youthworker* 14, no. 6 (1998): p. 49. Fields recounts his own tendency toward pragmatism, describing his early years in youth ministry: "Our programs changed every time I spied on another youth ministry."

2   Doug Fields, "Healthy Youth Ministries Have Spiritually Healthy Leaders," in *Purpose Driven Youth Ministry* (Grand Rapids, MI: Zondervan Publishing House, 1998), p. 30.

3   Ray S. Anderson, "A Practical Theology of Ministry," in *The Shape of Practical Theology* (Downers Grove, IL: InterVarsity Press, 2001), p. 62.

4   John R.W. Stott, "Your Mind Matters," *Youthworker Journal* XXII, no. 2 (November/December 2005): p. 20.

5   Ray S. Anderson, "Ministry As Theological Praxis," in *The Soul of Ministry* (Louisville, KY: Westminster John Knox Press, 1997), p. 32.

6   Fields, *Purpose Driven Youth Ministry*, p. 38.

7   Francis A. Schaeffer, "In the Spirit's Power," in *True Spirituality* (Wheaton, IL: Tyndale House Publishers, 1971), p. 59.

8   Anderson, *The Shape of Practical Theology*, p. 63.

9   Dorothy Sayers, "The Greatest Drama Ever Staged," in *Letters to A Diminished Church* (Nashville, TN: W Publishing Group, 2004), p. 1.

10 Richard Winter, *Still Bored In A Culture of Entertainment* (Downers Grove, IL: InterVarsity Press, 2002). See also Neil Postman, *Amusing Ourselves to Death: Public Discourse in the Age of Show business*, 2nd. ed. (New York: Penguin Books, 2005).

11 See Janet Elise Rosenbaum, "Patient Teenagers? A Comparison of the Sexual Behavior of Virginity Pledgers and Matched Non-pledgers" in *Pedatrics* vol. 123 no. 1 January 1, 2009: pp. e110–e120. and Melina Bersamin, Samantha Walker, Elizabeth Waiters, Deborah Fisher, and Joel Grube, "Promising to Wait: Virginity pledges and adolescent sexual behavior" in *The Journal of Adolescent Health* vol. 36 no. 5 May 2005, pp. 428–436.

CHAPTER 2
MapQuest: Charting a Course for MissionNext

NOT LONG AGO I WAS asked to speak at a family conference. As much as I love the itinerant nature of my ministry, it means I have to be rather selective in accepting opportunities that add to my travel schedule. The host picked up on my reluctance and began tempting me with a description of the beautiful mountain retreat. When he invited me to bring my family along, I was hooked.

The time came for us to pack up and head to the conference. "Honey, do you have the directions?" my wife asked. I pretended not to hear. Though rather vague, I did remember discussing directions on the phone with our host. I told him all I needed was the address and I'd find the place, but he had insisted I write down his directions. In the meantime, those directions had somehow disappeared.

I wasn't worried, though. *After all*, I thought, *I'll just use MapQuest. I can plug our starting point and final destination into the Internet powered application and, presto, it generates the route, calculating the mileage, travel time, and giving me maps and other details along the way.* So that's just what I did.

It worked like a charm until we got up into the mountains on some of the winding country roads. By this time we'd been driving all day—we were tired and hungry, and it was getting dark. But the route generated by MapQuest led us to a dead end: the conference center was nowhere to be found. I tried calling our host, but there was no cell phone service.

Finally we passed a squad car parked on the side of the road. I pulled over and asked the officers for help. I explained we were lost and had been driving around looking for the retreat site. Their squad car was equipped with a GPS system. They plugged in the address and came up with the same results. We all stood there scratching our heads. The sun had set and it was dark. It was well past dinnertime and we were late for the conference. My family was about to mutiny.

At that moment, one of the officers asked, "What did you say the name of the conference center was?"

"Trailhead Springs," I replied.

"Yeah, I've heard of that place," he said. "I think it's off of Deep Creek Road, about a mile from here. This address you have is wrong."

Thanks to the officer, we finally made it to the conference. Later that night, I sheepishly told our host what had happened. He explained that the address listed on the website was not the retreat address, which was why he had given me directions over the phone. I tried to get there relying on my own ingenuity to find the right way, rather than listening to the source. My wife and girls have never come so close to having me arrested.

Without the correct starting point or destination, we'll never get where we want to go. The whole journey is thrown off course. Too often we do ministry on autopilot—going on instinct or human ingenuity, without going directly to the source: God's Word. We must look to God in setting our grounds and goals for ministry to the emerging generation if we want to get where he is calling us to go.

Youth Ministry as Practical Theology

Poiesis and *praxis* are the Greek words Aristotle used to describe two different kinds of action.[1] *Poiesis* is an action that produces a product according to a design without regard to its future purpose or use. It's an assembly-line approach.

Imagine yourself working in a factory that produces cars. Your job is to assemble the fuse box. Your eyes are trained on each set of components as they pass in front of you. You have no time or concern to look up and down the line at what comes before or after; you have been trained to do your particular action a very specific way.

In an assembly line your eyes are on the work right in front of you—

accomplishing the task immediately before you and doing your part with precision and uniformity, the same way every time. The parts and participants working further up or down the line are of little importance to your task. In fact, the ultimate product or its use is of little importance to your activity. You don't even know which model car your fuse box will inhabit. And your mind is not interested in who will one day drive the car or how it will serve them. Your concern is not with the design of the car, nor its ultimate product or purpose, but simply with your piece of the puzzle.

A lot of people approach next-generation ministry like an assembly line. They do things the way they've always done them with little theological reflection. It's complicated and costly to engage the emerging generation as a parent or youth pastor. Often we find ourselves turning ministry into a mechanism, rather than entering into the mess of broken lives—willingly wrestling with the implications of the gospel in our time and place. We can become experts at executing our particular programs, while ignoring our underlying assumptions and default goals.

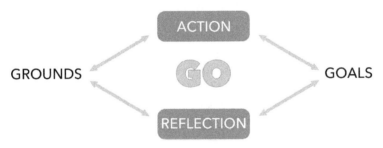

Figure 1. Praxis (grounds, goals, and ministry)

Praxis, on the other hand, keeps the *telos* (or ultimate purpose) in view. In *praxis*, the grounds for ministry (design) and the way one goes about ministry (action) are directed toward and informed by the ultimate goal of ministry (*telos*).[2] While *poiesis* is concerned with doing things the "right way," *praxis* is concerned with doing the "right things." A "praxeological" approach to next-generation ministry deeply engages the grounds and goals for ministry—looking to Christ in the power of his Spirit working with the Word to align and adjust the way we go about ministry to the next generation. This praxeological approach serves us in developing a meta-model for practical theology.

We can think of the meta-model as seen in Figure 1. Our grounds and goals bracket the way we go about ministry to emerging generations. Our grounds are the biblical principles and redemptive-historical precedents for youth ministry. Our goals should conform to God's vision, his purpose and direction, and eschatological destiny. Our grounds and goals then continually form and inform the way we go about ministry to adolescents and emerging adults.

A praxeological approach to youth ministry sees the ministry *itself* as inherently theological, both directing and illuminating our understanding and relationship with the Lord. Ray Anderson reflects this dynamic when he writes:

> Ministry cannot be construed solely as the practical application (or technique) that makes theological knowledge relevant and effective. Theological activity must emerge out of ministry and for the sake of ministry if it is to be in accordance with the divine modality. The "practice" of ministry, then, is not only the appropriate context for doing theological thinking; it is itself intrinsically a theological activity… Consequently, unless ministry takes a purely pragmatic turn, it is necessarily led to the theological activity of exploring the dogma of divine revelation given to us as the Word of God in Holy Scripture. This theological activity will be both exegetical and experiential.[3]

In the words of Thomas Aquinas, theology "is taught by God, teaches God, leads to God."[4]

The Apostle Paul writes, "Therefore since through God's mercy we have this ministry we do not lose heart" (II Cor. 4:1). It's easy to feel at times like a martyr in ministry to the next generation. But ministry is a mercy. Only in the crucible of ministry—entering the mess of others' lives—are we forced to confront our own brokenness and desperate need, and pressed to depend all the more on the grace of God and dig ever deeper into his Word. As we engage in the lives of others, we are privileged to catch glimpses of the divine in each person as unique reflections of the image of God, in turn illuminating our understanding and love for him through the people he has created. And as we encounter challenges we are forced to think, reflect, read, pray, discuss, wrestle, and repent. This is the pain and privilege of *praxis*.

False Dichotomies

Unfortunately, we tend to set up a false dichotomy in the world of next-gen ministry, separating the intellectual from the practical, illustrated in Figure 1.

We often fail to combine action with theological reflection. On one hand, some parents, leaders, and ministries tend to emphasize the intellect. They place a high value on proclaiming truth and transferring information. Their desire is that their youth emerge from adolescence with doctrinal vocabulary and definitions and a strong grasp of Bi-

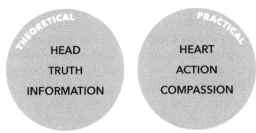

Figure 2. False Dichotomy in Next-Gen Ministry

ble content. These ministries tend to emphasize activities such as Bible studies, Sunday school, confirmation classes, catechism, and Scripture memory. They tend to cater to young people inside the church. Their teaching emphasizes information and theological discourse. They focus on the head. The truths of the gospel and the absolutes of Christianity stand in stark relief against the prevailing relativism and deconstruction inherent in this increasingly postmodern generation. Young people need assistance in developing a biblical world and life view that is robust and articulate. Recent studies indicate teenagers and emerging adults actually understand and can articulate very little about their own stated beliefs.[5] In increasingly post-Christian West and in underreached populations in the developing world, the story of Christianity and truth claims of Christ must be communicated and transferred to those with little biblical literacy.

On the other hand, there are parents, leaders, and ministries that tend to put emphasis on the practical. They place high values on behavior and Christian practice. They are interested in igniting passion, engendering compassion, and creating opportunities for youth to put their faith in action. These ministries usually stress activities such as: music and worship arts, fasting, service projects, mission trips, social justice, mercy ministry, fellowship gatherings, outreach events, and personal evangelism. They tend to pursue kids outside the church. Their ministries are heavy on emotion, practical application, and cultural relevance. They focus on the hands and heart.

Indeed, the gospel makes things better. Jesus transforms lives and has called his church to be an instrument of restoration in this broken world. Our youth need adults who will serve as models and guides in assisting them to reflect the reality of a relationship with Christ in every aspect of their lives, including emotions and actions. In a generation that is increasingly longing for meaning and purpose—to be a part of a movement bigger than themselves—the call to Christian action is compelling.

Of course there are dangers to this false dichotomy. When the pendulum swings, it is easy to overcorrect. Those whose emphasis is on more theoretical aspects of Christianity often (explicitly or implicitly) encourage young people to "intellectualize" their faith, downplaying the personal and relational aspects of life with Christ. In turn, this emphasis can contribute to legalistic and/or theologically arrogant individuals. Some kids emerge from this kind of ministry jaded and cynical, because they know all the right answers theoretically but have never learned how to integrate these truths into their lives and relationships. The tendency here is to focus on insiders and neglect the call to reach those outside the faith community. In an effort to preserve the integrity of the system of doctrine and pass the baton, a protectionist attitude may develop insulating them from peers in the community.

Those whose emphasis is on more practicable aspects of the faith often encourage young people to reduce faith to feelings and sets of behaviors, missing out on the rich heritage and theological truths which should form and inform all of life. Inherent in this emphasis is the issue of anti-intellectualism and disregard for tradition and rigorous Bible study. Some emerge from this sort of ministry with strong religious experiences and associations, but lacking in rich understandings and/or in abilities to articulate the fundamentals of what they believe. This leaves many without the tools and training to engage life with wisdom and discernment. The tendency here is to neglect the call to discipleship in an effort to be attractive, relevant, and relational.

As go adults, so go the youth. Many in next-generation ministry arrogantly see themselves as mavericks in the church. They feel they are doing the real work of ministry where it really counts: loving Jesus and young people, rather than getting caught up in and confounded by theology. Those who do pursue theological education are often less concerned about deepening their theology than about the pragmatics of their career—gaining credibility with parents and the church leadership or meeting denominational requirements.

In contrast, there have been many down through the ages who have overindulged on information but failed to live lives of real transformation:

> The Lord says: These people come near to me with their mouth and honor me with their lips, but their hearts are far from me. Their worship of me is made up only of rules taught by men. Therefore once more I will astound these people with wonder upon wonder; the wisdom of the wise will perish, the intelligence of the intelligent will vanish. (Isa. 29:13–14)

Jesus railed against the religious leaders of his day who had access to the law and the prophets but failed to live lives of repentance and humble service, and ultimately failing to recognize the Messiah himself.[6] As the writer of Proverbs counsels, "It is not good to have zeal without knowledge" (Prov. 19:2). True ministry flows from theology, and true theology results in ministry.

Paul's indictment of Israel is too often true of the Church today: "I can testify about them that they are zealous for God, but their zeal is not based on knowledge" (Rom. 10:2). This indictment comes from the same man who in his zeal as a religious leader persecuted the Church (Phil. 3:6). If anyone understood the dangers of zeal without knowledge, it was

Paul. He makes it clear in Ephesians 2 that the believer's faith, while not based on his works, nevertheless will result in good works. James, in turn, describes the interplay of theology and action when he writes:

> Do not merely listen to the word, and so deceive your-selves. Do what it says. Anyone who listens to the word but does not do what it says is like a man who looks at his face in a mirror and, after looking at himself, goes away and immediately forgets what he looks like. But the man who looks intently into the perfect law that gives freedom, and continues to do this, not forgetting what he has heard, but doing it, he will be blessed in what he does. If anyone considers himself religious and yet does not keep a tight rein on his tongue, he deceives himself and his religion is worthless. Religion that God our Father accepts as pure and faultless is this: to look after orphans and widows in their distress and to keep oneself from being polluted by the world. (James 1:22–27)

A clearer indictment for those who would separate theology from ministry lies in James's words: "What good is it, my brothers, if a man claims to have faith but has no deeds? Can such faith save him? ...As the body without the spirit is dead, so faith without deeds is dead" (James 2:14–26). Just as Scripture makes it clear that our works—including our ministry to youth—flow from our faith, so our faith is fueled by our theology. Paul writes to the church in Corinth: "To be perfectly frank, I am getting exasperated by your infantile thinking. How long before you grow up and use your head—your adult head? ...Only mature and well-exercised intelligence can save you from falling into gullibility" (I Cor. 14:20, *The Message*).[7] In the words of Johann Kepler, we must "think God's thoughts after him."[8]

Christo-Praxis

There is no greater call to theological *praxis* than the testimony of Jesus, the living Word: "The Word became flesh and dwelt among us" (John 1:14).; In Christ, the truth was personified, knowledge embodied, the Word made flesh. The incarnation of Christ is the pinnacle of *praxis*. God was not content to give people a written revelation of himself. He gave them a living witness, inviting them into a personal relationship with him that would change their whole lives and the whole world. A relationship with Jesus is not life enhancing, it is life changing.

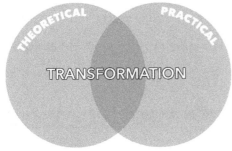

Figure 3. Christo-Praxis

Christ puts what has been broken back together. He confronts our tendency towards a false dichotomy, calling us to surrender ourselves wholly to him. God is not interested in mere information, let alone empty action. God is about transformation— engaging the head **and** the heart and the hands— thereby redeeming every aspect of our lives and ministries for his glory[9] (see Figure 3).

The sum total of God's revelation to man—the beginning, middle, and end of redemptive history, the author and hero of the divine drama—is Jesus Christ. "For from him and through him and to him are all things. To him be the glory forever. Amen" (Rom. 11:36). Again, Paul elevates the centrality of Christ when he writes:

He is the image of the invisible God, the firstborn of all creation. For by him all things were created, in heaven and on earth, visible and invisible, whether thrones or dominions or rulers or authorities—all things were created through him and for him. And he is before all things, and in him all things hold together. And he is the head of the body, the church. He is the beginning, the firstborn from the dead, that in everything he might be preeminent. For in him all the fullness of God was pleased to dwell, and through him to reconcile to himself all things, whether on earth or in heaven, making peace by the blood of his cross (Col. 1:15–20).

Our ministry *praxis* must be centered on Christ and in line with his kingdom trajectory. Such a "Christo-*praxis*" approaches theology holistically: as theoretical, personal, practical, and practicable.

31

MapQuest: Charting a Course for MissionNext

In the West, there has been a tendency to view this dynamic as a linear one (see Figure 4). The traditional understanding and assumption is that these aspects move in sequence from one to the next. This is often spoken of in terms of evangelism and discipleship. One hears the gospel, responds in faith, and then begins to live life in conformity to Christ.

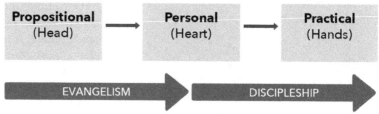

Figure 4. Linear Dynamic of Christo-Praxis

By the same token, there is not only a linear but also a circular dynamic within these facets (see Figure 3 again). God reveals himself in Scripture (propositional), yet we cannot fully understand his Word apart from knowing the living Word (personal). We cannot know Christ without the illuminating and regenerating work of the Holy Spirit. This work of the Holy Spirit transforms our lives from the inside out as we begin to progressively reflect the new reality of our relationship with Christ (practical). It is in this relationship that we grow in our understanding of God's truth and its radical and comprehensive call on every facet of our lives: head, heart, and hands.

Into the Mess

Jenny had a tough life. Her father was an alcoholic and her mother was clinically depressed. Jenny's parents were divorced so she split her time between them. Most of the time she preferred to stay with her mom because her father was verbally and physically abusive. But Jenny had called 911 several times when she discovered her mom barely alive from yet another suicide attempt.

I met Jenny when her father, reeking of alcohol, shoved her into our youth room one Sunday night, gruffly commenting, "She needs some religion." Jenny had a black eye and I could only wonder where that came from. She tried to mask her tears and set her jaded and cynical stare. She did not want to be there. The kids and leaders reached out to Jenny in friendship and love. They treated her as one of the community, even though she had never been to our church (or any church) before.

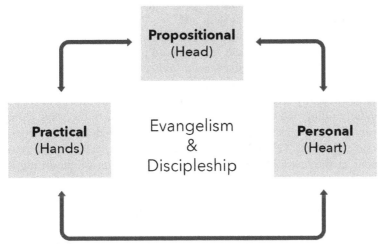

Figure 5. Circular Dynamic of Christo-Praxis

Amazingly enough, Jenny came back. She knew nothing about the gospel, and showed no interest in the Bible. She was loud and obnoxious and inappropriate; she was mischievous and at times downright manipulative. Sometimes it seemed like she was more trouble than she was worth.

Then came time for our youth missions trip. The plan was for only kids in the upper grades to go. In turn, these students would have to fill out an application including their testimony of faith in Christ and a description of their Christian life and practice. To my surprise, Jenny asked for an application. Not only was she too young, but most importantly she made no bones about the fact that she was unconvinced about Jesus.

For some reason, however, we decided to let her come on the trip. This was anything but linear! Here Jenny was going on a mission trip before she'd ever understood or embraced the gospel for herself. There she was serving the poor in the name of Jesus and sharing the gospel with little kids in the projects. Can you guess what happened? Before the end of the trip, Jenny came to me with tears in her eyes as we packed up from running our backyard bible club. "I've just prayed with little Shareen to ask Jesus into her heart. I've seen him at work all around me this week... In the people on the team and the people in the community. I want him in my life too. Will you pray with me?"

I'm crying as I remember the scene. God breaks in! From a human standpoint there is no reason Jenny should have even been on this trip. She was not a Christian. She was not old enough. What was she doing on a missions trip? But God had a mission for Jenny. And in his often creative and mysterious way he circumvents the conventions of human understanding and draws his people to himself. In some ways Jenny's story almost seemed backwards to me. But God invades lives in his own ways and times. We need to be open, sensitive, and flexible to the movement of the Spirit illuminating and engaging young people in myriad combinations and sequences of head, heart, and hands.

We are living theologies. Every act of ministry teaches us more about God, even as each act reflects what we already know of him. As Pete Ward puts it:

> Being with, however, is itself an expression of the gospel. As we spend time with young people, we find that we are a reflection of the love of God among them. The respect we show as we spend time getting to know groups and individuals is a witness to the presence of Christ among the group. The way we go about outreach among young people is therefore a sign of the gospel. We are the means by which Jesus becomes incarnated among a group of young people. To be "incarnational" as a youth worker is therefore to live out a spirituality that is deeply rooted in the life of Christ. We are imitators of Christ attempting, by the things we do and say, to offer young people an insight into the heart God has for them.[100]

Theology and practice should be inextricable. As we give ourselves to knowing God, we can't help but be moved to give ourselves away in ministry. After all, "all theology is missiology."

As we step out in the journey of ministry with young people, it's going to get messy. Spiritual formation is relational, not mechanistic. Any time we create a model or draw a diagram it is by nature reductionistic and limited. By the same token, these tools are helpful in giving us language and categories for conversation and interaction. As humans, our natural desire is to "get it right"—to live and work in balance. Those seeking to engage adolescents and emerging adults face the challenge of wrestling and living in the tension amidst pursuing growth in head, heart, and hands. It's important to be intentional as we look for teachable moments, creating opportunities for tweens, teens and twentysomethings to grow in each arena.

At the same time we must recognize that we'll never be able to achieve a perfect balance. Instead, we must embrace the tension and continually wrestle with it together with those we are called to love and lead. Ultimately, our trust is in the Lord to orchestrate, intervene, and intercede on each one's behalf as he authors each unique story. He is leading the expedition and he'll take us down unpredictable and wild pathways of his faithfulness to the next generation. Buckle in for the ride!

Questions for Reflection & Discussion

1. What things are appealing about the assembly-line approach to ministry with young people?

2. What are some underlying assumptions you have about the goals of working with young people? How does the supervising leadership seem to support your assumptions and goals?

3. During your youth, in what ways was your discipleship experience shaped by theoretical knowledge? In what ways was it shaped by practicable actions? In what ways might you be influenced currently by your previous discipleship experiences?

4. Describe some concrete ways that a focus on "Christo-praxis" might strengthen the current next generation ministry.

Notes

1   Aristotle, *Nicomachean Ethics*, trans. Martin Ostwald (Indianapolis: The Library of Liberal Arts and Bobbs-Merrill Educational Publishing, 1962), pp. 3–4.

2   Anderson, *The Soul of Ministry: Forming Leaders for God's People*, p. 27.

3   Anderson, *The Shape of Practical Theology*, p. 63.

4   Geerhardus Vos, *Biblical Theology: Old and New Testaments* (Grand Rapids, MI: Wm. B. Eerdmans Publishing Co., 1948), p. v.

5   Christian Smith and Melinda Lundquist Denton, *Soul Searching: The Religious and Spiritual Lives of American Teenagers* (New York, NY: Oxford University Press, 2005), p. 131, and Christian Smith and Patricia Snell, *Souls in Transition: The Religious and Spiritual Lives of Emerging Adults,* (New York, NY: Oxford Univeristy Press, 2009).

6   See Jesus' scathing indictment of the Pharisees in Matthew 23.

7   I Cor. 14:20, Eugene Peterson, *The Message* (Colorado Springs, CO: NavPress 2002).

8   Burton E. Stevenson, ed., *The Home Book of Quotations, Classical and Modern*, 10th ed. (New York: Greenwich House, 1984).

9   Romans 12:1–2: "For this reason…"

10 Pete Ward, *God at the Mall: Youth Ministry that Meets Kids Where They're At* (Peabody, MA: Hendrickson, 1999), p. 105.

CHAPTER 3

Base Camp: Grounds for MissionNext

CLIMBING MOUNT EVEREST IS COSTLY, takes time, and is unpredictable.

The key to a successful bid for the summit of any mountain is the base camp. Everest has four. Climbers spend some time acclimatizing to the altitude and conditions before setting off from Base Camp 1. Local Sherpas serve as guides and can be found at base camps to show climbers the way and assist them with navigating the treacherous terrain. Each successive base camp provides climbers with a source of much needed supplies and oxygen for the arduous trek. At these base camps, climbers can eat a hot meal, rest, and recover, renewing their strength for the next leg of the journey.

The weather on Mt. Everest is unpredictable and can make conditions dangerous and confusing. By returning to base camp, climbers can seek shelter from a storm and get reoriented for their next attempt at the summit. Many a climber has been lost on the mountain because they failed to return to base camp.

Climbing Everest sounds a lot like the journey of next-gen ministry. It is an adventure that is costly—requiring sacrifice and commitment to reaching and raising tweens, teens and twentysomethings. It takes time—walking with a few over the greater course of their lives. And it's unpredictable—navigating the terrain and enduring the storms of adolescence and the emerging adult years.

* * *

Jack and Diane are considering having children. They wonder, "Do we have any business bringing a child into this broken world?"

Base Camp: Grounds for MissionNext

On his sixteenth birthday, Bruce discovers his father's been having an affair and his parents are divorcing. He wonders, "Has God forgotten me?"

Cheryl weeps as she reads a letter from her twenty-something daughter, "Mom, I know he's a devout Hindu, but I'm going to marry him anyway."

Julie is exhausted from years of university ministry. Her colleague remarks, "You seem burned out."

Steve has never led a youth ministry before. He asks himself, "Why did I agree to do this? I don't have a clue!"

How would you approach these challenges? Where do you turn for guidance in ministering to youth and their families? What can anchor us amidst the storms of adolescence and emerging adulthood?

Ministry requires a base camp. We need a starting point in the journey of next-generation ministry—a firm foundation from which to venture out into the wilds of adolescence and emerging adulthood. Just as climbers spend time acclimatizing and preparing, we need to soak in God's Word and allow him to conform our hearts to his regarding the next generation. As climbers need a guide, we look to God to guide and direct us in our efforts at engaging the emerging generation, grounding our efforts in biblical precedents and principles.

Time and again we must turn and return to our base camp—to God and his Word—to renew our strength and realign our course. And we need a central theological *locus* as an anchor and shelter for our souls amidst the storms of adolescence. Without a base camp, we run the risk of being misguided and lost in our efforts at reaching and raising the next generation.

A Trail Guide: Following the Path of Next-Gen Ministry through His-story

Is there a biblical precedent for ministry to young people? How has God's hand in redemptive history demonstrated his concern for the next generation? We want our assumptions and approaches to any ministry grounded in God's redemptive work and his revealed will. We venture out in ministry to the rising generation because God does. He's our guide along the way. Let's journey with him along the path of youth ministry as we see it through the lens of the biblical story.

Before the Dawn of Time

Since before the dawn of time, God has been intimately and intentionally about the business of next generation ministry. In Psalm 139 we are told that God wrote all the days ordained for us before one of them came to be. The Alpha and the Omega (the Beginning and the End) has a personal interest in each child's development. He tenderly orchestrates each life from beginning to end, caring for and divinely tending to each stage of progress and development:

> For you created my inmost being; you knit me together in my mother's womb. I praise you because I am fearfully and wonderfully made; your works are wonderful, I know that full well. My frame was not hidden from you when I was made in the secret place. When I was woven together in the depths of the earth, your eyes saw my unformed body. (Psa. 139:13–16)

God is not concerned only with adults, seeing children and youth as unimportant until they reach a critical age. After all, in God's sight, we are all children (Rom. 8:15–17).

Through Creation and the Fall

From day one, God has had the next generation in mind. Embedded in the creation story is God's design that his people invest themselves in establishing future generations: "God blessed them and said to them, 'Be fruitful and increase in number; fill the earth'" (Gen. 1:28). This was not only God's "pre-fall" purpose for humankind, but it was re-established after the flood (Gen. 9:1, 7).

Even while pronouncing a curse on humankind, we see God's hand preserving and providing for future generations of his people: "And I will put enmity between you and the woman, and between your offspring and hers; he will crush your head, and you will strike his heel" (Gen. 3:15). Right from the outset, God telegraphs his great plan of redemption—protecting and preserving his children through his Son. The dual implication of the use of the word "offspring" is important to understand. God would not only give victory over the evil one to his children, but it would be Jesus, his divine Son, who will achieve the victory.[1] As the offspring of the woman, Jesus both identified with his children and represented them in his atoning death and resurrection. As a result, each consecutive generation has been subjected to the curse and must be prepared to face the cosmic conflict—taking up their position in the company of the victorious by trusting in the victory won in Christ. God's desire for his children is that they be brought up seeing their story in the context of his great story, embracing their place as his children by embracing his Son, Jesus Christ.

This will not be easy, nor will it come naturally. Sin entered the world, the curse was pronounced, and the conflict has been raging against the raising of the next generation. In Genesis we read, "To the woman he said, 'I will greatly increase your pains in childbearing'" (Gen. 3:16). The whole task of raising the next generation—of parenting them through all the stages of life—has been frustrated by the curse.[2] The implication is that from the time of the fall onward it would be a painful struggle to raise and parent children, in the birth experience and beyond. Not only would childrearing be painful and burdensome, but work in the world would be toilsome and demanding, further pulling at the fabric of the family and siphoning off the resources and relationship required of parents in nurturing their children:

> To Adam he said, "Because you listened to your wife and ate from the tree about which I commanded you, 'You must not eat of it,' cursed is the ground because of you; through painful toil you will eat of it all the days of your life. It will produce thorns and thistles for you, and you will eat the plants of the field. By the sweat of your brow you will eat your food until you return to the ground, since from it you were taken; for dust you are and to dust you will return." (Gen. 3:17–19)

From the outset, the stage was set for youth ministry: we who are parents need to have others, and ultimately God, come alongside us in the task of raising the next generation. Parenting is painful and difficult. We need help.

Through the Flood

God's interest in youth and family ministry has always been at the epi-center of his plans for all humankind. By Noah's day, God saw that the thoughts of man's heart were "only evil, all the time" (Gen. 6:5). God restored his creation by preserving a remnant through the flood. It is im-portant to note that Noah's sons were all born during the time it took to build the ark. In other words, they all grew up with the purpose and plan of God as central to their family's mission. The persecution and ridicule Noah experienced would have formed the backdrop to their growth and maturity, further sealing the lived-out conviction and commitment of their father. What an impact this must have made on these boys as they grew into the men God would use to establish the next generation of his people! And what a picture of the call to us in youth ministry today: coming alongside students and families in order to help them see their lives as wrapped around the mission of God in the world. Peter makes it clear that Noah and his family were a picture of God's redeeming a peo-ple for himself, the great family of God, the covenant community (I Pet. 3:20–22). Commenting on I Peter 3, John Calvin wrote, "…humankind would rush on to their own destruction, but that the Lord would in a wonderful way deliver his very small flock."[3]

Through Abraham's Call

God's faithfulness continued through the generations that followed. In Genesis 12 we read of the call of Abram and God's promise to future generations to bless them and make them a blessing:

> The LORD had said to Abram, "Leave your country, your people and your father's household and go to the land I will show you. I will make you into a great nation and I will bless you; I will make your name great, and you will be a blessing. I will bless those who bless you, and whoever curses you I will curse; and all peoples on earth will be blessed through you." (Gen. 12:1–3)

Yahweh "covenanted" with Abraham, making a promise to his de-scendants saying, "I will establish my covenant as an everlasting covenant between me and you and your descendants after you for the generations to come, to be your God and the God of your descendants after you" (Gen. 17:7). Even circumcision, as the sign and seal of God's covenant promises to the next generation, was to be applied not only to adults but to children, demonstrating God's future orientation toward—and hand upon—the next generation.[4]

> Then God said to Abraham, "As for you, you must keep my covenant, you and your descendants after you for the generations to come. This is my covenant with you and your descendants after you, the covenant you are to keep: Every male among you shall be circumcised. You are to undergo circumcision, and it will be the sign of the covenant between me and you. For the generations to come every male among you who is eight days old must be circumcised, including those born in your household or bought with money from a foreigner—those who are not your offspring. Whether born in your household or bought with your money, they must be circumcised. My covenant in your flesh is to be an everlasting covenant." (Gen. 17:9–13)

In Genesis 21–22, we read the story of the birth and sacrifice of Isaac. God provided Isaac in Abraham's old age as the fulfillment of his promise of an heir. Then he turned around and demanded the right to Isaac's life, so that Abraham could demonstrate his faithfulness by sacrificing his son. God then demonstrated his faithfulness to his promises by rescuing Isaac and providing a ram, which prefigured Christ, the ultimate substitutionary sacrifice for all his people:

> I swear by myself, declares the LORD, that because you have done this and have not withheld your son, your only son, I will surely bless you and make your descendants as numerous as the stars in the sky and as the sand on the seashore. Your descendants will take possession of the cities of their enemies. (Gen. 22:15–18a)

God similarly claims the rights to *our* children; we recognize they are "on loan" from him. Ultimately, our trust must be in his provision and redeeming work for them. We are stewards called to trust our children to his purposes, relinquishing our rights to them while not neglecting our responsibilities. Following God's example, we train our eye on the next generation and not for their sake alone. This begins with our children's inheritance in the Lord, and then extends that to the nations, as the promise in Genesis 22 continues: "...and through your offspring all nations on earth will be blessed" (Gen. 22:18b). God's mission in the world is generational as well as geographic. His hand in history demonstrates his ministry to and through youth and their families.

It is important to note that even Abraham recognized his need for help in raising Isaac. Initially, his parenting demonstrated a reliance on himself.[5] In time he came to prayerfully, humbly, and dependently trust in God, and solicited the help of others to come alongside him in providing for Isaac and his descendants (Genesis 24).

Across biblical history we see how God worked *through* families, blessing wombs and raising up each generation to carry on his purposes according to his plan. Time and again God worked *in spite of* families, as exemplified by Abraham, Isaac, Jacob, and Joseph. Though Isaac seemed to have failed to pass the baton of faith to his sons, still God overruled and preserved his people and plan through Jacob. Though Joseph was sold into slavery as a youth and carried away to a foreign land, God's sovereign hand was on his life. God used Joseph to accomplish his own sovereign purposes in spite of the family's dysfunction and rejection:

> But Joseph said to them, "Don't be afraid. Am I in the place of God? You intended to harm me, but God intended it for good to accomplish what is now being done, the saving of many lives. So then, don't be afraid. I will provide for you and your children." And he reassured them and spoke kindly to them. (Gen. 50:19–21)

God is the great Youth Minister—preserving, chastening, guiding, and superintending the lives of his young people. Moses was preserved from genocide and kept connected to God's people even when ripped from his home as a baby (Exodus 2). Rescued as a child, Moses was used by God to rescue his people from slavery. God protected the firstborn of his people Israel at the Passover (Exodus 12). Samuel was a gift from God, dedicated to God, and raised not by his parents but by Eli in the temple (I Samuel 1). Namaan's little servant girl, though taken from her family at an early age, was used by God to be a missionary to her master; but on the other hand, God chastened the youth who mocked him by making fun of his prophet Elisha (II Kings 2, 5). King Joash, though raised well, failed Israel. Though he respected his earthly father figure, he failed to transfer this allegiance to his heavenly Father, revealing the consequences when children do not make faith their own.

God continued to demonstrate his hand in the lives of the young by making Josiah king at eight years of age and using him to bring his people back to himself (II Kings 23). Even in the face of tragedy, God revealed his sovereign hand at work to Abijah, the son of Jereboam: he was mercifully allowed to die and be buried before the judgment occurred in which all the people were killed and devoured by animals (I Kings 14). This compassionate act of God demonstrated that even in apparent tragedy, God's eye was on his chosen children (II Kings 14:12–13). By the same token, God preserved and used Daniel together with Shadrach, Meshach, and Abednego to stand strong and make an impact, even though they were probably less than ten years of age when taken into captivity (Daniel 1).

Perhaps David is the ultimate Old Testament example of God's work in the life of a young person. God had David anointed as a youth, and then demonstrated his faithfulness time and again to David by enabling him to defeat the lion and the bear, and ultimately helped him save Israel from slavery through the defeat of Goliath (I Samuel 17). God chose and used a simple shepherd boy, one neglected and mocked by his older brothers and untrained, inexperienced, and unarmed, to be his people's champion. God left no doubt that he was to receive the credit for David's success. God is the one who empowers and defends his young.

God's passion for the next generation forms the final words of the Old Testament. Malachi prophesied of the coming day of the Lord: "He will turn the hearts of the fathers to their children, and the hearts of the children to their fathers" (Mal. 4:6). This refrain was picked up in the opening chapters of the New Testament in connection with the Messiah's arrival and ministry as fulfillment of the prophecy (Luke 1:17). This refers to more than just a father's heart toward his own children but encompasses the turning of the older generation to the younger.

A Trail Guide: Following the Path of Next-Gen Ministry through His-story

Through the Incarnation

In the New Testament, God continued to have his hand on the young. He anointed John the Baptist while he was still in Elizabeth's womb (Luke 1:11–25, 41). God chose an unwed teenager to be the mother of our Savior, graciously giving Mary a heart for and allegiance to God above that of her parents, her fiancé, and the culture (Matt. 1:18–25; Luke 1:26–38). With the birth of Jesus, God made his entrance into human history as a baby, growing through all the normal stages of human development. Jesus experienced, understood, identified with, and validated every aspect of human experience, including adolescence: "Jesus grew in wisdom and stature, and in favor with God and men" (Luke 2:52).

As a youth of only eleven years (according to Jewish reckoning), Jesus demonstrated his own shift in allegiance and identity from his earthly parents to his heavenly Father, from his nuclear family to the family of God: "Didn't you know that I had to be in my father's house?" (Luke 2:41–50). Jesus' core identity as the Son of God was fully formed as a young man of about 30 years of age, which was evidenced when he says, "Who are my mother and brothers? Those who do the will of my father in heaven, these are my mother and brothers" (Matt. 12:46–50). The shift from dependency on earthly parents, begun as a youth, was completed in his manhood. In turn, Jesus validated and elevated the call to youth ministry by beckoning the children to come to him and chastising his disciples for considering them to be unimportant: "Let the little children come to me, and do not hinder them; for the kingdom of heaven belongs to such as these" (Matt. 19:14).

God's hand in history demonstrates his ministry to youth and families. The stories of his faithfulness toward, and focus on, the next generation form the framework of his calling on the church, God's covenant community. We are to be his family on earth, his instrument for shepherding the next generation. The church is called to be the community in which adolescents and emerging adults are encouraged to discover and embrace their core identity as children of God: transferring their ultimate allegiance from their earthly parents to their heavenly Father… from their nuclear family to the family of God.

Base Camp: Grounds for MissionNext

The Church as Base Camp

Throughout redemptive history God reclaimed and restored his people, calling out a remnant to be his instrument in reaching the next generation and gathering the nations.[6] Beginning with Adam and Eve, then down through Abraham's descendants and the establishing and preserving of his chosen nation, Israel, God's plan culminated in Christ and the establishing of the church. God's enduring intent, though once found only in seed form, now blossomed in the coming of Christ and the work of the Holy Spirit amidst his people. Generational and geographic boundaries were destroyed, social and cultural divisions bridged.[7]

His call on the church is to maintain its future hope in the return of Christ and the consummation of history, while participating in his redemptive work in the world. This call can be met only by faithfully passing on the baton of faith to the next generation, calling young people to take up the mantle of his mission. Our desire must be to see each one touched by the ministry of Jesus and participating in his mission as members of his family.

Supply Source

The base camp is a source for oxygen, food, water, and a place to find shelter and rest. The church is the believer's base camp, mediating God's truth and love through his people. The church is our source of identity and community—the people of God receiving the provision of God and resting in the promises of God. For this reason, next-gen ministry should extend from the church even as it leads young people to find their identity and community in the church.

Jesus was and is both fully human as well as fully divine. Nothing in his humanity was negated by his divinity. He lived the life we were meant to live and, by so doing, he grew through the full range of human experience—emotionally, developmentally, physically, relationally, and cognitively. His life is ours by imputation, but is also given as a model for our imitation; Jesus lived the life we were meant to live. His life leads us in recovering our full humanity. From an early age—12 years old by Jewish reckoning (11 years old by our modern western accounting)—Jesus demonstrated the shift in allegiance that must occur in every child's life.

In his gospel, Luke recorded the story of the youth, Jesus, travelling with his family to Jerusalem for the feast of the Passover:

> After the Feast was over, while his parents were returning home, the boy Jesus stayed behind in Jerusalem, but they were unaware of it. Thinking he was in their company, they travelled on for a day. Then they began looking for him among their relatives and friends. When they did not find him, they went back to Jerusalem to look for him. After three days they found him in the temple courts, sitting among the teachers, listening to them and asking them questions. Everyone who heard him was amazed at his understanding and his answers. When his parents saw him, they were astonished. His mother said to him, "Son, why have you treated us like this? Your father and I have been anxiously searching for you." "Why were you searching for me?" he asked. "Didn't you know I had to be in my Father's house?" But they did not understand what he was saying to them. Then he went down to Nazareth with them and was obedient to them. But his mother treasured all these things in her heart. And Jesus grew in wisdom and stature, and in favor with God and men. (Luke 2:41–52)

Jesus never sinned. His attendance in the temple courts was not an act of rebellion or irresponsibility; instead, Jesus demonstrated the shift in allegiance that each of us should make and so foster in our young: the shift in core identity and allegiance from our earthly parents to our Father in heaven and from our nuclear family to the family of God, the church.

There is a temptation today to see the church the way the people of God in the Old Testament so often did, as an end in itself. Parents are guilty of the same when they focus only on their nuclear family, neglecting the kingdom purposes of God. Churches perpetuate such a stance when they focus solely on catering to members rather than reaching out to those who have yet to know the love of Christ. The covenant community is the beginning point of missions, not the end. If made the end, we have missed the point.[8]

Base Camp: Grounds for MissionNext

Mission Headquarters

Just as the base camp is a source of supplies, it is also the headquarters for the mission. At base camp, climbers revise their plans, study their maps, review their mission, and secure a guide before launching out toward the summit. The church is our headquarters for mission. God has called us to reach the nations and the next generation. Our base camp propels us forward in pursuit of this vision.

This is the purpose Jesus came to fulfill: inaugurating the kingdom reign of God over all people and all of life. The Father's great commission to the Son redounds with this theme: "I will also make you a light for the gentiles, that you may bring salvation to the ends of the earth" (Isa. 49:6). Jesus was the ultimate prophet, calling the people of God back to their original purpose: to reach the nations and the next generation. We see this clearly in the account of Jesus cursing the fig tree:

> The next day as they were leaving Bethany, Jesus was hungry. Seeing in the distance a fig tree in leaf, he went to find out if it had any fruit. When he reached it, he found nothing but leaves, because it was not the season for figs. Then he said to the tree, "May no one ever eat fruit from you again." (Mark 11:12–14)

Jesus used the tree as an object lesson—cursing it for not fulfilling its purpose. The tree may have been leafy and green, alive to itself, but it failed to offer life by producing fruit. Jesus used the fig tree as a picture of the failure of God's people to fulfill God's purposes: neglecting to offer life to the nations and the next generation.

Immediately following the cursing of the fig tree, Jesus entered the temple, chasing out the moneychangers and merchants who had set up shop in the temple courts. Jesus reacted zealously in spite of the fact that these people were allowed to conduct business in and around the temple, and provided a necessary service for many who needed to acquire sacrificial animals after travelling some distance to worship (Deut. 14:24–26). His anger was not over *what* they were doing. What they were doing was not wrong; it was *where* they were doing it and what they were not doing that angered Jesus. They had set up shop in the outer courts of the Temple: the court of the Gentiles. They made the area so overcrowded that there was no room for the Gentiles to gather to witness the worship of God in the adjacent temple courts.

The Jews had selfishly considered their own convenience and self-perpetuation at the expense of their God-given purpose of reaching the nations. Jesus reminded them of God's original intent for them by quoting, "Is it not written: My house will be called a house of prayer for all nations? But you have made it a den of robbers" (Mark 11:17). They were robbing people not of their money but of life—life with God. After clearing the temple of the moneychangers, Jesus fulfilled his Father's purpose by welcoming in the outcast and injured, the alien and the orphan, the Gentile and the child. He ministered to them and received their enthusiastic worship:

> The blind and the lame came to him at the temple, and he healed them. But when the chief priests and the teachers of the law saw the wonderful things he did and the children shouting in the temple area, "Hosanna to the Son of David," they were indignant. "Do you hear what these children are saying?" they asked him. "Yes," replied Jesus, "have you never read, 'From the lips of children and infants you have ordained praise'?" (Matt. 21:14–16)

Jesus' indictment of the Pharisees is one we must accept for ourselves in the church today. We need to examine ourselves and see if we are guilty of failing to reach the Gentile (geographic) and the child (generational). This account makes it clear that the two are intimately entwined with the core purpose of God's missionary work in the world for which the church is his chosen instrument.

At the birth of the New Testament Church during Pentecost, we read that people from every nation were gathered and heard the word of the Lord in their own tongue as Peter preached the gospel. God's mission for the Church involves the reaching of every nation and generation: "In the last days I will pour out my Spirit on all people. Your sons and daughters will prophesy, your young men will see visions" (Acts 2:17). Peter called to those gathered, "Repent and be baptized every one of you, in the name of Jesus Christ for the forgiveness of your sins. And you will receive the gift of the Holy Spirit. The promise is for you and your children and for all who are far off—for all whom the Lord our God will call" (Acts 2:39).

Acts 2:42–47 describes the early church as a community centered on the Word of God, the worship of God, and the work of God. Biblical youth ministry flows from this communal call. Parents are not left on their own to raise and reach the next generation; rather the church as an extended family has the responsibility to bring children in and raise them up. The church is the core community, the prime place of identity as God's children, called according to his purpose.

It is the church that is called to care for the widow and orphan as exemplifying true religion (James 1:27). At the heart of the church's mission is a concern for the persecuted, downtrodden, oppressed, and helpless of which widows and orphans are representative. In a world of broken homes, deadbeat dads, absent and unavailable fathers (and mothers), and abandoned and persecuted youth,[9] the call to look after the widow and orphan takes on new implications and deep significance.

It is in the church that young men are to be trained by older men and younger women, by older women. This responsibility to invest in and equip the next generation is shared by the community, and is not limited to the nuclear family (Titus 2:4–8). Paul's relationship with Timothy is a beautiful example of the work of youth ministry in the early church.

In his letter to the Ephesian church, Paul writes:

> But to each one of us grace has been given as Christ apportioned it.... It was he who gave some to be apostles, some to be prophets, some to be evangelists, and some to be pastors and teachers, to prepare God's people for works of service, so that the body of Christ may be built up until we all reach unity in the faith and in the knowledge of the Son of God and become mature, attaining to the whole measure of the fullness of Christ. Then we will no longer be infants, tossed back and forth by the waves, and blown here and there by every wind of teaching and by the cunning and craftiness of men in their deceitful scheming. Instead, speaking the truth in love, we will in all things grow up into him who is the Head, that is, Christ. From him the whole body, joined and held together by every supporting ligament, grows and builds itself up in love, as each part does its work. (Eph. 4:7–16)

Next-gen ministry is the task of the church as each member uses their gifts to build up the body and see young people come to maturity in Christ. The church is the body of Christ, and "each member belongs to all the others" (Rom. 12:5). The responsibility for fulfilling God's mission in reaching every nation and emerging generation rests on the shoulders of God's people, the church. It takes the combined gifts and unique calling of each member working in concert to accomplish God's will.

In Paul's second letter to the Corinthian church, he reminds them that the church is a community of people reconciled to Christ and one another, and has been given the task of representing Christ in reconciling the world to him (II Cor. 5:16–20). This is our call, not as isolated individuals or families, but as members together of God's family.[10] The call is to reach "all"—all nations and all generations—people from every tribe, language, and tongue, men and women, young and old. Next-gen ministry, therefore, is at the core of the church's mission: MissionNext.

God, in turn, ordains pastors and leaders in the church. He is the one who establishes the roles and responsibilities within the family of God. It is our responsibility to discern and affirm his gifts and call in the lives of members in the body. The instructions given in II Timothy and Titus 2 make it clear that there are to be elders who shepherd the local church in discerning God's direction. These elders set apart members for particular ministry focal points within the overarching ministry of the church. For example, Paul and Barnabas were commissioned for a specific ministry and sent out by the church in Antioch (Acts 13:1–3). Likewise, members of the church are enjoined to use their particular gifts in conjunction with the rest of the body:

> Just as each of us has one body with many members, and these members do not all have the same function, so in Christ we who are many form one body, and each member belongs to all the others. We have different gifts, according to the grace given us. If a man's gift is prophesying, let him use it in proportion to his faith. If it is serving, let him serve; if it is teaching, let him teach; if it is encouraging, let him encourage; if it is contributing to the needs of others, let him give generously; if it is leadership, let him govern diligently; if it is showing mercy, let him do it cheerfully. (Rom. 12:4–8)

Base Camp: Grounds for MissionNext

From these passages there is a precedent for churches to set apart gifted and called people for the particular focus of reaching the next generation. This ministry is rooted in God's character and work. He has been overseeing and orchestrating his work in and through the lives of young people in each generation throughout redemptive history. The church, as his representative in the world, is called to be his instrument in carrying on his ministry to all nations and all generations. This necessitates a shift in understanding from seeing ministry to young people as the sole responsibility of the nuclear family on the one hand or as relegated to a disconnected parachurch model on the other. Instead, ministry to young people is the responsibility of the church family—moving primarily from parents to being shared by a passionate, gifted, and called community. It must be pulled from the periphery and brought back inside the church.[111]

The heart of the global church ought to be wrapped around the next generation, calling adults to pour out their resources and their lives. The adult community is charged with investing in the future of the church by relinquishing their rights and selfish pursuits in order to lift up the rising generation. By bowing our wills and wants in humble service and support of Christ's call to young people, we can offer shoulders for the next generation to stand on.

This is contrary to the world's message and the instinctive motives of our own hearts. While the nuclear family is the core unit and beginning point of missions within the church family, we tend to make the "Christian family" an end in itself. Just as an acorn isn't complete unless it is planted and grows into an oak tree, one cannot understand the family until one understands its purpose.

The world beckons us to put ourselves first, then our children, then others as an afterthought and with nothing but our leftovers—if at all. Instead, God calls us to begin with his glory (not our own) and his mission (not our purposes or plans). His heart for the world then forms and informs the way we lead our families, while diminishing our own self-interests. This stands in stark contrast to the world's priorities. If God has established the grounds for youth ministry, he also has established its goals. A biblical approach to next-gen ministry will look to him not only for precedent, but also for its ultimate purpose. Let's fix our eyes on the horizon as we set out from base camp.

Questions for Reflection & Discussion

1. In what ways could a leader counsel a youth worker who has lost sight of the "base camp?"

2. What are a couple specific ways this chapter has strengthened your concerns for next-gen ministry? Mark some paragraphs that particularly struck you. Share these places for discussion in your team.

3. Describe one way God's work in the OT motivates your own ministry service.

4. In what ways could the ministry help parents to strengthen their teenager's allegiance to God?

5. In what ways could the church look even more like a base camp?

Notes

1 Vos, *Biblical Theology*, pp. 43–44.

2 Matthew Henry, "Sentence Passed on Eve," in *Commentary on the Whole Bible, vol. 1, Genesis to Deuteronomy* (Peabody, MA: Hendrickson Publishers, 1998), p. 25. Bruce Waltke, *Genesis* (Grand Rapids, MI: Zondervan, 2001), pp. 94, 105. See also C. John Collins, *Genesis 1–4* (Phillipsburg, NJ: P&R Books, 2005).

3 John Calvin, *Commentaries on the First Epistle of Peter*, trans. John Owen (Grand Rapids, MI: Baker Book House, 1979), p. 117.

4 Louis Berkhof, *Summary of Christian Doctrine* (Grand Rapids, MI: Wm. B. Eerdmans Publishing Co., 1998), pp. 170–171.

5 Genesis 16 gives the account of Abram and Sarai conspiring to have a child through Hagar rather than trusting in the Lord to provide.

6 Christopher J.H. Wright, *The Mission of God: Unlocking the Bible's Grand Narrative* (Downers Grove, IL: IVP Academic, 2006). CF George W. Peters, *A Biblical Theology of Missions* (Chicago, IL: Moody Press, 1972), pp. 129–130.

7 Susan Hunt, *Heirs of the Covenant: Leaving a Legacy of Faith for the Next Generation* (Wheaton, IL: Crossway Books, 1998), p. 33.

8 James Montgomery Boice, *Foundations of the Christian Faith: A Comprehensive and Readable Theology* (Downers Grove, IL: InterVarsity Press, 1986), p. 650.

9 Patricia Hersch, *A Tribe Apart* (New York: The Random House Publishing Group, 1999), p. 19.

10 Gilbert Bilezikian, *Community 101: Reclaiming the Local Church as Community of Oneness* (Grand Rapids, MI: Zondervan Publishing House, 1997), p. 62.

11 "The Changing Face of Adolescence: A Theological View of Human Development," in *Starting Right: Thinking Theologically About Youth Ministry*, ed. Kenda Creasy Dean, Chap Clark, Dave Rahn (El Cajon, CA: Zondervan Publishing House and Youth Specialties Books, 2001), p. 61.

CHAPTER 4

To Infinity and Beyond:
Goals for MissionNext

"Men wanted for hazardous journey. Low wages, bitter cold, long hours of complete darkness. Safe return doubtful. Honor and recognition in event of success." (Ernest Shackleton)

"To infinity…and beyond!" (Buzz Lightyear)

PIXAR ANIMATION'S BUZZ LIGHTYEAR IS the beloved space ranger from the Toy Story films. His famous line, "To infinity and beyond" has become a cultural catch phrase amongst millions of fans.

Of course, Buzz is just a toy, not a real space ranger (as becomes clear through the story). But at the beginning of the film he believes he's the real thing. He is unaware that his space suit is plastic and his gadgets are nothing more than stickers and LED lights. When told by the other toys that he is indeed *not* a real space ranger, Buzz determines to prove them wrong by demonstrating that he can fly. Tension builds as Buzz mounts the bedpost, spreads his plastic wings shouting, "To infinity and beyond!" and leaps into the air. As he plummets toward the floor in free fall, something amazing happens. Seemingly by chance, a perfectly timed chain reaction of events coincides, keeping Buzz airborne: he lands on a ball bouncing him back up into the air which launches him onto a matchbox car speeding through a loop then up a ramp, shooting him onto a toy plane in flight; the plane takes him for a spin round the ceiling and sends

To Infinity and Beyond: Goals for MissionNext

him flying across the room, where he lands in perfect form on the bed. "See," he says with confidence, "I told you I could fly." "That wasn't flying," replies Woody, "That was falling with style." In this movie, and in each successive sequel, Buzz discovers his mission. He—along with Woody and the other toys—have a purpose to pursue, a goal to achieve: a quest which brings them together and focuses their efforts and energies. Time and again Buzz takes flight (falling with style) in an effort to further the mission at hand.

What are the goals that drive your ministry? How are we to pursue God's mission in the lives of adolescents and emerging adults?

Emerging generation ministry needs be grounded theologically, but also guided by Christ's kingdom trajectory. We need a firm foundation from which to launch and a goal to guide our efforts. Our vision should be from God, not of our own ends. Our goals must be aligned by his purposes and plans: the temporal desires and eternal destiny he intends for his people.

As fallen humans, we are powerless to pursue or effect God's goals in our own ability and ingenuity. Like Buzz, we *want* to see ourselves as heroes—capable of more than we really are. The truth is, when it comes to next-gen ministry, we are all just "falling with style." God, in his providence and grace, sovereignly orchestrates and superintends events—enabling us to soar not in a power of our own, but in reliance on his Holy Spirit. He is the author of purpose and the power supply. Confidence in him keeps us humble, but also releases us to jump into next generation ministry with abandon. May you experience the joy of free falling in the grace of God, buoyed by his Spirit, as you soar in life and ministry "to infinity and beyond!"

Mission

Let's discover God's mission for our ministries to young people. As we set out from base camp let's stay focused on the summit; our ministry to adolescents and emerging adults based in biblical precedent, and directed toward God's ultimate purpose.

It is imperative that we identify where we are heading and the ultimate goal of ministry to the rising generation. We need to adopt the vision—the *telos*—that will drive the engine of our efforts and inform how we direct our efforts. The *Westminster Shorter Catechism* begins by asking, "What is the chief end of man?"[1] Aristotle begins his *Nichomachean Ethics* by wrestling with the question of whether or not there exists a *telos* that is big enough to direct one's course:

> Every art or applied science and every systematic investigation, and similarly every action and choice, seem to aim at some good; the good, therefore, has been well defined as that which all things aim. But it is clear that there is a difference in the ends at which they aim.... Of medicine the end is health, of shipbuilding, a vessel, of strategy, victory, and of household management, wealth.... Now, if there exists an end in the realm of action which we desire for its own sake, an end which determines all other desires; if, in other words, we do not make all our choices for the sake of something else—for in this way the process will go on infinitely so that our desire would be futile and pointless—then obviously this end will be the good, that is, the highest good. Will not the knowledge of this good, consequently, be very important to our lives? Would it not better equip us, like archers, who have a target to aim at, to hit the proper mark?[2]

Unless we begin with our *telos*—our end-goal, our purpose—in view, we'll miss the target. Without a God-defined destination, we'll find ourselves misguided, off course, and lost in the journey of ministry. Instead, let us take care to establish the direction of our ministry according to God's ends—his ultimate purposes to govern our *praxis*.

So the question remains: "What are God's goals for next-gen ministry?"

They are really no different than his goals for the church. Ministry to the young is a facet of the overarching ministry of the church, and must not to be set apart from it. Otherwise, we run the risk of perpetuating a false dichotomy that already pervades the modern church: the separation of youth ministry from the core ministry of the church. In essence, the church needs to return to its prime calling to the next generation. Some of us need to repent of the disconnected, peripheral, and often independent way in which we have attempted to go about ministry to tweens, teens and twentysomethings.

This approach to youth ministry was inherited from parachurch organizations of the past (and present) that emerged largely in reaction to the failure of the institutional church to reach the next generation.[3] In this vacuum, societies and organizations arose to engage the young people the church was failing to reach, and to pursue the calling of the church to reach the nations. Mainline churches in the West were jettisoning the truth of God (by denying the authority of Scripture and deity of Christ), as well as the mission of God to reach the nations and the next generation. In turn, while the evangelical church has taken up anew the mantle of next-gen ministry, it often has been guilty of running youth ministry on the *periphery* of the church, as opposed to viewing it as *integral* to the life and mission of the church. Therefore, in order to know God's goals for any ministry to young people, we must understand them in light of God's goals for the church; that is, embodying his heart and pursuing his desires for his people.

Passion

God's heart for his people—including emerging generations—is revealed throughout Scripture, as we saw in the previous chapter. The overarching theme of his pursuit of his people is captured in the refrain resounding throughout Scripture (from the Pentateuch to Revelation) and down through the ages: "I will be your God and you will be my people."[4] In redeeming a people to himself, God time and again reveals his heart for the young. God is the great youth pastor, expressing time and again his passionate heart toward the next generation. In tracing God's hand in history we've seen already many stories and examples of God's faithfulness toward the next generation. In these passages we read explicit statements of his heart for the young. The psalmist declares, "One generation shall praise your name to another" (Psa. 145:4); and "The children of your servants will live in your presence; their descendants will be established before you" (Psa. 102:28).

God cares for those who have no parents to love and lead them in his ways; he grafts them into his family and provides those who would care for them. He is "a father to the fatherless, a defender of widows, is God in his holy dwelling. God sets the lonely in families" (Psa. 68:5–6a). We're living in a world of abandoned kids,[5] where parents often are rarely present physically, emotionally, or spiritually. This verse gives hope and serves as a challenge to the church today to be God's instrument in the lives of young people.

The Lord makes it clear that in his economy, children are more than a mere responsibility—they are a blessing. They are not an inconvenience as the culture so often treats them; rather, they are gifts to be treasured, ones to be invested and delighted in (Psa. 127, 128). Acknowledging God's divine fathering of children sets us free to pursue the next generation with confidence and hope knowing that he is the one who builds the house. We can partner in the work of God from a place of rest, rather than trying to raise the next generation without him or for him.[6] After all, God is the one who tenderly and intentionally creates each child. His hand is on his children's lives from beginning to end: "For you created my inmost being, you knit me together in my mother's womb. ... All the days ordained for me were written in your book before one of them came to be" (Psa. 139:13–16). For this reason we can trust God and entrust our children to his care.

God's heart for young people is demonstrated in the affirmation of his covenant love through the prophet Isaiah: "All your sons will be taught by the Lord, and great will be your children's peace" (Isa. 54:13). The covenant-keeping God gives us great hope as we trust his promises to the next generation:

> As for me, this is my covenant with them, says the Lord. My Spirit, who is in you, and my words that I have put in your mouth will not depart from your mouth, or from the mouths of your children, or from the mouths of their descendants from this time on and forever, says the Lord. (Isa. 59:21)

By the same token, God makes it clear that both parents and children stand on their own before God: "Every living soul belongs to me, the father as well as the son—both alike belong to me. The soul who sins is the one who will die" (Ezek. 18:4). Children are not mere extensions of their parents, nor are they inextricably tied to the repentance or rebellion of previous generations. The covenant blessings are not automatic or mechanistic, but relational. God desires relationship with each successive generation and each individual child.

At the close of the Old Testament, God promises: "I will send the prophet Elijah before that great and dreadful day of the Lord comes. He will turn the hearts of the fathers to their children, and the hearts of the children to their fathers" (Mal. 4:5–6a). God's heart for the next generation is the last word of the Old Testament and the first word of the New. It is inextricably tied to the ministry and mission of Christ, the coming Messiah (Luke 1:17).

Jesus is the express image of the Father, the divine Son of God, sent to reveal his heart for the world and accomplish his work. He demonstrates God's heart for children when he said, "Let the little children come to me and do not hinder them, for the kingdom of heaven belongs to such as these" (Matt. 19:14). Jesus gives the strongest of warnings to those who would cause one of his little ones to sin: "It would be better for him to have a large millstone hung around his neck and to be drowned in the depths of the sea" (Matt. 18:6). There is a special place and priority in the heart of God for the young. In the opening chapters of the New Testament church, Peter expresses God's heart for children in his call to the people to repent and be baptized: "The promise is for you and your children and for all who are far off—for all whom the Lord our God will call" (Acts 2:39).

In light of these verses it is clear that God has a special place in his heart for youth. It is incumbent upon the church to conform its heart to his by cultivating a passion for the next generation and pursuing his purposes in their lives.

Purpose

This chapter begins with the question framed by the Westminster Divines: "What is the chief end of man? The chief end of man is to glorify God, and enjoy him forever."[7] God's glory is our good. God's desire from the dawn of time has been that we would live our lives with him and for him. The conclusion of the great doxology found in Romans declares that "from him, and through him, and to him are all things. To him be the glory forever" (Rom. 11:36)!

The key to spiritual formation is helping young people understand that their lives are formed by and found in God. He is the great author of human history, and our lives are wrapped up in his story. This means next-gen ministry is about leading young people to know the author of the story, God the Father. This knowledge is gained by understanding general and special revelation, by embracing the hero of their lives (Jesus), and by the illumination of the Holy Spirit working through the Word.

A Bigger Story

Hiro Nakamura was an average employee of Yamagato Industries, working as a computer programmer, and bored with his life as a single twenty-something in Tokyo, Japan. To escape the monotony, Hiro turned to his love of fantasy and sci-fi. He longed for adventure and felt he was made for more—until one day, he discovered his special powers, teleporting to New York City five weeks into the future. There he spied a comic book at a newsstand, *9th Wonders*, and found that it mirrored (and even predicted) the events of his life—he was living out the storyline. The comic genre he loved became his life. Hiro's quest expanded in twists and turns as audiences eagerly anticipated each episode of the 2006 NBC television show *Heroes*.

Our ministry to young people must acknowledge that students are born with hearts and within a culture that leads them to see themselves as the hero of their own small story. It is no wonder that more and more adolescents and emerging adults are finding their lives empty and pointless—uninspiring and boring, hopelessly frustrating—and themselves as isolated and alone. The answer is to help them see how thrilling and life-giving it is to find their story caught up in a much larger tale; to see themselves both as smaller yet more significant than ever before.

Christian author and scholar J.R.R. Tolkien captures this in the conversation between Bilbo and Gandalf at the close of *The Hobbit*:

> "Then the prophecies of the old songs have turned out to be true, after a fashion!" said Bilbo. "Of course!" said Gandalf. "And why should not they prove true? Surely you

don't disbelieve the prophecies, because you had a hand in bringing them about yourself? You don't really suppose, do you, that all your adventures and escapes were managed by mere luck, just for your sole benefit? You are a very fine person, Mr. Baggins, and I am very fond of you; but you are only quite a little fellow in a wide world after all!"[8]

Rather than being the hero in their own two-dimensional comic book that is read and discarded, young people need to be invited into the great drama of redemption—the grand meta-narrative, the epic novel that God is authoring, except that this is no work of fiction: life is an adventure in which God is the hero, yet we are integral to his plan of redemption. His story is our story. In this light students will find they are "smaller" but "weigh" more, humbled yet infused with significance and purpose.[9]

As Jesus becomes the center of their lives, they begin to walk with him and live for him. Life is realized as a grand adventure—the epic quest of discipleship—looking to Christ to love, lead, and use them to accomplish his work in the world, the extension of his kingdom reign and rule in every heart and over all of life.[10]

It means knowing both what is true and what to do, and thinking God's thoughts after him. In Paul's letter to Timothy we read, "All Scripture is God-breathed and is useful for teaching, rebuking, correcting and training in righteousness, so that the man of God may be thoroughly equipped for every good work" (II Tim. 3:16–17). The writer of Hebrews states: "For the word of God is living and active. Sharper than any double-edged sword, it penetrates even to dividing soul and spirit, joints and marrow; it judges the thoughts and attitudes of the heart" (Heb. 4:12). In his letter to the church in Colossi, Paul lifts up the lordship of Christ over all of life: "He is before all things, and in him all things hold together. And he is the head of the body, the church; he is the beginning and the firstborn from among the dead, so that in everything he might have the supremacy" (Col. 1:17–18).

Integration, in turn, involves growing in a personal, intimate, and vital relationship with Jesus. The great story becomes *my* story, as the truth is mediated and illuminated through a relationship with the Truth personified. The truth becomes my truth, as what is in the head makes its way into the heart. My life is one with Christ's: "For you died, and your life is now hidden with Christ in God" (Col. 3:3). "And God raised us up with Christ and seated us with him in the heavenly realms in Christ Jesus" (Eph. 2:6). Jesus said, "Then you will know the truth, and the truth will set you free" (John 8:32). This is more than propositional knowledge, this is relational knowledge born of intimacy and experience, what the Bible calls "wisdom, " that is, truth internalized and applied.

Transformation is the result. My life progressively takes on the characteristics of Christ as he loves and leads me. My heart's new motivation expresses itself through my will: "To this end I labor, struggling with all his energy, which so powerfully works in me" (Col. 1:29). The sanctifying work of the Holy Spirit works in tandem with my spirit as I strive to become more of whom God created me to be, more of my true self, living a life of repentance, dependence, and abandon.[11] In his letter to the Romans, Paul calls us to lives of transformation:

> Therefore, I urge you, brothers, in view of God's mercy, to offer your bodies as living sacrifices, holy and pleasing to God—this is your spiritual act of worship. Do not conform any longer to the pattern of this world, but be transformed by the renewing of your mind. Then you will be able to test and approve what God's will is—his good, pleasing and perfect will. (Rom. 12:1–2)

What better description of the transformed life of abandon to the Lord, than Paul's words to the Philippian church:

> But whatever was to my profit I now consider loss for the sake of Christ. What is more, I consider everything a loss compared to the surpassing greatness of knowing Christ Jesus my Lord, for whose sake I have lost all things. I consider them rubbish, that I may gain Christ and be found in him, not having a righteousness of my own that comes from the law, but that which is through faith in Christ— the righteousness that comes from God and is by faith. I want to know Christ and the power of his resurrection and the fellowship of sharing in his sufferings, becoming like him in his death, and so, somehow, to attain to the resurrection from the dead. (Phil. 3:7–11)

To Infinity and Beyond: Goals for MissionNext

Only as we are transformed by the work of Christ will we begin to live out his command to "love the Lord your God with all your heart and with all your soul and with all your strength and with all your mind; and love your neighbor as yourself" (Luke 10:27).

These three facets of spiritual formation take place within the context of the formative family of God, his covenant community the church.[12] His people are charged with telling the story, living the story, and inviting others into the story. As such, the church is entrusted with leading each one to individually and corporately pursue the four purposes of the church: celebration, growth, love, and impact. The second chapter of Acts paints a picture of the church living out the purposes for which God intended it:

> They devoted themselves to the apostles' teaching and to the fellowship, to the breaking of bread and to prayer. Everyone was filled with awe, and many wonders and miraculous signs were done by the apostles. All the believers were together and had everything in common. Selling their possessions and goods, they gave to anyone as he had need. Every day they continued to meet together in the temple courts. They broke bread in their homes and ate together with glad and sincere hearts, praising God and enjoying the favor of all the people. And the Lord added to their number daily those who were being saved. (Acts 2:42–47)

Next-gen ministry is at the core of the overarching mission of the church and should therefore focus on leading students into a relationship with Christ, incorporating them into the body of Christ, and equipping them to live with and for Christ. This cannot happen effectively unless next-gen ministry is seen as a prime responsibility and central to the ministry of the church.

Celebration

The early church was marked by a commitment to public worship: "They devoted themselves … to the breaking of bread and to prayer… Every day they continued to meet together in the temple courts… praising God" (Acts 2:42–47). Ministry that is faithful to the Lord's desires for his people will be involved in leading adolescents and emerging adults into a lifestyle of worship, celebrating God's Word and work in all of life. Corporate worship with the people of God will be emphasized and encouraged, as will private worship. Both will embody the perspective that every facet of life is to be lived in worship of God (John 4:23–24; Rom. 11:36).

For example, many churches have a "Youth Sunday" once a month. The young people in the church are given the opportunity to plan the order of service, lead the music, read Scripture, offer testimonies, etc. Other churches endeavor to involve young people in participating in the worship every week—enfolding them and apprenticing them into the leading of corporate worship. Adolescents and emerging adults can be seen playing their instruments as part of the band or ensemble, singing in the choir or music team, running the sound or projection, greeting and seating members, sharing testimonies before the congregation, leading in congregational prayer, collecting the offering, passing out handouts, participating in drama or dance, setting up or taking down the space, employing their creativity and artistry throughout the life of the church, and the list goes on.

Churches ought to encourage and instruct in private worship. Some churches post devotional readings on their website which follow along with the teaching series. Parents encourage their teens to see all of life as worship as they encourage family prayer and scripture reading, and as they spontaneously and naturally reference the Lord and rejoice in him throughout the day. Adults can provide "running commentary" on life for the adolescents around them, pointing out connections and practicing the presence of Christ along the way. As adults model lifestyles of devotion—consistently walking with Jesus in dedicated private times of prayer and reflection—the young people around them will be more likely to imitate and adopt these practices in their own lives.

Growth

In Acts 2 we read that the early church, "devoted themselves to the apostles teaching" (Acts 2:42). Likewise, a commitment to the reliability and authority of Scripture as the inspired Word of God is foundational to a biblical next-gen ministry (Psa. 78:2–6). Students are exposed to faithful and consistent teaching, preaching, and Bible study. Next-gen ministry is particularly concerned with equipping adolescents and emerging adults to interpret and apply God's Word to all of life, taking into account the relevant issues and developmental needs of tweens, teens and twenty-somethings. We must recognize that "change [growth] takes place when the truth is served in the context of relationships"[13] (Josh 1:6–9; Deut. 6:4–9).

Churches and ministry organizations can pursue growth in the lives of their young people by engaging them in a variety of ways. Common to many are weekly small group Bible studies led by spiritually maturing adults who have a love for Christ and young people and have some training and ability at engaging adolescents in wrestling with the Word and applying it to their lives. The key is to ask good questions, to assist emerging adults in probing the scriptures and allowing the scriptures to probe their hearts. The goal is to help young people make connections and integrate their faith and life. As students grow and mature in their faith, adults can apprentice them in leading bible studies with peers or younger children in the church and community. The pastor, campus minister, youth worker or adult leader must take teaching and preaching seriously and strive in prayerful and effective preparation and delivery which pursues language, illustration, and application relatable to the youth in their community.

The power of the one-to-one relationship cannot be overstated. Those in the rising generation need adults who will take them seriously and pursue relationships of purpose in their lives: adults who actually spend time in their world and live life openly before them, while wrestling through the challenges of their lives with biblical wisdom, prayerful concern, and sacrificial service—in turn, celebrating joys and rejoicing in God's faithfulness and provision along the way. Intentional and intensive moments of growth often take place in the unique setting of conferences, camps and retreats. Of course, it is important to model and train young people how to read, interpret and apply the Bible on their own and in the context of community—encouraging them to own and pursue their personal spiritual growth. As young people are engaged in these opportunities consistently through adolescence they will be more likely to carry on these patterns through emerging adulthood and into their adult years.

Love

An atmosphere of godly love and acceptance will pervade biblical next-gen ministry. It will be marked by a sense of community as members of the body of Christ, learning what it is to pursue true fellowship in the Lord: "They devoted themselves to… the fellowship…. All the believers were together and had everything in common…. They broke bread in their homes and ate together with glad and sincere hearts" (Acts 2:42–46). This means that *leadership* sets the tone for authenticity and transparency. Only in a ministry that proclaims and rests in God's grace will students be free to struggle and free to be honest with themselves, each other, and the Lord. In a culture of performance, tweens, teens and twentysomethings have very few relationships with adults who do not have an agenda for them, demand they be "competent," or assume they want or need relationships with adults.[14] Those adults are rare who have no agenda but that they encounter Christ; no goal but God's. Here we find the rule of love propels the reign of love as the community of Christ pursues the cause of Christ.

One youth pastor constantly declares to the kids, "Our job as leaders is to love you! That's it!" Do young people in the church feel loved? Adolescents and emerging adults will learn how to love others more by the way we love them than by being told to do it. Do adults look youth in the eye? Do they smile at young people?

Godly love and acceptance tears down barriers between the generations as the older delights in the younger. Playing together, laughing together, enjoying a meal together in groups and one-on-one; these expressions of fellowship and hospitality mean the world to those in the rising generation—communicating value and creating space for redemptive relationships to be formed and fostered. One minister I know tries to be a catalyst for the formation of spiritual friendships between students as he intentionally and prayerfully arranges clusters of kids with key adults who facilitate regular gatherings: going to the movies, sleeping over at one's house, grabbing a meal together, even serving at a soup kitchen or some other service project together.

What would it look like for adults to put down the cell phone, turn off the computer or TV and stop whatever is occupying and distracting them to attune to the young people in their lives? How might we practice being present by allowing time for casual conversation? Many adults don't know how to talk to kids unless they are formally teaching or following a curriculum. Adults can learn to ask good questions and actively listen. They can seek to find out what a young person is into and join them in it, rather than reinventing alternatives or requiring they leave themselves at the door.

Tweens, teens and twentysomethings need safe places with spiritually maturing adults who will care, counsel and keep confidence (as appropriate). Young people need to learn how to open up their lives to others as they celebrate and are celebrated, even as they share their burdens and learn to carry the burdens of others. Honesty and vulnerability must be modelled and fostered—striving for ministries where adolescents and emerging adults can take off their masks and be authentic before the Lord and each other.

Impact

The early church was a community used by God to make an impact by serving others and seeing others saved: "Selling their possessions and goods, they gave to everyone as he had need... And the Lord added to their number daily those that were being saved" (Acts 2:45–47). A biblical youth ministry exists to impact the world for Christ and his kingdom (not to perpetuate or protect its own kingdom).

The church is called to reach out in the love of Christ and proclaim the gospel to those who have yet to know and embrace Jesus as Lord and Savior.[15]

One campus ministry encourages groups of students to spend their spring and summer holidays serving in mission overseas. Many church youth ministries will take their teens on a weeklong mission trip to another country or domestic community. Getting adolescents to get their hands dirty in making a difference in the lives of others expands their worldview and helps them think outside themselves. It's often in these intensive moments that young people are confronted with their own ugliness and need for repentance and growth, and increased dependence in

Christ. After all, *God is always just as interested in what he wants to do in us as through us.* Exposure to a variety of service and cross-cultural mission opportunities is just as much about the *development* of the young person being apprenticed in ministry as it is about their *deployment* in ministry. Of course, care must be taken to partner with local leaders, churches and ministries that have the capacity and vision for this kind of collaboration, and to whom we defer for direction and coaching in where and how we can guide our youth to relate as learners in helpful and respectful ways that honor the host culture and preserve the integrity of the local ministry dynamic.

One youth group committed to serving every Sunday morning at a women's shelter—providing and serving breakfast, and offering blankets, smiles and listening ears. Another group of students partnered with a sister congregation in their city to provide tutoring for underserved children in the heart of their city. One pastor encouraged the youth in his church to ask the principal of their public high school how they could serve the school. They ended up picking up trash and painting classrooms. The faculty and staff were so affected by this act of service that they invited the church to have an active presence in the life of the school.

Preparation for mission trips and service projects, as well as debriefing become critical opportunities to help adolescents and emerging adults reflect personally and experientially, wrestle with implications and integrate learning into their daily lives. Pastors, parents and ministry leaders will do well to be intentional about creating these opportunities around the events themselves.

What follows in this book is a template to assist in engaging these aspects of spiritual formation within the context of the church. **This book is not a ready-made plan for ministry or a recipe to follow for an effective ministry to emerging generations; rather, it is a philosophy of ministry based on careful theology and sound missiology, a lens through which you can examine and evaluate your own ministry and ministry plans.**

In these ways, next-gen ministry, as a ministry of the church, will be about the Great Commandment (Matt. 28:18–20) and the Great Commission (Matt. 22:36–40)—pursuing God's purposes for his people by engaging adolescents and emerging adults in these facets of spiritual formation.

Questions for Reflection & Discussion

1. Why is it hard for you to embrace your limits? What idols would you need to confess and turn away from?

2. Why do you think it is so prevalent that ministry leaders live out of their own efforts instead of a humble reliance on the Lord's provision?

3. What are ways in which you need to repent of being disconnected and peripheral in your ministry to young people?

4. Evaluate your church's mission and your youth ministry's mission; how are they alike and dislike?

5. How can you, in a conversation with a student, encourage them to be a part of a grander story rather than the lead in their own small story?

To Infinity and Beyond: Goals for MissionNext

Notes

1   Westminster Assembly, "The Shorter Catechism," in *The Westminster Confession of Faith and Catechisms* (Brevard, NC: The Committee for Christian Education and Publications for the Presbyterian Church in America, 1983). The Shorter Catechism was completed by the Westminster Assembly on November 5, 1647.

2   Aristotle, *Nicomachean Ethics*, pp. 3–4.

3   Mark H. Senter, III, *The Coming Revolution in Youth Ministry: And its Radical Impact on the Church* (Wheaton, IL: Victor Books, 1992), p. 142; *When God Shows Up*, p. 212. See also Mark W. Cannister, "Youth Ministry's Historical Context: The Education and Evangelism of Young People" in *Starting Right: Thinking Theologically About Youth Ministry* (Grand Rapids, MI: Zondervan, 2013), p. 87.

4   Leviticus 26:12; Jeremiah 7:23; Ezekiel 36:38; Hebrews 8:10; Revelation 21:3.

5   Chap Clark, *Hurt 2.0: Inside the World of Today's Teenagers* (Grand Rapids, MI: Baker Academic, 2011), p. 43.

6   Schaeffer, *True Spirituality*, p. 59.

7   *Westminster Shorter Catechism*, question 1.

8   J.R.R. Tolkien, *The Hobbit* (London: George Allen and Unwin Ltd., 1937), p. 301.

9   C.S. Lewis, *The Weight of Glory* (New York, NY: Touchstone, 1996), p. 39.

10   Brennan Manning, *Abba's Child, rev. ed.* (Colorado Springs, CO: NavPress, 2002), p. 76.

11   Dallas Willard, *Renovation of the Heart* (Colorado Springs, CO: NavPress, 2002), p. 243.

12   *Ibid.*, p. 233.

13   Larry Crabb, *Inside Out* (Colorado Springs, CO: NavPress, 1988).

14   David Elkind, *Ties That Stress: The New Family Imbalance* (London, England: Harvard University Press, 1994), pp. 118,167. See also Tim Kimmel, *Grace Based Parenting* (Nashville, TN: W. Publishing Group, 2004), p. 213.

15   Rodney Clapp, *A Peculiar People: The Church as Culture in a Post-Christian Society* (Downers Grove, IL: InterVarsity Press, 1996), p. 158.

PART II. NAVIGATING THE LANDSCAPE

ONLY KEN AND JOHN WERE left. The others in their hiking party had gradually dropped out along the way. Their hiking route would take them 4 miles south along the Continental Divide, climbing up to 12, 889 feet above sea level to the peak of Mt. Ida. From there, they planned to head down to Rock Lake—another 2 miles.

Ken Killip loved the outdoors, but had never been here, nor in places this rugged before. John York was familiar with this country and knew the way. Before long they found themselves off the trail and navigating by compass, map and topography. But the difficult terrain and the heavy load began to take their toll on Ken. Before long, lagging behind, he lost sight of John and they were separated by weather. Gonzales recounts, "Because he'd been following York, he had not been checking his topo-graphical map, and that is not a good way to create a reliable mental map. Now his brain was unconsciously trying to form a mental map of the route from a position he didn't really know to a destination he'd never seen before."

As Ken's exhaustion and stress grew, he perceived less and less. "He saw less, heard less, and began to miss important cues from his environ-ment." Without a compass, neglecting his map and failing to take note of the landscape, Ken began climbing a steep slope thinking it was Mt. Ida. He was sure he'd soon be on the other side drinking from the cool fresh water of Rock Lake.

By this time, Ken had been hiking for 12 hours. It was after 5pm and he'd drunk the last of his water about 3 hours before. It was getting dark and cold and the rain was relentless. At last, Ken reached the top. But to his dismay, he was in the wrong place. The lake he expected to see on the other side wasn't there. His bearings were off. The image in his head and the reality of the world around him did not match up. He was disoriented and discouraged. Gonzales notes, "Killip now teetered on the invisible dividing line between two worlds: He was in a state of only minor geographical confusion… but he didn't have the big picture. He knew what was behind him. He did not know what was ahead of him. He could see into his past, but he had lost that vital ability to perceive the world and therefore to see into his own future."[1]

Refusing to believe he was lost, Ken ignored the landscape and forged ahead. Before long he found himself blundering through dense forest in total darkness, while trying to convince himself he wasn't lost. At last, confused and disconnected from the world he knew, Ken felt increasingly anxious and unsettled. Frantically, he tried scrambling up a scree slope to get a better view. In his panic, Ken failed to pay attention to the landscape—he lost his footing and couldn't catch himself. Careening down the slope, he tumbled and landed in a crumpled heap at the bottom. The next days were marked by further disorientation, injury and exposure.

At this point his perspective began to change. His third night in the wild, Ken began to engage his surroundings. Rather than pressing on in misperception, blindly following his own mental map, Ken began to attune to "and even wonder at the world in which he found himself. He had at last begun to model and map his real environment instead of the one he wished for."[2]

On his fifth and final day, a helicopter pilot spied his blue parka hanging on a tree and called in ground rescue to his location. Gonzales recounts his interview with Ken Killip: "'I lost thirty pounds in five days,' Killip told me. His knee injuries required two operations. Today, he still goes into the wilderness, but 'now I carry a survival pack and a map and a compass everywhere.'"[3]

Ken found himself in unfamiliar territory and failed to pay attention to the landscape. As a result he found himself lost, discouraged, exhausted and wounded. His story serves as a reminder for those who would venture into the wilds of ministry among the emerging generation. After establishing base camp and setting our sights on the summit, we must turn our attention to navigating the landscape of adolescence. Wise explorers study the topography before beginning the trek. While on the journey they are continually aware of the environment—endeavoring to adjust and accommodate to their surroundings as they negotiate the terrain. We must do the same.

God and his Word never change; the world constantly does. The rate of change is increasing exponentially. We cannot make assumptions about the experiences of adolescents today—naïvely thinking their journeys are little different from our own. Rather, we are called to enter into the world of teens and twenty-something's as cross-cultural missionaries—seeking to understand and engage as we build bridges of relationship in the gospel.

Questions for Reflection & Discussion

Based on the story of Ken's treacherous hiking experience:
1. How are you (mis)perceiving the world in which you live?

2. What needs to be in your ministry "survival pack?"

3. What protects you from finding yourself in unfamiliar territory and not paying attention to the landscape?

4. What are some practical steps you can take to engage the culture of adolescents and emerging adults? Why don't you take them?

Notes

1 Laurence Gonzales, *Deep Survival: Who Lives, Who Dies, and Why* (New York, NY: W.W. Norton Co., 2004), p.154.
2 *Ibid.*, p. 169.
3 *Ibid.*, p. 170.

CHAPTER 5
"We're Not in Kansas Anymore!"

"WE'RE NOT IN KANSAS ANYMORE, Toto" is the line made famous in the 1939 film, *The Wizard of Oz*—based on the beloved children's novel by L. Frank Baum. Dorothy and her little dog Toto have been swept up in their house by a tornado, only to find themselves deposited in the strange and wonderful land of Oz.

The director captures the viewer's imagination with powerful effect. Up to this point in history, movies had been filmed in black and white. But *The Wizard of Oz* was one of the first films to employ the new color technology. The director, with creative genius, depicted rural Kansas in black and white. Imagine the arresting effect on those original moviegoers as they watched Dorothy awake to the Technicolor world of Oz. From monochrome to living color… The movie experience would never be the same. Dorothy's infamous line had a profound double-meaning: a shift had happened; no one was in Kansas anymore!

The journey of next-gen ministry is marked by transitions. We must tune in to the shifts that have taken place over time in order to better understand where young people are today. We're not in Kansas anymore!

Understanding the history and emergence of both adolescence and recent approaches to next-gen ministry sheds light on present-day circumstances, providing insight for ministry to young people and their families in current contexts. We cannot know where we are or where we are going if we don't know where we have been.[1] Destiny is directly related to history. A praxeological approach to next-gen ministry will strive for a working knowledge of its historical context. This involves examining and understanding the history of society and culture; the local community

"We're Not in Kansas Anymore!"

and individuals within the community; one's denomination and church; and the field of next-gen ministry itself. Jesus authored and entered human history, and God continually directs his people to look back at his hand in history to understand where they are today, to avoid the mistakes of the past, and to celebrate and emulate his work in the lives of those who have gone before.

Adolescence as we know it is a relatively modern phenomenon. In this section we will look at the emergence of adolescence as a distinct period of human development. By examining the history of adolescence from its inception to the present time, we will come to a better understanding of the unique nature and issues of ministry to emerging generations. In turn, we will survey the history of modern youth ministry to glean insight from the past and a platform for future development of ministry to tweens, teens, and twentysomethings.

Families and Farms

Adolescence is an artificial phenomenon as opposed to a natural one. In many ways it is a result of the fall—a social invention, developed by default.[2] Society once had two essential stages of development: childhood and adulthood. Almost universally, across cultures and throughout time, ushering children into adulthood has been the responsibility of the adult community.[3] About 100 years ago, that began to change.

Prior to the industrial revolution, families in many parts of the world were much more involved in life as a singular unit. The nuclear family was the hub of business, education, and the home. For instance, if the father was a farmer, then the family lived in a farmhouse on the property, and parents and children would work the farm and maintain the home together. If the parents owned a shop, then their house was usually in the back of the store, and all of the family members were involved in different aspects of running the business and keeping the home.

In addition, children would be educated and apprenticed within this close community context. These conditions provided tremendous opportunity for children to grow up among loving and nurturing adults who provided models of behavior and attitude, apprenticing young people into maturity and usefulness. Issues of identity, belonging, and purpose were clearly lived out—unquestioned—and reinforced by the monocultural context and tightly knit community.[4] Parents were present in the lives of their children, and clear rights of passage marked the transition from childhood to adulthood. Until about 1900, "adolescence" (such as it was) in the West lasted from about 14½ to 16 years of age—barely two years.

In discussing adolescence, it is helpful to recognize that this developmental period begins in biology and ends in culture. Social scientists mark the beginning of adolescence by calculating the median age of onset of puberty in a given population (typically measuring the onset of menses in the female population, as this tends to be reported most accurately); and in turn, they measure the end of adolescence when the young person is embraced and acknowledged as a fully functioning, interdependent member of the adult community.[5]

From the Farm to the City

The term *adolescere* (literally meaning "to grow up into") was coined by Jean Jacques Rousseau in the 1780s. However, it wasn't until 1904 that Stanley Hall used the term in the way we apply it today.[6] This took place around the turn of the 20th century concurrent to the dawn of the industrial revolution in the West. With mechanization, farming and small businesses gave way to industry and the growth of city centers. Parents began commuting to work in factories, rather than living and working at home.[7] Children were separated from parents and other adults in the community, as the adults went to work. In this milieu, it became necessary for society to provide supervision and education for the young in the absence of parents, which led to the birth of public schools.

Children therefore spent less time with their parents, especially their fathers. They were no longer apprenticed in work, nor educated in the home. They became less involved in intergenerational relationships. They were removed from close contact with adults and less involved with younger children and siblings, finding themselves corralled into age-based grade groupings.

For example, in North America, this was most clearly seen in the development of the public school system—which in turn became a mech-

"We're Not in Kansas Anymore!"

anism for delivering the predominant secular humanism emerging from Darwinism and the Enlightenment. The values and traditions parents held often were undermined rather than reinforced by what was being taught in the schools. Close personal relationships with adults were exchanged for a sea of peers and usually only one supervising adult/teacher. And that relationship was primarily based on academic performance, not personal and character development.

In this era, families were still largely intact (divorce had yet to reach the epidemic proportions seen today). Because of the influence of traditional values, or (as Francis Schaeffer called it) the last of the interest off of North America's founding heritage,[8] mothers were still typically at home. While fathers went to work, and children went off to school, mothers kept the homefront a place of safety, security, and rest. In many ways, they absorbed the stress and strain of both their husband and children.[9]

Adolescence began to emerge as a distinct stage of development. In the absence of parents, and gathered together on school campuses, students began to create their own music, language and styles of dress. These were followed by underlying values, customs, and norms. By 1970, the age of adolescence was extending from around 13 years of age to around 18, lasting five years with the end marked by graduation from high school, the military draft, and, for many, marriage.

From the City to the Web

The more recent technological revolution brought with it further fragmentation of society. The pace of change, the flow of information, and the tools and skills necessary to navigate a technologically advanced world have left stress and strain in their wake. In many parts of the world, activity and entertainment options pull at the fabric of the family. Adult involvement and influence continues to diminish as the media becomes the dominant voice, dividing families even in their homes and cars, where a television, computer, or game system may be found in each room and DVD players and iPods in the car. Smart phones and personal devices used for text messaging, and social networking, further isolate young people from adults, and, in many ways, from each other. Kids are more connected technologically than ever before, and yet relationally they are more isolated and alone in their own disconnected virtual worlds.

In turn, adults have fewer boundaries between work and home. Use of the same technology—mobile devices, telecommuting, and email—allows work to push its way into the home.

Other pressures have further isolated parents from their children. High mobility and a lack of job security (in contrast to earlier generations where a father may have stayed at the same job for his entire career) increases the pressure to perform and often means staying late at the office, working on weekends, or engaging in work-related travel. This is coupled with the mass exodus of mothers from the home in the wakes of the sexual revolution and the women's liberation movement. Even those who aren't pursuing another career often fill their time with social and volunteer obligations. Some even see their homes and parenting as a competitive pursuit, treating their house like a museum and their children like trophies on display or thoroughbreds to be raced and shown for their owner's fame.[10]

Waking Up in Oz

Today, many young people find themselves in a culture of isolation. Adult stress, pursuits, and pleasure may trump a commitment to nurturing the next generation.[11] Parents are tempted to "tax" their families—especially their children—in an effort to make up for the deficit in their own lives, to pay for their careers and leisure. In the 1990s, the term "latch-key kid" was coined in the U.S., as students increasingly found themselves coming home to an empty house while their parents were at work or commuting. One columnist interviewed parents as to the number one trait they longed for in their tweens (nine to 11 year olds). The overwhelming reply was independence.

Independence—during a time when children most need to know they can depend on adults. As a result, many adolescents experience being systemically abandoned on the journey to adulthood. With globalization, this reality has become common around the world. They are on their own to find the "yellow brick road" and follow it to adulthood. Thus, adolescence now begins around age 10 and lasts until the late twenties, even pushing into the early thirties: a 20-year journey to be walked alone. Let's

"We're Not in Kansas Anymore!"

call these formative years of development the "10/30 Window."

TABLE 1. Lengthening of Adolescence[12]

Period	Onset of Adolescence (yrs)	Entry into Adulthood (yrs)	Duration (yrs)
Pre-1900s	14.5	16	1.5
1970	13	18	5
Today	10	30	20

While adolescence is a 20 year journey, it is marked by three distinct phases[13]: early, middle, and late adolescence or emerging adulthood. As parents, pastors, and concerned adults seek to understand and attune to these developmental dynamics, they can become more effective in ministry to the young people in their lives and communities.

TABLE 2. Stages of Adolescence[14]

Stage of Adolescence	Beginning Age (yrs)	Ending Age (yrs)	Approx. Duration (yrs)
Early Adolescence	9–10	14–15	5
Middle Adolescence	14–15	19–21	5
Late Adolescence	19–21	28–30+	10

Early Adolescence

Early adolescence begins now as early as age 10 (though it is still marked by the onset of puberty—which has also moved up to younger years); it ends at approximately 15 years old. For this reason more and more churches are developing "tween" ministries, recognizing that their 10, 11, and 12 year olds no longer fit in a traditional children's ministry model.

Early adolescents, while in transition, are nonetheless more child than adult. During this stage children need to feel safe and secure, highlighting the importance of surrounding early adolescents with an atmosphere of love and acceptance. They desperately need to feel emotionally and physically safe and to sense that they fit in with their peers. How they are treated publicly—especially how well they are received—goes a long way toward reaching this age group.

The question on their hearts is: "Do you like me?" If early adolescents sense that you genuinely delight in them (and they *can* tell), they will feel connected. In fact, this is why it is so important to have a high ratio of mature adult leaders in early adolescent ministry. It takes the sensitivity, patience, and understanding of an adult to come alongside these often awkward and uncomfortable young people.

The nuclear family remains a strong place of security and identity for early adolescents, who are more likely to participate in family-based activities. During this time children will be more likely to engage in parent-child discussions than will their older siblings. This is a good age group to encourage parents to serve as leaders in the ministry. For many, this phase of life is remembered as the most difficult; "today it's so threatening that adult presence and support is a godsend to kids."[15]

Early adolescence is marked by the "I": all he really knows is how he feels and what he wants at the time. In many ways, an early adolescent is like the director *and* the lead in her own production, viewing all others as props and extras. Thirteen year-old Kelly told me, "I know everyone is looking at me the moment I step into the youth room."

Relationships and cognition are marked by concrete thinking versus abstract thought. For this reason, concrete, hands-on activities and play-based opportunities for learning and relationship building are key. As concrete thinkers, this is a prime time to help kids in their acquisition of biblical knowledge, memorization of Scripture, and learning of key terms and definitions. It is a good time to begin teaching kids the forms and patterns of Christian practice and body life, so that, as they progress through adolescence, these patterns will be in place and they can begin to fill in the forms with deeper understanding, personal application and ownership.

This is also a key time for initial transformative religious commitments. The vast majority of Christians recall their conversion experience took place in late childhood or early adolescence. This crucial season of growth in young lives is one the church would do well to approach seriously and intentionally.

Zack was one of those kids leaders loved to death, but who could also be the death of them. Like so many students in his youth ministry, Zack came from a broken home. His mom was bi-polar and his dad was always working (when he wasn't drunk). Zack's mom came to a church looking for financial assistance, and it was then that Zack first encountered the youth minister.

As an early adolescent, Zack was playful and always had a ready smile. As this pastor got to know him, he talked about his dad in glowing terms: how his father had promised to build a canoe with him and how they had plans to go camping and fishing together. The youth minister asked Zack from time to time, "So, how's the canoe coming along?"

"Well, my dad had something come up this weekend, but he said we'd work on it next weekend." As the weeks, months, and years went by, however, the canoe was never finished.

Meanwhile, Zack and his pastor got to know each other. Anytime the church's early adolescent ministry had something going on, he was there. He attached himself to this pastor, and it was sometimes hard and even annoying to manage his constant demand for attention. The youth pastor played the guitar... so sure enough, Zack picked up the guitar. Zack took up soccer when he found out his pastor liked the sport.

As much as this pastor loved the guy, Zack also drove him nuts. He was always the loudest, most obnoxious, and rudest student in the youth group. The leaders frequently had to address his behavior and discipline him. In the guys' small group Bible study—which was already like trying to herd cats—Zack was the one you could count on to distract everyone, taking them on rabbit trails and asking questions that had nothing to do with the passage or with spiritual things at all.

Whenever they spent time together, the pastor tried to steer the conversation towards matters of the heart, but Zack just wanted to kick the soccer ball, play the guitar, or tell funny stories. The minister would offer some spiritual commentary on the movie they had just seen together, and Zack would respond with, "Can I listen to your iPod?" It sometimes made the youth pastor wonder if he was cut out for early adolescent ministry; it just felt like he was getting nowhere.

But when Zack got caught shoplifting, his mom called the youth pastor, and he and Zack talked and prayed about it. When he was caught using pornography, the pastor was the one who walked him through it. Then one day, Zack came up to him after youth group. "Can I play you a song I wrote?"

"Of course—I'd love to hear it!" his pastor responded enthusiastically, while preparing himself for another juvenile song about bodily functions.

To his surprise, the lyrics were a sweet love song to Jesus—a young heart's response of faith and commitment to his Savior.

The pastor cried. It had been three years of walking with Zack. With tears in his eyes, this pastor embraced him, "That was beautiful, man. When did you write that?"

"I dunno… Couple nights ago, I guess. I just wanted you to know I 'did it.'" With that, he jumped up and headed out the door, calling over his shoulder, "Come on! Let's kick the soccer ball!"

That's early adolescence.

Middle Adolescence

The concept of middle adolescence emerged on the scene in the mid-1990s. This stage of adolescence begins around age 14 or 15, and ends around ages 19–21. Middle adolescence is marked by several unique factors, including clusters and layers.

Clusters

During this stage, young people become much more abstract in their thinking. As a result, middle adolescents are able to reflect on their lives and often find themselves increasingly feeling abandoned by the adults and the institutions that once were there for them. In the face of this pain, middle adolescents band together in "Clusters."

Clusters are friendship groups that create a sense of a surrogate family. Clusters are not the "clíques" of yesterday; they are neither as loosely bound nor as permeable as clíques. In fact, while the clíques of the past were often about students advancing up the social ladder or sharing similar interests, Clusters are about finding a place of social safety and a sense of belonging to help them weather the raging storms of adolescence.

This clustering effect takes a variety of forms around the world, sometimes (though not always) within youth sub-cultures or as gangs. Each member's loyalty and commitment to the Cluster is implicit; in turn, members of a Cluster tend to subordinate their personal convictions to the will of the collective whole. Clusters develop their own sense of world view, values, and norms. If students have had and maintain close connections to their family in which strong convictions have been born, they have a much greater chance of connecting with a Cluster of like-minded students. However, even students with a well-developed sense of core convictions will often subordinate their will to the Cluster's will.

A youth minister in Sierra Leone, Africa says, "Kid's are banding together in what they call 'clíque gangs' when there is as one youth put it, 'no other means to survive.'" Another pastor working with the emerging generation in Romania writes, "Our youth form their own surrogate families... they're trying to find a safe place.". A third pastor in Bogota, Colombia expressed his concern over the dark, online communities known as suicide "cultures" in which kids across the city find a sense of belonging—to the point of participating in synchronized suicide.

Therefore, the idea of one cohesive student community is a myth. Youth ministers, parents, churches, and other organizations engaging teens must recognize clustering as the basic building block of mid-adolescent society. While there may be varying manifestations of this reality in communities around the world, it is fast becoming a global issue. Rather than ignoring it or working against this phenomenon, adults must acknowledge and engage Clusters with the gospel.[16]

Some ministries divide students arbitrarily into small groups based on geography, school, age or grade. Instead, in sensitivity to the clustering dynamics of mid-adolescence, ministry leaders might try to accommodate Clusters, allowing for existing affinity groups and making room for students to self-select the smaller groups in which they participate.

In turn, adults need to look for opportunities to connect with Clusters of adolescents. This requires a willingness to risk rejection, coupled with a sensitivity and respect for the individuals in the Cluster. Remember, adults are viewed with suspicion by most middle-adolescents—it will take time, proximity, and perseverance to build trust.

One afternoon the deacon looked out of the office window at the church and saw a group of mid-adolescent boys skateboarding in the parking lot after school. These guys were doing some cool tricks off the steps along the walkway. One of them had a camcorder and they were taking turns recording their stunts. Though not naturally comfortable with teenagers, the deacon felt he should go and meet them. As he walked across the parking lot he overheard their conversation:

- "Dude, Billy is doing some mad !@#$ out of his trictionary!" [Translation: Billy is doing some great tricks from his repertoire.]
- "Hey, Dan. Climb that basketball pole and get a B.E.V. of that kickflip." [Translation: get a birds-eye view from the camera.]
- As the deacon got closer they noticed him approaching and immediately stiffened, as though they knew what was coming:
- "Man, here comes the donut shop." [Translation: here comes the cops.]

"Hey guys" he greeted them. They eyed him with suspicion—waiting to be kicked off the church property. You should have seen their surprise when the deacon asked if could watch them and offered to run the video camera. Dan and the other skaters explained to him that they'd been run off from every other parking lot they tried to skate in.

Over time, other leaders from the church began to spend time with these guys. Some of the church interns were accomplished skaters themselves, and joined in with them while other adults hung out, talked, and watched them skate—cheering for them and bandaging them up when they got hurt. In time, they even started participating in the church's youth ministry activities.

Over the coming months, by God's grace, they all professed faith in Christ. The church even started a new believers' discipleship group with them as a Cluster. Eventually this Cluster started a campus club extension of the youth ministry on their public school campus! The faculty and staff couldn't believe that this former group of "slackers" and "kids at risk" were so radically changed. God invaded their Cluster. The deacon, who crossed the parking lot, couldn't help wondering if they were a bit like Jesus' first rag-tag disciples—a Cluster for Christ.

Most Clusters are not this permeable or open to such transformation. More often than not, Clusters exert a level of power over the members of the group. Because the Cluster tends to dominate each member's individual will, spending time with individuals one-to-one or in gatherings apart from their Cluster is key to deepening personal relationships. In fact, it may come out that some kids do not really feel that safe within their own Cluster—accepting the submersion of themselves as a small price to pay for a place of belonging.

One ministry had been involved in Carrie's life for a few years now. She always kept group members at arm's length—participating up to a point, but resisting going any deeper. At 16 years old, Carrie seemed to finally be opening up and showing a real commitment to the church and sense of deep belonging in the community. She began talking about her Cluster—sharing the drama and moral dilemmas she was facing—and really wondering how God wanted her to respond. But she never brought anyone from her Cluster to youth group or church. One night, her youth pastor finally asked her, "Hey Carrie, why don't you ever invite your friends to come with you?"

She looked him in the eye, and with a conflicted look on her face she replied, "I just can't have them here. You have to understand… This is my safe place." Carrie wasn't yet ready spiritually or developmentally to wade into the complexity of integrating these competing arenas of her life.

Layers

Within the fracturing and compartmentalizing of so many societies around the world, today's adolescents face increasing demands under the numbers of roles and relationships they must navigate. As Chap Clark states in *Hurt*, "Today's mid-adolescents have been forced into living according to the layers that define them."[17] As a result, egocentric abstraction is a mark of the mid-adolescent. According to Clark:

> They have the ability to think and reflect on life and others, but they do not yet have the ability to rise above the immediacy of their experience The pain is so raw, the daunting nature of the task before them so discouraging, and the intense sense of aloneness and vulnerability so palpable that the only way a mid-adolescent can deal with their life experience so far is through egocentric abstraction. To be blunt, a mid-adolescent is at least somewhat aware that their life impacts others even as others impact them, but they don't have the resources or energy to care.[18]

As a result, egocentric abstraction leads the mid-adolescent to develop multiple "selves" that vary according to the role, relationship, or responsibility.[19] To the adults in their world, mid-adolescents may seem to be suffering from a multiple -personality disorder. Mid-adolescents are now able to think abstractly and marshal abstract and complex processes of thinking and logic in order to function within each layer of their lives, but are unable to integrate their thinking across "Layers."

For this reason, mid-adolescents often appear disingenuous and lacking in commitment, when in fact they are genuinely committed and consistent within each layer. Mid-adolescent students need adults in their lives who will patiently walk with them—helping them recognize incongruities, and encouraging them toward integration and integrity. They need adults who will patiently encourage and challenge them to discover and develop their identities and core values, worldviews and convictions, and nudge them along to become the cohesive, whole person they are meant to be in Christ. Consequently, adults must take care not to force mid-adolescents into "superficial or feigned levels of premature commitment and responsibility."[20]

Jason and Laura were the ideal student leaders within the college ministry. Jason was 19 years old and Laura was 18. Both were from well-respected families within the church, and each had come to embrace their faith as their own, expressed in membership in the local church. Jason and Laura were at the center of the student ministry team—a group of young people who demonstrated servant leadership, and worked together to help run the campus ministry.

Though they had been dating for two years, they both had signed purity pledge cards and never showed inappropriate affection—and they made a concerted effort not to use their relationship as an excuse to be exclusive, but invested in other friendships and small groups within the campus ministry and the Christian college they attended. In fact, when not at school, they seemed to always be at church. Jason and Laura were always the first to welcome new students. They could always be counted on to lead worship, volunteer for prayer, head up the next fundraiser, or stay late to help stack chairs. Laura was known for memorizing Scripture, and Jason's Bible knowledge was well beyond his peers. (They even made some of the adults look bad!)

Jason and Laura were the obvious pick to lead the student-led youth conference—a weekend bringing together hundreds of young people from across the city to worship and study God's Word together. In fact, in an effort to challenge teens to take responsibility and step-up their game spiritually, the adult leaders involved had decided that they would only serve as consultants and observers at this retreat, allowing the students themselves to run the event entirely.

Imagine everyone's shock when Jason and Laura were caught sleeping together at that very retreat. Moments after they stepped from the stage in front of hundreds of their peers—leading everyone in songs of praise and prayers of commitment, sharing their testimonies of God's work in their lives—Jason and Laura stole away to have sex together.

Finally exposed, they admitted that this had been going on for quite some time. In fact, it took that exposing event to create the dissonance needed, together with loving adult involvement, to focus their attention on the inconsistency in their lives. Sadly, for every story like Jason and Laura's, there are many more that go undetected and unassumed as adults ignore the Layers in kids lives and see what they want to see, often putting kids at risk themselves by assuming too much and asking too much before kids are developmentally and spiritually ready and resourced.

Late Adolescence

Late adolescence, also known as emerging adulthood, begins anywhere from 19 to 21 years of age and ends as the adolescent transitions into adulthood, around thirty years old. During late adolescence the individual is discovering his true self by experiencing the integration of the many "selves" of early adolescence into one cohesive and consistent whole.

The late adolescent moves from the "Me" ("all I really know is what I want and need in the moment") to the "Me/You" relationship—able to think and act abstractly in relationships with others and the world around them. Now they begin to leave the Clusters of mid-adolescence and move into more traditional cliques, or quasi-permeable social groups. The late adolescent *still* has a limited view, but is able to have it expanded by education and experience.[21]

Community becomes possible in a mutual sense of the word, though late adolescents are still often reticent to connect in genuine community.[22] This means that today's twenty-something needs "foundational teaching, directive adult leadership, and careful theological reflection and mentoring."[23] While the rare exception exists, we must take care not to forget that twenty-somethings are still adolescents. This is the end stage of adolescence, and the adult community plays a critical role in guiding emerging adults into adulthood. It's our job to help them *land* and *launch*: land in the context of interdependent adult relationships firmly rooted in Jesus Christ, and launch with responsibility and full participation into life—engaging God's world and living their lives in line with his kingdom calling.

Bob and Darren meet almost every week for coffee. Bob is in his 40s and Darren is in his 20s. They have journeyed together for the last nine years. Darren was in 11th grade when they first met. Friends brought him to church where Bob attended and volunteered in the youth ministry. Bob recalls what Darren was like back then: "Like most of his peers, Darren was self-absorbed and easily bored. He flitted from girlfriend to girlfriend, and was preoccupied with skateboarding and video games. He viewed everybody and everything as an asset—only valuable as long as they met his own needs for fun or affection."

Though Bob had a family and career of his own, he faithfully served the young people in his church—volunteering a few hours a week in next-gen ministry. At the ministry leader's suggestion, Bob invited Darren to join a small group of teenage guys he led in Bible study on Sunday nights. Even as Darren went on to College, Bob stayed in touch with him and they would get together over breaks.

In fact, Darren began volunteering in the youth ministry alongside Bob. Bob remembers Darren during the college years: "Darren changed majors like he changed girlfriends in High School. Every time we talked, he had a new idea of what he was going to be and do—but he was growing in his relationship with Christ and beginning to serve him with a genuine heart for others. In fact, he even began to serve me and my family: helping me with yard work and projects around the house—even on his breaks from school."

Darren says of Bob: "Yeah, he didn't feel like a youth leader or bible study teacher anymore, even though we still talked about Jesus and the Bible. He just asked me a lot of questions and listened a lot. Come to think of it, his questions really made me think and sometimes challenged me... But I didn't always let him know that! He doesn't know how much I was listening to him and watching him—especially on breaks and stuff when I was around his family and helping around the house. Or when we served together on youth retreats and things."

After graduating from College, Darren got a job in his hometown; that's when he and Bob started meeting together one-on-one each week. As Darren puts it: "Best thing about it is there's no agenda. I don't feel like Bob sees me as his ministry or project or something. I'd say we really are friends now. I mean, Bob shares his life with me and asks me to pray for him."

Bob says, "You could call it a mentoring relationship, but it's growing into more of a mutual friendship as well. Darren asks me questions about my struggles in marriage and parenting. He's definitely his own person now, but I can tell he's analyzing what I'm saying and looking for wisdom and insights from my life and experience as he figures things out. And I'm learning from Darren too. His perspective and feelings about things, and the questions he asks me, can really make me think. And he and his wife are so sweet with my kids."

Darren's parents remain distant and aloof, but in Bob he's found an adult willing to journey with him: Consulting with Darren through dating, engagement and the first years of marriage; encouraging Darren to form a small group Bible study with fellow twentysomethings in the church; praying with him and processing family of origin issues; apprenticing him in ministry; celebrating his triumphs and grieving his disappointments; and just being present on the road to adulthood.

When Darren and his young bride were expecting their first child, Bob and his wife were the first people they told.

Follow the Yellow Brick Road

The yellow brick road led Dorothy and her companions to the Emerald City. It's important for the church to retrace its steps, to find the "yellow brick roads" of the past and learn the various ways we have gotten to where we are today in the world of next-gen ministry. With the emergence of adolescence came the development of much of what constitutes youth ministry today. Since that emergence, ministry practitioners have continually been reacting to both the continuous development of adolescence and culture in the world, and to the successes and blind spots of previous generations' responses.

The first generation of next-gen ministries emerged in response to various social problems present in society. In 1780, a newspaper editor in Gloucester, England noticed a number of young boys causing trouble in his neighborhood as he walked to work each day. Realizing that these boys' families could not afford the private education of the upper classes, Raikes designed a series of literacy classes to be taught out of local homes, using Christian volunteers and the Bible as the textbook.[24] Taking its name from the only working day children had off each week, "Sunday School" spread throughout the UK and North America. Seeing a similar problem among working men in London who had few options in terms of housing and recreation (gambling houses, saloons, and brothels among them), Sir George Williams opened the Young Men's Christian Association (YMCA) in 1840 to give men (and later women) space for Bible study, recreation, and rest from society's pressures. Beginning in the mid-1800s in both Britain and the US, local churches and community governments began to partner together to organize young people against the vices of society.[25] Using almost military pomp, these societies gathered students with colorful banners, oaths, badges and sashes, chants, and conferences to fight for Christian morality in wide and focused (temperance societies, suffrage societies, etc.) ways, sometimes even combining with local Sunday School programs in their endeavors.[26]

Patterns would emerge, however, in this first generation, that are still with us today. Denominations—realizing the effectiveness of Raikes' Sunday School program—began transitioning Sunday Schools in their communities from literacy programs serving the unchurched and underprivileged into the theologically distinct, denominationally resourced entities that still exist today.[27] As YMCAs added additional facilities such as gymnasiums and bowling alleys, rather than being subsumed under increasing church authority as with Sunday Schools, they began to blend into the communities they served, first limiting and then eliminating any explicit Christian focus.[28]

Towards the late 1800s, a second generation of next-gen ministries would emerge. These ministries realized the passion and benefit that organizing young people could produce, but spurned earlier attempts at using such groups for community-building or social justice, in favor of more overtly evangelical approaches. Aided by emerging educational theories that encouraged the raising of children as believers in Christ (rather than evangelizing them as non-believers),[29] and by increases in technology that allowed various ministry practitioners to share ideas with one another, various societies emerged that channeled students' energies into study of doctrine, right living, and a desire to go on mission for Christ. One of these practitioners was Francis Clark, a young pastor who designed "The Society for Christian Endeavor" in 1881. Christian Endeavor was imagined as a society for young people that utilized the uniforms, oaths, and social underpinnings of earlier societies,[30] but led students in evangelistic zeal and spiritual disciplines.[31] As the society grew to millions of students by the turn of the century, Clark created and trained a network of staff members, and published regular newsletters and curricula for local chapters, akin to later parachurch ministries.[32] Around the same time, the Student Volunteer Movement for Foreign Missions attracted thousands of students to its conventions, and produced hundreds of missionaries.[33]

Unlike some earlier programs, these movements tended to focus on older teens and college-age students. As adolescence became more and more a distinct stage of development, ministers from a variety of denominations noted the emergence of theological liberalism, and how ill-equipped churches were to train young people in orthodox Christianity. As a result, the second generation of youth ministry was welcomed (and, as with the first, eventually emulated by denominational bodies along theological lines[34]).

A lot happened in the 50 years following Clark's success—a world war (and the specter of another to come), economic depression, increasing theological liberalism, and mandatory high school in the United States all contributed to the decline of organized societies and transitioned into a third generation of next-gen ministry that would respond to such changes in two very different forms, which in some ways are still with us today.[35]

One form saw the explosion of adolescence coincide with massive leaps forward in technology. Technologies like radio (and later television), combined with a newfound amount of time and money in the hands of teens, led some practitioners to be able to reach hundreds and thousands of youth. For instance, in 1931, Percy Crawford began the "Young People's Church of the Air," a radio ministry directed at young people.[36] Crawford would in 1940 inspire Jack Wyrtzen to also create a radio station, where he would broadcast live open-air preaching in New York. Torrey Johnson would do the same in the Midwest. By 1945, Wyrtzen and Johnson would combine their ministries to form Youth for Christ, a teenage evangelistic crusade ministry (who would ironically hire a young man named Billy Graham as their first staff member).[37] Such ministries would reshape the concept of working with teens to feature skits, shorter sermons, newly composed youth worship songs, and entertainment—all elements of the stereotypical youth program today, and all shaped by the constraints of technology and the evolving felt needs of adolescence.[38]

Conversely, at the same time another form of ministry was emerging—or re-emerging, as the case may be. Likewise influenced by the changes in adolescent culture, the youth societies of the past, with their pomp and heavy focus on morality and discipleship, morphed into more evangelistic endeavors that catered to students investigating faith, originally called "youth fellowships."[39] In 1933 Evelyn McClusky began the Miracle Book Club, a simple Bible study for students at the high school by her home.[40] McClusky's approach, which might be compared to relational evangelism today, caught like wildfire, and like Clark before her, McClusky trained a network of leaders, and disseminated curricula nationwide. The Miracle Book Club would become an incubator for a generation of youth leaders,[41] including Francis and Edith Schaeffer (whose own influential next-gen ministry, L'Abri, would revolutionize the world), and a young pastor named Jim Rayburn. Having been told he was not needed at the very local church that hired him, Rayburn saw the local school as his parish and created Young Life clubs—incorporating the same language, games, entertainment, and accessible Bible studies as large crusade meetings, but in a relational small-group setting. Interestingly, Youth for Christ also set up clubs as a supplement to their crusade emphasis, and by 1960 had refocused their efforts into these local clubs (now called Campus Life) as crusade attendance waned. Still other club ministries would form around extra-curricular affinities, such as the Fellowship of Christian Athletes, founded in 1954.[42]

The success of the club model would transform next-gen ministry as never before. Unlike previous generations of ministry, where denominational bodies would try to reproduce entire programs with their own specific theological bent and national control, the transition into the fourth generation of youth ministry occurred mainly at the local level. Individual churches, wishing to reach their own local schools and teen populations, began to woo club staffers (many of whom were young college students, seminarians, and ministers living on next to nothing) into newly created positions within the local church.[43] This individual would often use this "junior" position within the church as a stepping-stone on the way to becoming a full pastor. Their task would be to reproduce exactly what they were already doing, but with the resources of a specific local church, and with the intent of incorporating teens from the ministry into the local church as they were converted. This birthed the "youth group," the model still in use today in most churches. However, such views would also result in next-gen ministry to be perpetually viewed as an outsider ministry or necessary evil, what Stuart Bond calls a "One-Eared Mickey Mouse"—a ministry that is not completely a para-church entity, but never fully integrated into the full church body.

As the newly minted youth worker became a common position in churches, such practitioners were now cut off from larger organizations which had before provided them with training and resources such as ideas and curricula. New businesses, often run by practitioners themselves, emerged to fill this gap. In 1968 two former Youth for Christ workers, Mike Yaconelli and Wayne Rice, began selling ideas for next-gen ministry out of the trunk of their cars (this became Youth Specialties).[44] Another youth pastor, Tom Schultz, in 1970 began to publish a magazine of similar resources called *Group*. Such companies, and many more, continue to serve next-gen workers at the local level. Today, many Christian colleges and seminaries offer courses on youth ministry, and some offer undergraduate and graduate degrees in youth ministry. A number of diverse organizations and institutions have capitalized on the big business that is the modern youth ministry machine.[45] The mega-church movement has also led to the mega-youth movement, resulting in large and prestigious youth ministries in churches where multiple staff members, interns, and big budgets undergird enormous programmatic enterprises. These ministries are often envied and seen as the ideal. Churches across North America and around the world try to copy these programs and paradigms, often lacking the resources or the contextual criteria for these models to work (see figure 6).

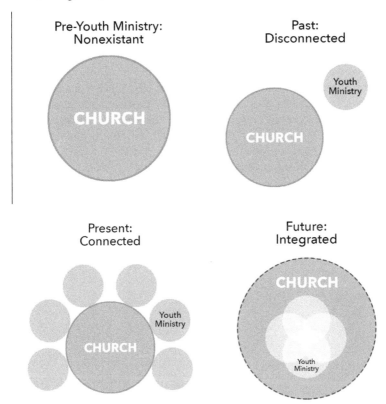

Figure 6: Youth Ministry's Connection to the Church

Thankfully, there are signs that a fifth generation of next-gen ministry is forming. More and more next-gen ministers no longer see their position as a stepping-stone, but as a life-long calling. Many are seminary trained and serve as ordained pastors to youth and their families, sometimes as a part of a larger role as ministers of education. Some ministries are adopting models other than the suburban 'club' model that dominated the 20th century in response to aforementioned changes in adolescence, often to respond to a more diverse and global population. Nonetheless, many church's approaches have not changed over the years, despite the fact that adolescence is changing and evolving. The ways of doing ministry inherited from early para-church models cannot remain the same when these methods are unchecked by Scripture and out of touch with the time, place, and people they purport to serve. By the same token, what is true and good needs to be retained and not simply discarded. A healthy approach to ministry among the 10/30 Window must take into consideration the shifting landscape of adolescence if parents, pastors and churches are to deeply engage and effectively reach each consecutive generation. A gospel-centered, "glocal" approach will see the church through each era and each context, and will attune to the issues tweens, teens and twenty-somethings face today. With that in mind, leaders must continue to survey the landscape of adolescence and emerging adulthood and note the shape of the shifting world around them, and the shifting world inside them.

Questions for Reflection & Discussion

1. How has the church's history of ministry to young people shaped where we are today? What are some best practices we've inherited? How can we continue to build on the past?

2. Reflect on your own experience and your local community. List some of the changes taking place that contribute to the distancing of the older generation from the rising generation.

3. Describe how your church ensures young people feel valued? How might you grow in this area?

4. Can you recall a time when a young person you know was led to live out of "superficial or feigned levels of premature commitment and responsibility" (p. 93)? Describe the tension between calling young people to higher levels of commitment and responsibility on the one hand, and sensitivity and patience with their pace of maturity on the other. Brainstorm ways you and your leadership team might help guide young people though this tension?

Notes

1 John W. Whitehead, *Grasping for the Wind: The Search for Meaning in the Twentieth Century* (Grand Rapids, MI: Zondervan Publishing House, 2001), p. 273.

2 Thomas Hine, *The Rise and Fall of the American Teenager: A New History of the American Adolescent Experience* (New York, NY: Harper Collins, 1999), p. 33.

3 Suzanna Smith, "Family Theory and Multicultural Family Studies," in *Families in Multicultural Perspective*, ed. Bron B. Ingoldsby and Suzanna Smith (New York, NY: Guilford Press, 1995), p. 9.

4 Paul G. Hiebert, *Cultural Anthropology, 2nd ed.* (Grand Rapids, MI: Baker Book House, 1995), pp. 214–218.

5 Ibid., pp. 140–141.

6 Stanley G. Hall, *Youth: Its Education, Regimen, and Hygiene* (New York, NY: Appleton and Co., 1906).

7 Hine, *The Rise and Fall of the American Teenager*, p. 138.

8 Francis Schaeffer, *How Should We Then Live? The Rise and Decline of Western Thought and Culture*, 50th anniversary ed. (Wheaton, IL: Crossway Books, 2005), p. 205.

9 Elkind, *Ties That Stress*, p. 43.

10 David Goetz, *Death by Suburb* (New York, NY: Harper Collins, 2006). Goetz states: "Parenting is today's most competitive sport."

11 David Elkind, *All Grown Up and No Place To Go: Teenagers in Crisis* (Cambridge, MA: Perseus Books, 1998), p. 134.

12 *Source*: Clark, *Hurt 2.0*, pp. 26–29.

13 Thomas P. Gullota, Gerald R. Adams, and Carol A. Markstrom, *The Adolescent Experience*, 4th ed. (San Diego, CA: Academic Press, 2000), pp. 18–19.

14 *Source*: Chap Clark and Dee Clark, *Disconnected: Parenting Teens in a MySpace World* (Grand Rapids, MI: Baker Books, 2007), p. 156.

15 Chap Clark, "Youth in an Age of Delayed Adulthood," *Youthworker* (November/ December 2000): p. 41.

16 Clark, *Hurt 2.0*, pp. 73–86.

17 Ibid., p. 64.

18 Clark and Clark, *Disconnected*, p. 61.

19 S. Harter et al., "The Complexity of the Self in Adolescence," in *Readings on Adolescence and Emerging Adulthood* (Upper Saddle River, NJ: Hall, Prentice, 2002), p. 112.

20 Clark, "Youth in an Age of Delayed Adulthood," p. 41.

21 Craig Dunham and Doug Serven, *TwentySomeone: Finding Yourself in a Decade*

of Transition (Colorado Springs, CO: Waterbrook Press, 2003), p. 98.

22   Ibid., p. 164.

23   Clark, "Youth in an Age of Delayed Adulthood," p. 41.

24   Mark W. Cannister, "Youth Ministry's Historical Context: The Education and Evangelism of Young People," *Starting Right: Thinking Theologically about Youth Ministry* (Grand Rapids, MI: Zondervan, 2001.), p. 78.

25   Mark H. Senter, III, *When God Shows Up: A History of Protestant Youth Ministry in America* (Grand Rapids, MI: Baker, 2012), p. 57.

26   Ibid., p.118.

27   Cannister, p. 79.

28   Senter, p. 112.

29   Cannister, p. 81.

30   Senter, p. 124.

31   Ibid., p. 144.

32   Ibid., p. 159.

33   Justo Gonzales, *The Story of Christianity* (San Francisco, CA: Harper and Row, 1984).

34   Cannister, p. 85.

35   Thomas Bergler, *The Juvenillization of American Christianity* (Grand Rapids, MI: Eerdmans, 2012), p. 212.

36   Youth for Christ International, "History of Youth for Christ," 2003. http://www.yfci.org/yfci/history.php (accessed February 20, 2007).

37   Cannister, p. 88.

38   Bergler, pp. 49–53.

39   Senter, p. 198.

40   Ibid., p. 216.

41   Cannister, p. 87.

42   Senter, pp. 219–226.

43   Senter, p. 249.

44   "The Story of YS." http://www.youthspecialties.com/about/history/ (accessed March 26, 2016).

45   Senter, p. 252.

CHAPTER 6
Shift Happens

In 2008 Karl Fisch, Scott McLeod, and Jeff Brenman uploaded a video to YouTube titled, *Did You Know?* It quickly went viral. The arresting statistics and descriptions of our rapidly changing world led to their video garnering the nickname "Shift Happens."[1] Here are some of the observations they made:

Did You Know?

- If you're one in a million in China... there are 1,300 people just like you.
- China will soon become the #1 English speaking country in the world.
- The 25% of India's population with the highest IQs is GREATER than the total population of the United States. TRANSLATION: India has more honors kids than America has kids.

Did You Know?

- The top 10 in-demand jobs in 2010... did not exist in 2004.
- We are currently preparing students for jobs that don't yet exist... using technologies that haven't been invented... in order to solve problems we don't even know are problems yet.
- The US Department of Labor estimates that today's learner will have 10–14 jobs by the age of 38.

Did You Know?

- 1 out of 8 couples married in the U.S. last year met online.
- Today, the number of text messages sent and received everyday exceeds the total population of the planet.
- It is estimated that 4 exabytes (4.0×10^{19}) of unique informa-

tion will be generated this year. That is more than the previous 5,000 years. The amount of new information is doubling every two years...

- For students starting a 4-year technical degree this means that half of what they learn in their first year of study will be outdated by their third year of study.

Did You Know?

- During the course of this presentation, 67 babies were born in the U.S. 274 babies were born in China. 395 babies were born in India.

So what does it all mean?

Great question—and even more so when we recognize that these statistics are already out of date! We are living in exponential times. The church must wrestle with the realities of a rapidly changing world. Nowhere is this more important than in engaging the next generation. We must take care to navigate the shifting landscape of adolescence on the journey of next-gen ministry.

Understanding the importance of the adolescent cultural context, and focusing on the key characteristics of global youth culture, lead us to see ministry to tweens, teens and twentysomethings as a cross-cultural missional endeavor of the church. Adults who accept the challenge to reach the 10/30 Window must become students of the culture, not only gaining an understanding of the dominant adult culture, but specifically acknowledging and engaging youth culture.[2]

Consensus continues to build on the existence of a global youth culture that is distinct from the dominant adult culture.[3] If the church is to have an impact on the next generation, the adult community of faith must enter and engage the youth culture as cross-cultural missionaries. Next-generation ministry leaders will approach ministry among the 10/30 Window just as we approach global missions: with an eye toward globalization and contextualization, seeking to bridge the generational/cultural gap with the gospel. Missions is both geographic and generational. This is "MissionNext."

What Is Culture?

According to Paul Heibert, culture can be defined as "the integrated system of learned patterns of behavior, ideas, and products characteristic of a society."[4]

Edward T. Hall offers the following characteristics of culture:

> ...anthropologists do agree on three characteristics of culture: it is not innate, but learned; the various facets of culture are interrelated—you touch a culture in one place and everything else is affected; it is shared and in effect defines the boundaries of different groups...there is not one aspect of human life that is not touched and altered by culture. This means personality, how people express themselves (including shows of emotion), the way they think, how they move, how problems are solved. ... However, ...it is frequently the most obvious and taken-for-granted and therefore the least studied aspects of culture that influence behavior in the deepest and most subtle ways.[5]

Bill Romanowski sees culture as a "collection of beliefs, values, and assumptions that makes up a kind of master plan for living and interpreting life."[6] Culture includes the attitudes, values, goals, and practices of a society or people group.

Flip the Iceberg

Cultural expert Ruth VanReken urges leaders to "flip the iceberg." What does she mean? As those who believe in the *Imago Dei*—that all human beings are created in the image of God—then at the most profoundly fundamental, deepest level we share in what is most essential: All of humanity is created, and therefore every person is creative, intelligent, relational, emotional, sexual, physical, familial, worshippers, etc. This gives hope for connection across cultural and generational divisions. It enables people to engage the world of the other and, in turn, to open their hearts to them—to honor, respect, and discover the beauty in each other's culture and generation, and to start from a place of solidarity rather than difference. Such a platform reduces fear and anxiety in the lives of adults who don't know how to engage younger people. This posture communicates welcome and safety to one other; as a result, it actually engenders greater interest in the differences, not as divisions, but as opportunities to know and love adolescents and emerging adults—to love neighbor as oneself.

Visible Part

Ways of life
Laws and customs
Institutions
Methods
Techniques
Rituals
Language

doing

thinking

Norms
Roles
Ideologies
Beliefs
Philosophy

feeling

Values
Tastes
Attitudes
Desires
Assumptions
Expectations
Mythes
Etc.

Hidden Part

Figure 7: The Weaver Cultural Iceberg (Drs. Robert Khols/Gary Weaver)

If the church is going to engage in MissionNext, moving toward the 10/30 Window as God's agent in in shaping the beliefs, values, attitudes, assumptions, and practices of the emerging generation, then it is imperative that adults become students of youth culture.

Culture is not static; it is changing all the time. Leaders must always be engaging the culture to stay abreast of changes and to continually take the unchanging Word to a changing world.

And no culture is changing as fast as the youth culture.

"Welcome to McWorld, May I Take Your Order?"

I've learned to travel light. Between my backpack and my roll-aboard, I can pack enough for up to two weeks abroad. I do have to be pretty mercenary about what I collect along the way. That's why I love my smart phone camera: you can snap a bunch of pictures and they won't take up space in the suitcase.

So among other things, I collect pictures of menu items from McDonald's restaurants around the world. Weird, huh? But I've found it to be a fascinating study in globalization. You can find McDonald's restaurants on every continent and in over 50 countries.

I snapped a picture of the banana pie and the seaweed-seasoned fries in Malaysia (not to mention their seasonally specific menu for Ramadan, which was taking place while I was there). I got a shot of the McOz burger (with beetroot and pineapple) in Australia. I snapped one of the Maharaja Mac off the menu in India (you can get it in vegetarian, chicken or lamb; no beef, because cows are sacred to the Hindus). I grabbed a green tea milkshake to wash down my Shaka Shaka chicken and teriyaki burger in Japan. In the Philippines you can get a McSpaghetti and chase it with a Taro milkshake. I've checked out the Bulgogi Burger (marinated pork) in South Korea, and the Samurai Pork Burger on the menu in Thailand. In Brussels I snapped a pic of the Croquet McDo (a ham and cheese sandwich)—and of course Belgians say they invented "frites" (what McDonald's calls "French fries" every where else in the world). In Greece diners can get the Greek Mac (same as Big Mac) and a Shrimp Burger. In Hungary they order McBuri (hash browns) along with *langos*, a popular Hungarian breakfast food. In Scotland they serve Iron Bru (a Scottish soda), and in England I've seen a mincemeat and custard pie. In Chile, I spied the McPalta (pork and avacado burger). And the list goes on.

What is amazing about McDonald's is how they maintain consistency across town and around the world, while at the same time accommodating and adapting to unique local cultures. This is a picture of *glocalism*—the convergence of the global and the local.[7]

Enrique travels extensively, researching global youth culture and training next-gen ministry leaders around the world. Occasionally he'll show a slideshow featuring pictures he's taken of street art or graffiti. "When asked where they think I took these pictures, common answers are New York, L.A., and Chicago. I love the reaction when I tell them the list includes: Belgium, Chile, Ireland, Japan, Philippines, Mexico, Colombia, Germany, and India, to name a few." So much of the styles and practice of graffiti reveals the radical extent of a youth culture that is no longer bound by nationality or geography, but has become a global phenomenon.

Walt Mueller calls youth culture "the soup the emerging generations swim in every day."[8] Paul Borthwick echoes this when he writes: "Increased secularization, postmodern thinking, and our post-Christian culture have set youth in a culture distinct from that of adults."[9] Globalization and high mobility are two key factors that have joined forces together in creating a growing global youth culture.[10] It is incumbent upon those who would reach the next generation to understand the key characteristics of the global youth culture.

Globalization

Malcom Waters defines globalization as "a social process in which the constraints of geography on social and cultural arrangements recede and in which people become increasingly aware that they are receding."[11] Globalization involves the spread of Western culture and capitalism through "settlement, colonization, and cultural mimesis[12]"[13] (imitation). Tom Sine observes that globalization is "homogenizing us into one huge McWorld macroculture in which every place looks like every other place. Local cultures, which often reflect more of the values of God's kingdom than does the invading global commercial culture, are disappearing at an alarming rate."[14] Nowhere is this homogenization seen as clearly as in the global youth culture. At the same time, it is important to recognize that, beneath the surface, there are deeper cultural currents which are particular to each context.

"Welcome to McWorld, May I Take Your Order?"

Technology and media have continued to shrink the world and break down boundaries between groups, allowing information to flow and giving instant access to ideas, images, music, movies, and fashion that once took years to migrate from one area of the world to the next. Through the Internet and common usage of the English language, communication is expanding in an unprecedented manner among young people around the world. Thanks to digital media and social networking sites like YouTube, Instagram, Twitter, and Facebook, adolescents and emerging adults scattered all over the world are instantly aware of what is happening with others like them everywhere else.

While hiking in the Himalayas, I made my way through a small village of thatched huts, passing a tween boy leading his goat along while talking on his mobile phone.

A teenager showed me YouTube videos on his laptop as we hung out in the Pilipino slum where he lived.

In the past few days, I've gotten Facebook updates from students in Colombia, Japan, Tanzania, France, and Turkey.

Young Brits are learning dance steps from Bollywood. Emerging adults on the Yangzee are learning English through YouTube videos. German youth are quite taken with *anime* from Japan.

Artists like Maya Arulpragasam (stage name: M.I.A.) are sweeping-up awards in film and music across continents. She has roots in Sri Lanka and was raised in London. M.I.A. combines hip-hop, reggae, and South Asian influences in her music. She is an icon of the new breed: kids growing up in a world without borders.

The influence of local cultures and communities is diminishing. Monocultures are disappearing as the emerging generation matures amidst the conflation of cultures. And no one country has the corner on the youth culture market anymore. International marketers are paying attention—they are becoming gurus at cross-cultural "missions" as they effectively capitalize on the export and import of pop culture around the world, captivating the lives of global youth.[15] Where is the church in it all?

Postmodernism

The evangelical church saw success in engaging modernity. Many of our

Shift Happens

youth and university ministry models and methods follow the same linear logic, argumentation, and scientific approach to apologetics and outreach that were effective with previous generations. The Four Spiritual Laws and other modes of evangelism grew from their particular context—the modern era.

But the emerging generation are growing up in an increasingly post-modern era.

Postmodernism rejects much of modernism's approach to understanding life. Assumptions in postmodernism are found on Table 3. Tying these principles together is a radical individualism that both flows from and forges a sense of isolation and disconnection. Postmodernism reinforces how alone today's youth really are.

Some, like Harold Netland in his book *Dissonant Voices*, posit that postmodernity cannot endure. They see it as a worldview without an agenda—simply a rejection of modernity, rather than a stand for something. (Yet it has endured for half a century!)

Others see postmodernity as a *changeling* by its very nature: it is pragmatic, and conforms to the cultural context. For example, it can be found wrapped around social justice or ecology and global warming, while some years ago it centered on political movements (e.g. the student anti-war movement of the 60s, and the anti-globalization efforts of the 80s).

Table 3. Postmodern Assumptions to Engage with the Gospel[16]

Principle	Belief
Rejection of absolute truth	"Truth is relative and up to me to define for myself."
Loss of meta-narrative	"There is no big story to make sense of my own. Meaning and purpose are up to me to create for myself."
Pragmatism	"With no grand story and no governing rules, decisions are made based on what works for me."
Pluralism	"With no story and no truth to bring cohesion, options abound. Life is a smorgasbord of values, beliefs, religions, etc., there for my sampling."

"Welcome to McWorld, May I Take Your Order?"

Deconstruction	"Anyone or anything that tries to make a truth claim is to be eyed with suspicion and reduced to remove its claim on me."
Materialism and Hedonism	"Since it is up to me to forge meaning and purpose in life, I try to satiate myself with the pursuit of things and pleasure. If it feels good, do it."
Rejection of materialistic-scientism (reality is matter and energy—predictable and controllable	"I am sceptical of non-theistic unified truth claims like evolution, but am open to non-deterministic views of reality"
Self is mystical and above plane of material reality Stresses importance of living in the "now"	"I am open to the existence of metaphysical realities and spirituality" "I am action oriented, and appreciate the significance of being present in the moment"

Judy is an emerging adult living in Sydney, Australia. Over a flat white latté she remarks, "I've read parts of the Bible and the Koran. I like some of the Ten Commandments, but I don't agree with others. You're entitled to your own opinion, just don't try to force it on me."

Aaron just returned to London after spending four months in India during a gap year: "It's a very spiritual place. I'm not sure what I believe, but I definitely think there is more to life than getting the job and the girl and gettin' me own place and all."

Mamun left Bangladesh at seventeen to live with his uncle in New York. He describes his rationale: "Bangladesh was little opportunity for me. Here I live in my Uncle's basement and attend university. I will get engineering job and live the American dream."

Daciana is a sixteen-year-old from Ukraine. She confesses, "I like the boys. There's no reason not to, right? I mean, what's point anyway? They use me... I use them. Everyone gets what they want."

A rejection of modernity is not a rejection of the gospel—and adults must take care not to equate the two. Every generation, every culture, and every operant worldview reflects both the beauty of the Creator and the brokenness of the fall. It is important that those who engage younger generations not demonize postmodernism, taking up a reactionary or com-

115

bative stance. Rather, by looking closely at the underlying longings—even the things postmoderns reject—leaders can find opportunities for gospel connections.

For instance, while postmoderns tend to reject absolute truth, they *are* often open to discussing spiritual things and don't see religion as taboo. In turn, the loss of meta-narrative sets up a dissonance in many, as they long for a bigger story to bring cohesion and meaning to their lives. For many young people the drama of redemption is captivating and compelling in a postmodern world.

Any contemporary approach to engaging the emerging generation must address the assumptions of postmodernism. Without commonalities, there are no points of contact for the gospel—and our message is unintelligible. But without pointing out biblical contrasts, syncretism always results. By identifying and engaging worldview beliefs, values and assumptions we can better build bridges for the gospel in our relationships with the young people in our lives. Tim Keller notes:

> "Because of our cultural blinders, we must not only speak to the people over the bridge; we must listen to them as well. We need to listen to what they are saying and take seriously their questions, their objections to what we are sayng, and their hopes and aspirations. More often than not, this interaction with a new culture shows us many things taught in the Bible—things we either missed altogether or thought unimportant, possibly even the way in which we misread the Bible through the lens of our own cultural assumptions."[17]

Imagine what it would be like if the older generation were to take this approach with the rising generation? Not only making the effort to bridge the generation gap in order to speak to them, but also to listen? To take their questions seriously? Inviting young people to voice their objections, and share their hopes and aspirations? What correctives in our biblical understanding might we receive? What truth and beauty might we, in the older generation, discover through the eyes of the young?

Glocality

With globalization comes homogeny; with high mobility comes diversity.

"Welcome to McWorld, May I Take Your Order?"

Today's global youth are growing up in a pluralistic world in both the descriptive and prescriptive senses of the term. While youth used to grow up in fairly closed systems of cultural segregation, now those communities are far more permeable. The world of the emerging generation is characterized by glocality:

- Interracial relationships and marriages
- Multi-ethnic communities
- High mobility and expatriation
- Immigration and the increase in refugees
- Multilingual education
- Ease of travel and increased world tourism
- Multinational business

These combine to forge a new world where young people are growing up amidst an increasingly diverse population.[18] That is why it is important to keep in mind that, beneath the surface of the global youth culture, there are deeper cultural currents that are particularistic in each context. Understanding and engaging local customs, norms, particular cultural beliefs, values, and assumptions must not be neglected by those ministering to young people in each given context. Engaging the global and the local realities of young people today is the work of glocal youth ministry.

Jenna's mother is Anglo and her father is Chinese. She grew-up mostly in Mexico, with a few years in the United States. After graduating from high school she moved from Mexico City to Chicago for university—at the same time her parents were transferred to the Philippines. She's just started dating Ken, a Korean guy who moved to the States when he was fifteen.

When Jenna first showed up at the University of Illinois, she was not included in the diversity group on campus because she was "white." The classmates in her group project started making jokes about Mexican migrant workers, and didn't understand why she was bothered by this. She visited Ken's Korean church and was surprised when people assumed she spoke Korean, taking offense at her lack of "respect." The leader of the campus ministry assumed she was Pilipino since he'd heard that's where her family was. When her small group leader asked her, "So where are you from?" Jenna cringed, and thought for a moment before responding, "How much time do I have to answer?"

Shift Happens

Glocality brings a counterpoint to the global commonalities among those in the emerging generation. It's true that, in many ways, students around the world have more in common with each other than they do with the adults in their own culture. But by the same token, the uniqueness of each local community and each individual must be acknowledged and engaged.

In this blending world, global youth are far more tolerant of diversity and more comfortable with cultural differences. Emerging generations are increasingly free from the moorings of monoculture, leaving young people to define their own identity and choose allegiances for themselves. As a result, pluralism has set in.[19]

Nick lives in Greece with family. "My mother is orthodox and my father is an atheist. I was baptized and confirmed and I go to Mass with my momma."

He shared with his pastor about how he sometimes goes to a Baptist youth group with a friend from school: "The leaders are cool and I like what they say about Jesus."

Nick also has a Muslim friend from school. "We hang out. Ahmed is cool; very serious about what he believes. I've been to the Mosque a couple of times… When I pray I sometimes pray to God, sometimes Jesus and sometimes Allah. There are things I like about each."

Postmodernism and diversity lead to pluralism as young people feel free to choose from amongst religious beliefs, values, and cultures—resulting in their own personal syncretism. The new rule is "there are no rules." The greatest commandment is "thou shalt not judge."[20]

Abandonment

Perhaps the greatest common experience characterizing global youth culture is the issue of systemic adult abandonment. Gerard Kelly describes this alienation when he writes: "The irony of the 'new global youth club' is that the one thing young people most share the world over is this sense of lostness."[21] Counselor William Mahedy recounts seeing students he worked with (as part of a university ministry) exhibit the same symptoms as Vietnam veterans diagnosed with post-traumatic stress disorder. Home has become anything but a place of safety and security; instead it resembles a war zone for so many youth today.[22] While on the surface society looks very youth-centered with more money and resources, activities and entertainment, and material possessions aimed at young people, their overwhelming experience is separation and isolation.[23]

This systemic abandonment has been brewing over time. Chap Clark notes the key movements in the changing adolescent culture in the United States (see Table 4).

Table 4. Emergence of Adolescent Abandonment[26]

Date	Landscape of Adolescence	Generational Engagement
Pre-1940s	Open field	There was one dominant culture and no separate youth culture.
1940s–1950s	Path	Society began giving youth permission for their own path, but adults could walk with them if they wanted to.
Late 1950s–early 1960s	More identifiable road	Generational distinctives were more pronounced. Adults still could walk with youth.
Early 1960s–late 1970s	Well-worn ditch	Youth culture was independent and well established. Adults were no longer invited to enter the ditch.
1980s–1990s	Trench	Youth culture distanced itself, eyeing adults with suspicion. Adults tried to do ministry from the edge.
Today	Underground	Youth live one way with adults and another with their peers. Adults can no longer observe youth culture.

Any time a people group is oppressed, they grab onto each other and run for cover. According to Clark:

> Systemic abandonment has created an environment in which mid-adolescents believe they are truly on their own. As a result, they go underground; they pull away from the adult world. This causes a uniquely ordered society, a world beneath, a world in which rules, expectations, a value system, and even social norms are created to main-

tain an environment in which the middle adolescent can achieve the single most important goal of this stage of life: survival.[24]

Many adults are too busy pursuing their own needs and desires—and nursing their own stress and pain—to turn their attention to youth. David Elkind writes about this postmodern family imbalance:

These many ways of loosening the old constraints of the nuclear family have come about because parents have demanded relief from the stresses of family life that have accumulated in the modern period. Yet the crumbling of these divisions has been detrimental to most children and youth. Growing up is difficult when family rules, boundaries, and values are ambiguous and in flux. In the permeable family, therefore, the needs of parents and adults are better served than the needs of children and youth. This is the new postmodern family imbalance.[25]

This systemic adult abandonment of the young has become a global phenomenon. Families, communities, schools, organizations, institutions, and governments build their own empires on the backs of the young, rather than offering shoulders for the emerging generation to stand on. While it looks different in different pockets and places around the world, the net effect is the same: students are increasingly marginalized, alienated, and even commodified by the adults in their world.

Fumio is 16 and lives in Japan. His day begins at 5:00 a.m. when he gets ready for school. Fumio packs three meals and heads out the door at 5:30 a.m. to catch a train to "cram school." Here he tries to get ahead as much as he can, eats the breakfast he's packed, and catches a train to his regular school. After a full day of school, Fumio jumps a train to cram school again. Here he eats the dinner he packed while trying to pack in more knowledge. Then he rides the train home, walks in his family's apartment at 8 p.m., quickly greets his mother, and heads to his room to do his homework and study (he hasn't seen his father all day—Dad left for work before Fumio left the house and isn't home yet). He falls asleep around midnight, only to wake up and do it all again tomorrow—six days a week.

Japan has consistently ranked at the top of countries with the highest suicide rates in the world. Is it any wonder that this is so, with the intense performance pressure and high level of competition, coupled with a lack of adult nurturing relationships?

While playing soccer not far from their village in Uganda, Akiiki and his friends were abducted by a group of LRA (Lord's Resistence Army) soldiers. Over the following months, Akiiki and his friends would be systematically indoctrinated into the terrorist cult, made to witness atrocities, brainwashed, and forced to participate in brutality. Akiiki doesn't remember what it was like to be known and loved and cared for. He both fears the older soldiers and craves their attention.

Deon knows nothing about his father, except that he left his mother and is now in prison somewhere. His mother was 12 when she had him, but she is too busy working two jobs and taking classes at the local community college to pay much attention to him. They live with his grandmother in Baltimore, Maryland in the U.S. Deon is 14 and has already spent time in juvenile detention. His older half-brother, Lebron, is finally showing some interest in Deon at the urging of his gang.

Carlos works with street kids in Zona 18, Guatemala. Perched on the steep rim around the city's garbage dump, Carlos and his team have set up a school for children and young teens. "These kids have nothing. They are literally living in the dump. Most of them have been abandoned by their parents, or they cannot attend public school because they have to work to earn money for the family by washing windows, or just picking through the trash for food and things to sell. We have 12 year olds raising five year olds here…."

As different as these stories are, one theme remains the same for youth around the globe: they've have been abandoned by the adults in their world.

Some argue that in certain places, or at certain socio-economic levels, young people seem to receive every resource and opportunity from adults. For some, parents and social systems provide educational opportunities, extra-curricular activities, entertainment options, and material possessions. So why is it that upwardly mobile suburban youth share such a kindred connection with urban young people? For example, hip-hop continues to dominate as the most popular genre of music among kids of upper-middle class, white, North American suburbanites. The music and

fashion communicate an underlying sense of marginalization and abandonment, anger and hurt. While geographically separated, kids stand in
solidarity with each other on an experiential-emotional level. Regardless
of external circumstances, both have been deprived of adults who care
deeply for them and are committed to nurturing them. In the end, the
net effect is the same.

Parents can cover their children with every protection (i.e. wipe them
down with hand sanitizer and cover them with helmet, knee pads, and
elbow pads); they can send them to the best schools; they can clothe
them in the latest fashions and buy them the latest game system; they can
equip them with the best computer and handheld device; they can secure
extra tutoring and coaching; they can allow them to live at home rent
and responsibility-free into their twenties; but they can still fail to engage
their hearts and souls, neglecting to intentionally guide and direct them
into adulthood. In and of themselves, these things are not necessarily
inappropriate to offer our children. But intentional parenting involves
resisting the temptation to pat ourselves on the back for all we are providing our kids, while unwittingly engaging in just another subtle form
of abandonment.

In some contexts, adolescent sophistication belies the fact that young
people are deeply lacking in maturity and self-sufficiency, tempting adults
to believe that teenagers don't need them.[27] Adolescents the world over
have learned to distrust adults, believing that they possess an agenda for
the relationship, or regarding adults as those who will repeatedly fail them
(or even use them). As a result, adolescents often seem cold and unre-
sponsive to adult pursuit, which, in turn, reinforces adult rejection of the
young.[28]

What's Next in Cross-Cultural Missions: MissionNext

Young people will only open up to those who have come into their world.[29]
Look at the work of Jesus. Laying aside his rights and privileges, he took
on human flesh and "pitched his tent" among us—identifying with every facet of human culture and experience (John 1:14). The incarnation,
coupled with Christ's commission to "go" (in Matt. 28:19), compel us to
move toward the 10/30 window by entering the world of adolescents and
emerging adults with the good news of the gospel—the people of God

thinking theologically and acting glocally in reaching teens, tweens, and twentysomethings. This is MissionNext.

Contextualization

Christ entered human history in a particular cultural context. His life-style, dress, and teaching reflected the culture he had come to reach. He capitalized on the language, history, customs, and practices of his generation, finding images, symbols, and opportunities for sharing the gospel. He affirmed that which was good, and challenged cultural prac-tices that were out of accord with his Father's will. In both his teaching and lifestyle, Jesus was both deeply culturally embedded and radically counter-cultural. We are called to the same. This is in essence the work of contextualization.[30]

To do so, we are compelled to follow the apostle Paul as he followed Christ, and look to his example in engaging the different people groups of his day. Paul was the prototypical missionary of the early church. Take his ministry in Athens: rather than speaking without knowledge, Paul began by spending time in the Athenian community, observing their culture and absorbing their poetry and philosophy, art and religion. He spent time both in the commercial marketplace and the marketplace of ideas. He approached the people with familiarity and respect. He sought to build a bridge for the gospel by finding points of connection, common themes and language, insights and truths he could affirm, and showing Christ as the ultimate fulfillment of what they lack and long for (Acts 17).

Tim Keller points to Paul's ministry as a model for contextualization: "Paul varies his use of emotion and reason, his vocabulary, his introductions and conclusions, his figures of speech and illustrations, his identification of the audience's con-cerns, hopes, and needs. In every case, he adapts his gospel presentation to his hearers... [The] speeches of Paul give us a strong biblical sense for engaging in careful contex-tualization. They remind us that there is no universal cul-ture-free formulation of the gospel for everyone. The Scrip-tures show numerous instances when the gospel truths are brought out in different orders, argued for using different premises, and applied to hearts in distinctive ways. It is

clear that Paul does not feel an obligation to give the whole
gospel picture to his audience in one sitting. He puts the
pagan Gentiles on a very gradual ramp and works to establish foundational principles without necessarily getting to
the work of Christ right away. And yet, while these gospel
principles are never expressed in the same way to all, it is
clear that they have the same content—the nature of God
as just and loving, the state of our sin and lostness, the reality of Christ's accomplishment of salvation on our behalf,
and the necessity of receiving that salvation by faith and
through grace."[32]

The church has struggled to arrive at a singular working definition
of contextualization; instead, there is a wide spectrum of ideas of what
contextualization looks like. Any conservative, evangelical definition will
include sensitivity to the culture as a tenet that supports fidelity to Scripture.

Christian contextualization can be thought of as the attempt to communicate the person, works, Word, and will
of God in a way that is faithful to God's revelation, especially as put forth in the teachings of Holy Scripture,
and that is meaningful to respondents in their respective
cultural and existential contexts. Contextualization is
both verbal and nonverbal and has to do with theolo-
gizing; Bible translation, interpretation, and application;
incarnational lifestyle; evangelism; Christian instruction;
church planting and growth; church organization; worship
style—indeed with all of those activities involved in carrying out the Great Commission.[33]

Paul Borthwick echoes this definition when he writes: "Youth ministers require the skill of missionaries, taking biblical truths and applying
them to specific cultures. Increased secularization, postmodern thinking,
and our post Christian culture have set youth in a culture distinct from
that of adults."[34]

Tom Sine encourages "mission executives, missiologists, and leaders
in local churches [to] make our best effort to anticipate how the context
in which we do mission work is likely to change in the future—before we

strategize."[35] Too often, ministries and ministers rely on models and programs that once were effective but now are outdated, rather than surveying the constantly changing cultural landscape of adolescence in order to adjust their approach to reaching the next generation. Mission agencies, churches, pastors, and researchers need to comprehend the unique nature of the global youth culture, specific youth sub-cultures, and the interplay with unique local cultures, in an effort to approach the 10/30 Window from a missiological perspective. Missions is not just about reaching other nations, but involves reaching the next generation right next door, and in the very next room. In this way, parents begin to see themselves as cross-cultural missionaries to their own children. Youth pastors, campus ministers and church leaders will see themselves as cross-cultural missionaries called to lead the church in engaging the emerging generation.

Integration

Cross-cultural missions—including generational missions—involve the work of contextualization on one hand and the work of integration on the other. In contextualization, individuals and people groups are engaged by bringing the gospel to bear on their unique identities. Integration refers to the importance of helping those same people come to see their lives as connected to God's people throughout history and around the world.

The church ought to celebrate the wondrous diversity among cultures and individuals, while also living in unity with fellow members of the body of Christ. Just as each individual is made in the image of God and reflects his imprint, so every culture and generation bears the mark of its Maker. There is beauty to behold, and truth to be affirmed, in each—even amidst the brokenness. In other words, authentic *glocal youth ministry* will seek both to infiltrate and integrate: engaging the emerging generation with the gospel and, in the transforming work of the gospel, see them integrated into the church universal, which is the covenant community, the people of God. This sense of identity and citizenship should supersede all other allegiance and bring about both a temporally present experience and an imminent expectation of the gathering of the nations when Christ consummates his kingdom at his coming.[36]

Questions for Reflection & Discussion

1. How do you think young people perceive the culture of your church/ministry?

2. List some of the ways you minister to adolescents and emerging adults (i.e. up-front teaching and preaching, small group discussions, activities and recreation, hospitality, one-to-one conversations, counseling, etc.). How can you engage them on the doing, thinking, and feeling levels of the cultural iceberg (p. 110)?

3. How have you seen the impact of postmodernism in your church and community? List some of the opportunities this presents.

4. What does "systemic adult abandonment of the young" look like in your cultural context? How can your church be a refuge in this culture of abandonment?

5. What counsel might you offer an emerging adult whose parents are overdoing it in terms of protection, activity and coddling?

6. How does your church strive to engage your context? Brainstorm some ways you can grow in the work of contextualization—of seeking to understand and engage the cultural realities of young people today.

Notes

1 http://shifthappens.wikispaces.com/

2 Walt Mueller, *Engaging the Soul of Youth Culture: Bridging Teen Worldviews and Christian Truth* (Downers Grove, IL: InterVarsity Press, 2006), pp. 109–111.

3 Fay Gale and Stephanie Fahey, "Youth In Transiton: The Challenges of Generational Change in Asia," in *The Association of Social Science Research Councils in Association with The Academy of the Social Sciences in Australia* (2005), p. 1.

4 Hiebert, *Cultural Anthropology*, p. 25.

5 Edward T. Hall, *Beyond Culture, 2nd ed.* (New York, NY: Doubleday, 1989), pp. 16–17.

6 Bill Romanowski, *Eyes Wide Open* (Grand Rapids, MI: Brazos, 2001), p. 42.

7 The term 'glocalization' was first popularized by Roland Robertson, *Globalization: Social Theory and Global Culture,* New York, NY: SAGE Publications, 1992.

8 Mueller, *Engaging the Soul of Youth Culture*, p. 113.

9 Paul Borthwick, "Cross-Cultural Outreach: A Missiological Perspective on Youth Ministry" in *Christian Education Journal* 3 (1999): p. 63.

10 *Ibid.*, p. 100.

11 Malcolm Waters, *Globalization* (London: Routledge, 1995), p. 3.

12 *Ibid.*

13 *Ibid.*

14 Tom Sine, *Mustard Seed vs. Mc World: Reinventing Life and Faith for the Future* (Grand Rapids, MI: Baker Books, 1999), p. 229.

15 *Ibid.*, p. 88.

16 Stanley J. Grentz, *A Primer On Postmodernism* (Grand Rapids, MI: Wm. B. Eerdmans Publishing Co., 1996), pp. 39–56, 138, 151.

17 Tim Keller, *Center Church: Doing Balanced, Gospel-Centered Ministry in Your City* (Grand Rapids, MI: Zondervan, 2012).

18 Mueller, *Engaging the Soul of Youth Culture*, pp. 91–93.

19 Harold Netland, *Dissonant Voices: Religious Pluralism and the Question of Truth* (Vancouver, B.C.: Regent College Publishing, 1997), pp. 8–10.

20 Harold Netland, *Encountering Religious Pluralism: The Challenge of Christian Faith and Mission* (Downer's Grove, IL: InterVarsity Press, 2001), pp. 212–215.

21 Gerard Kelly, *Retrofuture* (Downer's Grove, IL: InterVarsity Press, 1999), p. 151.

22 William Mahedy and Janet Bernardi, *A Generation Alone* (Downer's Grove, IL:

Shift Happens

InterVarsity Press, 1994).

23 S.S. Luthar and S.J. Latendresse, "Children of the Affluent: Challenges to Well-Being" in *Current Directions in Psychological Science* 14 (2005): pp. 49–53.

24 Clark, *Hurt 2.0*, p. 54.

25 Elkind, *Ties That Stress*, p. 3.

26 Clark, YFC721.

27 *Ibid.*, p. 12. Elkind cites Yale psychiatrist James Comer who states: "In my view, two massive sets of social and economic changes have occurred along parallel tracks, and they intersect most acutely at the point when young people attempt to make the transition form adolescence to adulthood. ... I see these two tracks as the following: a significant increase in the level and number of skills needed for successful adulthood, and a significant decrease in the ongoing support and guidance offered young people during their growing up years. These two trends have created a serous problem...indeed a crisis."

28 *Ibid.*, p. 167.

29 Borgman, *When Kumbaya Is Not Enough*, p. 32.

30 David J. Hesselgrave, "Contextualization of Theology," in *Evangelical Dictionary of Theology*, ed. Walter A. Elwell (Grand Rapids, MI: Baker Book House, 1984), pp. 271–272.

31 Mueller, *Engaging the Soul of Youth Culture*, pp. 200–213.

32 Keller, *Center Church*, pp. 101–102.

33 David Hesselgrave and Edward Rommen, *Contextualization: Meanings, Methods, and Models*, 2d ed. (Grand Rapids, MI: Baker Book House, 2000), p. 200.

34 Borthwick, "Cross-Cultural Outreach: A Missiological Perspective on Youth Ministry," p. 63.

35 Sine, *Mustard Seed vs.McWorld*, p. 217.

36 Paul-Gordon Chandler, *God's Global Mosaic: What We Can Learn from Christians around the World* (Downer's Grove, IL: InterVarsity, 2000), pp. 127–140.

CHAPTER 7
The Journey Within

CONSISTING OF A 2.4 MILE (3.86 km) swim, a 112 mile (180.25 km) bike and a 26.2 mile (42.195 km) marathon, the Iron Man triathlon is arguably the most grueling race in the world. Without taking a break, competitors must move through each leg of the event in under 17hrs or face disqualification. The race typically starts at 7 a.m. and ends at midnight—one brutally long day. Most people who enter the Iron Man consider it a personal accomplishment to even complete the race.

My friend Larry recently competed in the Iron Man; he said: "It's a race against the others... a race against the clock... but ultimately it is a competition with yourself."

The challenges of the landscape are matched by the obstacles within. Larry explains, "There comes a point in each Iron man's journey, where he has to overcome internal barriers or be overcome."

The demands of the Iron Man triathlon are mental and emotional as much as physical; what observers see on the outside rarely betrays the struggle within.

It is the same for adolescence. As important as it is to understand the broader cultural realities of the emerging generation, we must also be aware of the internal developmental realities of this season of life—the journey within.

Gaining an understanding of key factors of adolescent psychosocial development is vital to informing and shaping any ministry to the emerging generations. Jesus said, "I know my sheep and my sheep know me" (John 10:27). To better know the flock to which we are called, we must know the specific psychosocial developmental dynamics of adolescents.[1]

129

The Journey Within

God is concerned with the whole person throughout his or her entire life experience: "Love the Lord your God with all your heart, soul, mind and strength" (Luke 10:27); "You knit me together in my mother's womb" (Psa. 139:13); "And Jesus grew in wisdom and stature, and in favor with God and men" (Luke 2:52). Understanding how children grow and develop psychologically, physically, emotionally, and socially will help us in bringing the gospel to bear on the various challenges and opportunities each stage of adolescence brings. Such knowledge informs and shapes a our ministry's approach to evangelism, discipleship of tweens, teens and twentysomethings.[2]

Body and Brain

Adolescence is a period of unprecedented growth and development. Young people are subject to growth spurts and gangly features, voices that crack, and hair that appears in new places. It is the age of acne, body odor, and braces. Girls tower over guys (until guys catch-up and pass them!). Boys become men. Girls become women. Welcome to the world of adolescence. The rapid growth and physical changes are matched by equal if not greater internal changes.

Teenagers and emerging adults can behave erratically and be overly emotional. They may act responsible and sophisticated one moment, only to be completely the opposite the next. If sometimes it seems like they are mentally unbalanced, that is because, in one sense, they are: recent brain research—using magnetic resonance imaging (MRI), positron emission tomography (PET), and single-photon emission computerized tomography (PECT)—has allowed scientists an unprecedented window into the workings of the adolescent brain. Through this, researchers have discovered that, while the adolescent brain is the same size as the adult brain, a lot of growth is still taking place.

During adolescence, the brain first goes through a remarkable phase of development that is similar to early childhood. A large number of circuits are stimulated to further connect the brainstem, the limbic brain, and the cortex allowing them to function as one.[3] The neurons that fire most frequently become hardwired into the brain's neural circuitry. For instance, the circuit that manages strong emotional impulses in adolescents is strengthened by the encouragement and modeling of adults to think before speaking or acting. On the other hand, if young people are not held accountable for their impulsivity and attendant words and actions, developing this crucial adult skill will be that much more difficult.

The second process during this period of brain development is known as blossoming and pruning. The various neurological branches in the brain form strong connections when reinforced through experience. The branches that don't fire eventually shrink and whither away. For this reason, experiences during the adolescent years have a great influence over the forming and functioning of the brain. In essence, adolescence brings a unique window of opportunity for the brain to hardwire appropriate circuits through beneficial experiences.

This season of brain development brings great opportunities, but also great challenges. Even as positive experiences aid in wiring the brain in effective ways, so negative experiences can have a profound impact on brain development. "Adverse experiences during the blossoming and pruning periods have a greater negative impact than they might otherwise have, because when bad things happen, the brain is especially vulnerable to them, and can be more easily hurt."[4] Many experts believe this may help explain why victims of childhood and adolescent abuse can suffer from severe emotional problems even into their adult years.

The third process of brain development that takes place during adolescence involves myelination. Myelin is a fatty substance that forms a sheath around the axon—the main cable of the neuron. This protective insulation allows information to travel quickly along the electrical pathways in the brain. Without it, brain signals slow down and degrade, causing a breakdown in communication between parts of the brain and body. The first phase of myelination takes place in infancy. During adolescence, another phase of myelination is taking place. In certain parts of the teen brain, myelination actually increases 100 percent.[5] The circuit regulating emotion is still being myelinated during adolescence, which helps accounts for the erratic emotional responses often seen in teenagers.

Brain development during adolescence directly involves systems related to impulse control, relationships, and communication. The experiences young people have during this period of growth have profound implications for forming and reinforcing the wiring in their brains for years to come.

The Quest

Adolescence is a journey—a quest—that is reminiscent of Frodo's quest to save Middle Earth in Tolkien's classic series of fantasy novels, *The Lord of the Rings*.[6] At one pivotal moment in the story, Frodo finds himself in conversation with the elven queen, Galadriel. As they discuss his quest, she reminds him that "to be a ring bearer is to be alone." While the quest is Frodo's to complete, he is never truly alone. Ever-faithful Samwise Gamgee is always ready to encourage and support Frodo in his quest—not to mention the rest of the fellowship who, even unbeknownst to him, are fighting and sacrificing so that he will succeed.

The journey of adolescence can be pictured as a quest, with certain tasks to accomplish and questions to be answered along the way. In one sense, as with Frodo, the quest is a journey made alone. However, every adolescent needs a "fellowship" comprised of the community that surrounds each student as he or she embarks on and completes the quest. With the support and sacrifice of parents and a web of caring adults, the adolescent ultimately arrives at adulthood embraced and accepted as a fully functioning, interdependent member of the adult community.

Individuation is the concept social scientists use to label the quest of adolescence: the process of becoming an individual, of discovering and embracing one's personhood.[7] Just as any quest involves the completion of set tasks, so it is with the quest for individuation, which involves the tasks of defining and discovering a sense of identity, community, and trajectory.

Three Questions

Who Am I?

Identity refers to the sense of self as a unique individual. Adolescents must come to see themselves as distinct: they are no longer a mere extension of their parents or defined by others. Identity is achieved when adolescents have an internalized picture of who they are—their strengths and weaknesses, their dreams and desires—a sense of place in the world. The key question here is "Who am I?"

Adolescents and emerging adults may "reinvent" themselves or "try on" different identities, often coinciding with the different layers in their lives. This is a season of exploration and discovery—changes in fashion, music, interests, and pursuits give a glimpse of what's going on inside. For this reason, adolescents need adults to help affirm and define who they are. They need guidance in discovering who God made them to be as humans, as children of God, and in their unique personhood. They need the involvement of at least a few caring adults who have a settled sense of their own identity, who can walk with them and model before them what it looks like to be anchored in who you are in the Lord.

There are many voices in the lives of adolescents, each competing for their hearts and minds. The world tells them their identity is in what they have or what they wear or what they do—but the emerging generation longs for something deeper. They are wired for something more.

Where Do I Belong?

Community is the knowledge and experience of belonging. Adolescents must develop a sense of safety in family and community if they are to find a sense of belonging in the world at large. Those who don't have this experience of communal membership during adolescence struggle to feel like they fit anywhere, often becoming adults who still feel like "outsiders", forever carrying around a sense of rootlessness and restlessness in the background of their lives. The key question here is "Where do I belong?"

Adolescents and emerging adults are looking for places to belong. Partying and binge drinking are often more about "community" than they are about rebellion or addiction. The incessant need to be constantly connected through social media, and texting often comes from this underlying impulse. For some, sexual relationships and experimentation temporarily satiate this deeper hunger.

For this reason, the family needs to be a place of safety and security—of constant love and support and acceptance. In turn, adolescents need personal relationships with other adults besides just their parents—adults who value and respect them, and who include them as part of their lives.

133

The Journey Within

Do I Matter?

Trajectory or autonomy refers to a sense of personal power and purpose. Adolescents must develop an internal "locus of control." No longer are their lives dominated by external control (i.e., parents). Instead, adolescents begin to discover their own voice in the world. This is achieved as they take charge of their lives, learn to make significant decisions, assume responsibility for consequences, and experience a sense of ownership for their lives and destiny. The key question here is "Do I matter?"

Today there seems to be little emphasis on guiding young people into discovering their sense of calling—their unique "voice". Most students move through the machine of society and culture herded along like cattle. Every adult in their lives—if there are any—has an agenda for them. Parents want their kids to be comfortable, respectable and financially well to do. There is little challenge calling adolescents and emerging adults to risk and live lives of service by making a contribution in the world. Young people are growing up the world over with no concept of a bigger picture—no sense that their story is some how connected to a bigger story of which they are privileged to play a part.

Parents, ministry leaders, and adults in the church must be honest about the default goals we have for the rising generation. How have we acquiesced to the culture and baptized our worldly goals with spirituality? Does Jesus become the way for our youth to get good grades? Get good jobs? Find a husbands or wives? And what kind of lives are we living before the young people in our midst?

The emerging generation needs examples of adults who are living their lives in radical abandon to Christ's kingdom call—adults who have discovered their calling and invite young people to discover theirs.

Strength for the Quest

Attachment describes the adolescent's experience of connection and support.[8] Measured by communication, closeness, and trust, primarily within the family system, attachment also extends to the wider network of adults surrounding each child.[9]

A sense of family safety and security are critical for young people to develop the internal resources and strength for the quest of adolescence. Is the home relatively neat, clean, and orderly? Is family life predictable and routine? Are there boundaries of protection from intrusions on family time, priorities and space? Are emotional unrest and relational conflict characteristics of the home, or is the environment peaceful and loving?

The answers to these questions set the stage for the development of attachment between adolescents and the adults in their world. While adolescence is a quest that each youth must make alone, they can only do so from a solid foundation of relationships, which will provide the confidence and courage needed for the journey. No single relationship is as important as the adolescent's relationship with his/her parents.[10]

Strength from Mom

During childhood—from the womb until about 10 years old—the child's mother plays the dominant role in his/her life.[11] As a dependent, a child relies on his/her mother for nurture, safety, and security. The father is not absent in influence, nor exempt from it: his role during childhood is to encourage and support his wife in her role as nurturer. In turn, he too must relate to his children with tenderness and care. However, it is the mother who embodies and symbolizes the meeting of a child's needs for safety, security, and nurture. By around 10 years of age, this begins to change.

Strength from Dad

As children enter adolescence, they move from a stage of dependence to one in which they increasingly assert their independence. For this reason, their mother, who represented the childhood era, is now seen as someone to distance and distinguish themselves from.[12] Mothers often report feeling rejected by their early adolescent children, confused by the loss of closeness and conversation they had shared during the early school years. Early adolescents relate in unpredictable ways, sometimes reverting to the childhood role with their mothers when feeling overwhelmed or under nurtured. But a shift in attachment is underway. The father, who symbolizes adulthood, becomes the prime object of attachment as the adolescent embarks on the journey from dependence to independence.[13]

Young people are naturally wired to attach to their fathers as their safety net. The safety, security, and identity that were provided externally in childhood by their mothers must become internalized. The father's role is to provide external recognition, support, and encouragement in this task. Fathers function as scaffolding around a building under construction. The scaffolding offers some support and a platform for work to be done on the building, but the building stands or falls on its own foundation. It is imperative that fathers be present and actively involved in the lives of their adolescents.[14]

Fathers need to understand that their role, while different than it was during the childhood years, is extremely valuable to their child, and even critical to their development.[15] The voice of one's father—celebrating, supporting, cheering, and encouraging—is the most powerful earthly voice in defining who a person is. Dads must be there to offer guidance when needed and/or sought out. They must set boundaries as broadly as possible for their adolescents, gradually increasing freedom as they get older. In turn, fathers must hold their adolescents to well defined and appropriate consequences, neither constantly bailing them out nor abandoning them.

In essence, this father-adolescent relationship becomes the defining relationship of adolescence, exemplifying adulthood and encouraging young people to do the same. According to Clark, "A person's biological dad has more impact for positive or negative sense of self entering and through adulthood, than anyone else."[16]

Where's Dad?

Where are most fathers when their children are in the 10/30 Window years? Men tend to face the greatest career demands around mid-life. The stress and demands of their jobs and the burden of their mounting responsibilities, together with the realization of failed dreams and missed opportunities, siphon their energy and availability. Sadly, due to rampant divorce and broken homes, many fathers aren't present in the home physically, let alone emotionally.

The father of an adolescent girl finds she's not his "little princess" any more. The father of an adolescent boy finds his son doesn't want him to be "coach" any more. Conversations tend to revolve around grades or discipline. Anger or absence often characterize a father's relationship with his children. Fathers try to convince themselves that their tweens, teens, and twentysomethings don't want a relationship with them anyway; that they're too busy with activities, work, and friends. However, research confirms that adolescents and emerging adults long for a real relationship with their parents.[17]

In his book *To Own a Dragon*, Donald Miller shares his musings on growing up without a father:

> I began to wonder if those of us without dads aren't making mistakes in our lives we wouldn't make if we had a father to guide us. I wondered if there isn't a better paradigm for our existence—a way of being me, a way each of us could truly embrace if it were instilled in us by a man who spoke with altruism and authority. I wondered if people who grow up with great fathers don't walk around with a subconscious sense they are wanted on this planet, that they belong, and the world needs them. And I wondered this: Is there practical information we need to know about work, women, decisions, authority, leadership, marriage, and family that we would have learned if there were a guide around to help us navigate our journey? I wondered if some of the confusing emotions I was feeling weren't a kind of suspended adolescence from which the presence of an older man might have delivered me.[18]

Parents, and fathers in particular, must develop healthy attachments with their sons and daughters in the quest of adolescence. When researchers study adolescent attachment, they give particular attention to the child's perception of the relationship. Results show that the adult's perception of attachment has little impact on the child's growth and sense of identity through the teen years and beyond. However, the child's perception of the relationship makes all the difference.[19] This is a key principle to keep in mind: how young people feel about the relationship is what matters most.

All of these factors of attachment serve to strengthen children for the adolescent quest. However, it will take more than their mothers and fathers. The adult community surrounding each child has a huge impact on his or her ability to successfully navigate the adolescent journey.

The Journey Within

Strength from the Community

Research demonstrates that young people do best when surrounded by an adult community as they journey through adolescence.[20] Convergence and congruence are the key.[21] In other words, a group of adults share in a commitment to investing in the next generation's convergence. This commitment must extend in their message and purpose: harmony, agreement, and a sense of congruence. Adolescents need to be surrounded by an adult community that is committed to them and committed to the same message. In other words, young people need a community of adults in their lives all saying the same thing. Unfortunately, this is rarely the case.

In many communities, parents are often physically, if not emotionally, absent. Students are over-scheduled with school and activities keeping them away from home.[22] Even in the home, parents and children rarely spend time together, let alone eat meals together.

As a result, the adults that impact many adolescents' lives are teachers, coaches, or activity leaders of one kind or another. The ratio of students to adults in these contexts is typically too high for close, personal relationships to develop. Tragically, the dominant basis for these relationships is behavioral measurement: in a time of life when students need incredible support, encouragement, and a sense of unconditional love, they discover that almost every relationship they have with an adult is based on personal performance. The quest of adolescence is already riddled with stress and strain, with adults too often the worst contributors—diametrically opposed to the role they were meant to play.

In times past, youth have been seen as a society's greatest treasure and a resource to be invested in, nurtured, and protected. Today, adult abandonment is what marks their journey into adulthood. But with no adults there to cheer them on and catch them when they fall, the journey becomes too hard to take and too unclear to see. No wonder adolescence is lengthening. Young people are facing greater and greater demands with less and less resources to meet them, and yet are supposed to become adults without adults to show them the way.

Jump in the Pool!

Jump in the Pool!

Imagine if a father were to take his daughter down to a lake to teach her to swim. As they stand on the side of the lake, he explains, "Now honey, Daddy is going to teach you to swim. Are you ready?! Okay!" Now imagine him pushing her into the lake with no floatation and no instruction, as he turns and walks away. "You're on your own, sweetie. Figure it out. Let me know when you reach the other side." Ridiculous, right? At best she'll tread water; worst case, she'll drown.

No, instead he must get into the water with her. He can help her get acclimated, and encourage her to begin to put her face in the water. He then teaches her to stretch out in the water and begin kicking and taking strokes. Before long she is able to swim while he holds on to her. Then he takes away one hand, then the other. In time she is able to swim farther and farther away from him. Eventually, he finds himself standing on the shore, cheering her on as she swims to the other side.

Why is the journey of adolescence taking longer and longer? Because there are no adults in the pool. Kids around the world are being shoved into adolescence at an early age with no one to coach them and show them how to be adults. Its taking longer and longer to swim from childhood to adulthood, because young people are treading water and drowning along the way. There's no more important time for the church to jump in!

The Church as Safety Net

Chap Clark's description of the "tightrope of adolescence" illustrates well the adolescent quest as described in this chapter (Figure 6). The common path of human development involves leaving the safety, security, and dependence of childhood marked by mother attachment, initiating the onset of adolescence beginning at 10 to 12 years. From this point on, the youth must negotiate the precarious journey of adolescence—and do so alone. It is a journey of independence marked by father attachment. While mother embodied the dependence and nurture of childhood, father embodies what it means to be an adult. However, every father has limitations and experiences failure and brokenness. Both mother and father, together with extended family and the broader adult community,

139

The Journey Within

are needed to provide a safety net of support, guidance, and encouragement for adolescents as they make their way to adulthood. The tightrope has been negotiated successfully when the adolescent emerges as a fully integrated, interdependent member of the adult community. The church can be that safety net as we usher young people across the tightrope and into adulthood within the family of faith.

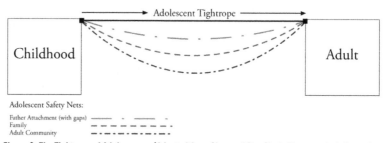

Figure 8: The Tightrope of Adolescence (Adapted from Chap and Dee Clark, Disconnected: Parenting Teens in a MySpace World, [Grand Rapids: MI: Baker Books, 2007], pp. 103-120).

Three Needs

Beyond basic tangible needs like food, clothing, and shelter, we can identify three *intangibles* every young person needs from the adults in their world in order to strengthen and equip them as they negotiate the quest of adolescence: good communication, a sense of closeness, and mutual trust in their relationships with parents and significant adults in their lives.

Communication

One of the chief complaints I hear from adults around the world is: "Young people never talk to me." Ironically, one of the main complaints I hear from young people is, "Adults don't understand me." Communication across generational/cultural lines isn't always easy, and it is certainly a two-way street. But it is incumbent upon the older generations to own the burden of responsibility in pursuing the younger, and to invite and encourage ongoing, healthy communication between parent and child, adult and youth.

140

An adolescent experiences good communication when parents and adults demonstrate that they are truly listening by being attentive, focused, and responsive. Asking good questions is key. The best questions are those that are: open-ended; clarifying; following up on answers; and demonstrating interest rather than interrogation. Adolescents can tell when a parent or adult takes active interest in their lives. Don't wait to be approached by young people—take the lead and beat them to it.[23]

Unfortunately, most parents' (especially fathers') conversations with their kids revolve around grades and discipline. Coaches are only interested in a young person's role on the team. Teachers rarely engage with students apart from their classroom behavior or curricular instruction. Ministry leaders are used to one-way forms of declarative communication (like preaching sermons), and when relating to young people they often drive the agenda of a Bible study or conversation by asking loaded or leading questions.

In contrast, parents and adults must take care not to treat those within the 10/30 Window as one-dimensional beings, neglecting to care about the whole person. Instead, young people need adults who take active interest in the multiple dimensions of their lives. It's up to adults to model good communication in their interpersonal relationships, so that adolescents and emerging adults will have examples to follow and environments which foster healthy communication skills. This requires that adults make an effort to be available to the young people in their lives. In fact, tweens, teens and twentysomethings need adults who will pursue them—taking the initiative by inviting and engaging them in friendly and meaningful dialogue. This kind of communication is foundational to meeting the needs of closeness and trust.

Closeness

As I survey young people around the world, one issue that constantly surfaces is a longing for uninterrupted, unstructured time with their parents (especially their dads). This seems contrary to a common perception of adolescence: that students want to distance themselves from parents and other adults. All people are wired for close personal relationships, especially within the parent-child bond. Attachment with parents, especially fathers—as has already been discussed—is key during adolescence.

The Journey Within

Because so many fathers are absent (or even abusive), other adult relationships become even more vital. This relational safety net provides strength and security a young person can lean on, and solid adult relationships they can launch from into adulthood themselves.

Adolescents perceive a close relationship when they experience a level of intimacy with their parents. This is exemplified by an experience of freedom, respect, and support when sharing their lives with the adults closest to them. Closeness is developed through shared activity, shared time, and shared stories. It is also fostered in celebrating triumphs and joys, grieving losses, and keeping confidences together. When parents and caring adults demonstrate a healthy level of transparency and authenticity, young people respond in kind. The key is to recognize that it is the adolescent's perception of the relationship that matters most. The parent or adult needs to attune to the young person—making an effort to see the relationship from his perspective and build a sense of closeness.

Trust

As described before, adolescence can be pictured as a construction project, with adult relationships as a scaffolding to provide support and serve as a sort of exoskeleton until the building can stand on its own. In the same way, adolescents need trusting relationships with parents and other adults in their world. These adults serve as needed support for young people as they become the men and women God made them to be.

Adolescents and emerging adults need to know that they can trust themselves and others. This trust is developed through consistency in their relationships with parents and other trustworthy adults. As they experience faithful adults whom they can count on, young people learn to trust others—and ultimately God.

They also need to learn to trust themselves. Young people are strengthened in their sense of self worth, competence, and personal agency when adults demonstrate trust in them. This gives them the ability to trust both others and themselves—equally vital to assuming adult roles and responsibilities. Of course, this means that adults must be prepared for young people to disappoint them and even to fail. Adults must assume a cost in these relationships. Likewise, adults need to create pathways for adolescents to turn from their sin, be forgiven, make restitution, and be restored to trust again.[24]

Three Gifts

"Children are an inheritance in the Lord." The emerging generations are more than a responsibility, they are a blessing. It is both the joy and the privilege of adults to do more than meet the needs of the young people in their midst; they must cherish and bless them as well. There are three important gifts to be passed from one generation to the next: Celebrating young people, grieving with them, and offering them the gift of repentance.

Celebrate

Adolescents need adults who will be their "biggest fans." In a world that is challenging and discouraging—where young people have little connection to genuinely caring adults—parents and other adults in the congregation have a wonderful opportunity to send a different message to the tweens, teens, and twentysomethings in their midst. Adolescents and emerging adults need to know that they are delighted in and enjoyed. Each one needs to be known and celebrated by a few key adults who love them in a unique and personal way.

This will mean being available and intentional—it will not happen by accident, nor without forethought. It takes intentionality and planning to spend time with young people. Running errands, grabbing coffee, sharing a meal, watching a ball game, working on a project, taking time to have a conversation before or after a church event, etc.—these are just a few examples of the ways adults can pursue adolescents and demonstrate that they are worth their time.

As kids get older and move into adolescence and emerging adulthood, the game changes. No longer can adults dictate the terms or times of the relationship. During adolescence, adults have to be willing to meet middle and late adolescents on their terms, and to be ready to respond when they are available. That calls for sacrifice: staying up late, turning off the computer or TV, or canceling an appointment. Adults must be prepared to make these kinds of accommodations in order to communicate value and priority of the young people in their lives. Learning to listen—and pursuing other forms of good communication—helps tweens, teens and twentysomethings see how much they are valued and enjoyed.

Surprise and delight the young people you are called to invest in. When was the last time you cancelled an appointment to spend time with your son? When was the last time you planned something special (and it needn't cost money) for your daughter? Introduce adolescents and emerging adults to the things you are interested in, but also be willing to discover their interests and join in them.

My father went to the U.S. Naval Academy where he lettered in fencing. As a young man growing up in Australia, my dad introduced me to fencing, but I took an interest in soccer. My dad had never played soccer before and knew nothing about the sport; but because of my interest, he not only came to most every game, he also read books on soccer, learned the rules, and even became a linesman—and later chaplain for the league—and served as my teams manager, just so he could be involved with me. He celebrated my uniqueness, my passions, my gifts and abilities, and so helped me to enjoy the person God had made me to be. I didn't have to be him. That continues to speak volumes to me about how my Father in heaven sees me as his cherished and valued son.

Often parents (in particular, but other adults as well) think that giving "presents"—in the form of material possessions or opportunities and activities—is the way to show young people that they are celebrated and loved. But more than these tangible presents is the gift of *presence*. Truly being *with* young people, in their lives and in the moment, is a powerful message of godly love and acceptance, especially in a world that tends to view people in a mercenary and mechanistic way. It's too often easier to give things than to give of ourselves—but relationships of love and support are what those in the rising generation are starving for. Celebrate his/her gifts, accomplishments, joys and character. Learn his/her "love language" (time, touch, gifts, words, service).

Grieve

Those in the emerging generation need adults who are willing to enter into their pain—and not to "fix it" or minimize it, but to honor their hurts and stand in solidarity with them in the brokenness of this world. That means taking the fall seriously and realizing that it is much more radical than we often perceive or want to recognize. Each generation bears its own burdens and pain. There is something powerful and validating to having older saints care about the hurt of younger ones. Adults can wipe the tears of the younger generation. That means adults will need to be in touch with their own pain.

II Corinthians 1 says, "We comfort others with the comfort we ourselves have received from God." In other words, you can't comfort another until you have been comforted; you can't be comforted unless you have been in touch with your own pain and turned to the Lord for his healing touch. Those in the church need to be careful not to slap a verse on the pain of another or "heal their wounds lightly" speaking "peace, peace when there is no peace" (Jer. 6:14). Dan is a Christian therapist who has counseled many youth and families. He once said, "As adults, we want to protect kids from pain. But what makes all the difference in people's lives is not how much pain they avoid, but how much support they receive through difficulty."

This also translates into allowing adolescents and emerging adults to wrestle with their faith during these important years. A lot of parents and ministry leaders get anxious when young people begin to question matters of faith and wrestle with their beliefs. Often, adolescents are silenced and not given permission to ask questions; instead, many parents and even church traditions place a premium on rote memorization and the transfer of information—showing more concern with giving young people the "right" answers than in asking good questions that help youth wrestle with and appropriate their faith as their own. For example, recent research in the U.S. has focused on the high numbers of churched youth who drop out of church attendance when they go off to college. A high correlation was found suggesting that students who were allowed to wrestle with their faith while in high school were much more likely to maintain church attendance and spiritual practices when they went off to college—while those that did not (or could not) tended to drop out of church during the college years.[25]

Repent

Michael is a therapist who counsels many youth and families. He shared that often when he is working with a struggling teen, he will also meet with the parent separately. "Sometimes I ask the father, 'Tell me what it's like when you have to apologize to your son?' And the way they answer speaks volumes about the dynamic in their relationship. If the father says something like, 'What do you mean? Apologize to my son? He's the problem. He's the one who needs to apologize to me.' That's an indicator that the father is unaware and unrepentant, and doesn't own his part in the problems of the family system and the struggles in his son's life."

Too often we think that, in order for young people to grow into repentant adults, we must give them lots of opportunities to repent to us. But actually, the way emerging adults learn to be repentant adults is by having adults in their lives who model repentance and are who willing to repent with them. No parent or ministry leader or caring adult can be perfect, but by God's grace we *can* be genuinely sorry and seek to change. That means offering a real apology, not tacking a "but" onto the end and then focusing on the adolescent's failure—that's not a real apology, but a ploy. Adults have to own their sin first in order for the young people in their lives to learn to own and acknowledge theirs.

Though parents will make mistakes and hurt their sons and daughters, owning their faults and failures and demonstrating repentance by apologizing, asking for forgiveness, and making restitution turns painful moments into times of healing and drawing near. Such actions do not push children away, as some might surmise, but bring them closer. In addition, the way fathers extend grace and forgiveness to their children communicates and fosters closeness in a powerful way.[26]

When my kids were younger I would read a book to them titled, *Anyway and Always*. The book chronicles God's covenant love down through redemptive history, concluding each chapter with God telling his people that in spite of their sin and rebellion, he loves them "anyway and always." I'll never forget one particular incident where I completely lost my temper with my girls and verbally blasted one in particular. She was crushed. God gripped my heart almost immediately and convicted me of my sin. I knew what I'd done had deeply wounded her tender heart. Sorry and deeply ashamed, I approached her, confessed my sin and asked for her forgiveness. In an amazing act of grace, she threw her arms around me and still with tears whispered in my ear, "It's ok, Daddy. I forgive you. I love you anyway and always."

Questions for Reflection & Discussion

1. It's easy to be tough on adolescents when they are experiencing the growing pains of the body and brain. Take a minute and remember some of your own awkward stories and situations in order to develop empathy towards the young people in your life.

2. Before seeking to answer the Three Questions (pp. 132–134), answer them for yourself. Compare your answers today with how you would have answered in your youth. How might you begin to incorporate these topics into conversations with young people?

3. How does your church value the role of parents in the lives of their tweens, teens and twentysomethings? Are there ways you can better support fathers in their unique role in their adolescent's life?

4. How do you think the young people in your life perceive your relationship with them?

5. How would you rate your ministry on meeting the Three Needs (pp.140–142)?

6. What are some ways you can incorporate the Three Gifts (pp. 143–146) into your ministry?

The Journey Within

Notes

1   Duffy Robbins, *This Way to Youth Ministry: An Introduction to the Adventure* (El Cajon, CA: Zondervan Publishing House and Youth Specialties Books , 2004), p. 183.

2   Dean, Clark, and Rahn, eds. *Starting Right: Thinking Theologically about Youth Ministry*, p. 60.

3   David Walsh, *Why Do They Act That Way? A Survival Guide to the Adolescent Brain for You and Your Teen* (New York, NY: Free Press, 2004), p. 28.

4   *Ibid.*, p. 36.

5   *Ibid.*

6   Tolkien, *The Lord of the Rings.*

7   Karina Weichold, Rainer K. Silbereisen, and Eva Schmitt-Rodermund, "Studying Links Between the Timing of Puberty and Psychological Individuation," *Paper presented at the biennial meeting of the Society for Research on Adolescence* (March 30–April 2, 2000), p. 2.

8   Chap Clark and Dee Clark, *Daughters and Dads* (Colorado Springs, CO: NavPress, 1998), pp. 58–59.

9   Elliott Currie, *The Road to Whatever* (New York, NY: Metropolitan Books, 2004), p. 274.

10 Smith and Denton, *Soul Searching*, p. 261. "Contrary to popular misguided stereotypes and frequent parental misconceptions, we believe that the evidence clearly shows that the single most important social influence on the religious and spiritual lives of adolescents is their parents. Grandparents and other relatives, mentors, and youth workers can be very influential as well, but normally, parents are most important in forming their children's religious and spiritual lives."

11 Clark and Clark, *Daughters and Dads*, p. 29.

12 *Ibid.*

13 Serge Saintonge, Pier Angelo Achille, and Lise Lachance, "The Influence of Big Brothers on the Separation-Individuation of Adolescents from Single-Parent Families" in *Adolescence* 33, no. 130 (Summer 1998): p. 2.

14 Dan Kindlon and Michael Thompson, *Raising Cain: Protecting the Emotional Life of Boys* (New York, NY: Ballantine, 2000), pp. 98–100.

15 Clark and Clark, *Daughters and Dads*, p. 57.

16 Chap Clark, "Strategic Issues in Youth and Family Ministry," (lecture, Fuller Theological Seminary, March 2005).

17 Madeline Levine, *The Price of Privilege* (New York, NY: Harper Collins, 2006), p. 31.

18   Donald Miller, *To Own a Dragon: Reflections on Growing Up Without a Father* (Colorado Springs, CO: NavPress, 2006), p. 34.

19   Clark, *Hurt 2.0*, p. 110.

20   William Damon, *The Youth Charter: How Communities Can Work Together to Raise Standards for All Our Children* (New York, NY: Free Press, 1997), p. 200.

21   Clark, *Hurt 2.0*, p. 172.

22   David Elkind, *The Hurried Child: Growing Up Too Fast Too Soon*, 3d ed. (Cambridge, MA: Da Capo Press, 2001), pp. 3–5.

23   Walsh, *Why Do They Act That Way?*, pp. 84–85.

24   Levine, *The Price of Privilege*, pp. 132–136.

25   Http://stickyfaith.org/articles/what-makes-faith-stick-during-college (accessed May 13, 2015).

26   Clark, *Hurt 2.0*, p. 175.

CHAPTER 8
Trailblazing: New Directions in Spiritual Formation

ALLISTER MCGRATH OBSERVES THAT WE are in danger of...
allowing ourselves and our churches to follow societal
norms and values, irrespective of their origins and goals.
To allow our ideas and values to become controlled by any
thing or any one other than the self-revelations of God in
Scripture is to adopt an ideology, rather than a theology;
it is to become controlled by ideas and values whose origins lie outside the Christian tradition—and potentially
become enslaved to them.[1]

Likewise, Tom Sine reminds us:
The church exists not only to meet our spiritual needs and
bring us into faith communities; it is also called to help
us transform our values from those of modern culture to
those of the kingdom. And the Bible reminds us that the
church exists not primarily for itself but for others. We are
called to place God's mission at the centre of our congregational life, as resident aliens who are intended by God's
grace, in spite of our brokenness, to be a rough sample of
his great homecoming celebration. And we are called to
share the good news of God's new order in word and deed
and by unmasking the values of the dominant culture.[2]

The rising generation is swimming in a soup of global youth culture,
one whose values, ideas, and goals ultimately run counter to the gospel.[3]

Trailblazing: New Directions in Spiritual Formation

During adolescence and emerging adulthood, our youth are in their most impressionable and formative season of life. The messages and experiences they are exposed to during the 10/30 Window will profoundly impact who they become as adults. It's vital the Church rally to reach the next generation around the world as the covenant community of God advancing the kingdom of God. Adult members of the community of faith can make an impact as they enter and engage the youth culture with wisdom and respect—seeking to affirm what is true and expose what is false. Of course, this can only be done through the power of the Holy Spirit working with the Word in and through his people as they faithfully reach out in relationship to love and lead emerging generations. As we in the church think more theologically about next-gen ministry, and as we seek to understand and engage the changing glocal realities of adolescence, we'll discover insight and implications for the spiritual formation of tweens, teens and twentysomethings.

What Is Spiritual Formation?

Spiritual formation (or discipleship) is the process of knowing and growing in a personal relationship with Christ. It is a work of God's free grace as the Holy Spirit regenerates the heart, enabling repentance and faith, leading the Christian on a journey of sanctification, that is, becoming more and more in love with, and like, Jesus.[4]

Spiritual formation doesn't happen in a vacuum. God has called his people to "go and make disciples of all nations" (Matt. 28). The church's mission is to serve as God's agent in reaching the nations *and* the next generation with the reality of a relationship with Christ. By the power and presence of the Holy Spirit and entrusted with the Word, God works in and through the covenant community to reach and raise his children.

In the past, some traditions have approached spiritual formation from a didactic, information-only stance, while others have emphasized the performance of various disciplines or duties. But spiritual formation is all-encompassing. It includes the heart, mind, soul, and strength; thoughts and emotions; relationships and actions. It is the "shalom" of God working in every aspect of human life. It is the lordship of Christ embraced in all of life, not in a merely intellectual or mechanistic way.[5]

What Is Spiritual Formation?

We can think of spiritual formation as being both descriptive and prescriptive. It describes the action of God in redeeming a people for himself and enables them to receive him as Savior and Lord.[67] It is prescriptive in that it is an ongoing work in which humans must respond in cooperation with the Holy Spirit, pursuing sanctification and growth in grace. In addition, this is progressive over the course of one's lifetime, culminating in the glorious restoration of all things.[8]

In fact, the Bible uses language linking physical growth to spiritual growth. In Ephesians 4:12–15, Paul uses images like "the body," "mature manhood," "stature," "no longer children," and "grow up." Peter writes, "Like newborn infants, long for the pure spiritual milk, that by it you may grow up into salvation" (I Pet. 2:2). John describes the phases of spiritual formation as movement from childhood, through adolescence, and into mature adulthood (I John 2:12–14). To "make disciples of all nations," involves recognizing that spiritual growth cannot be separated from human growth. They are meant to go together.

We participate in God's redemptive work in the world by pursuing the restoration of what was intended from the beginning: that human beings would grow up in a right relationship with God and his world. Participating in the spiritual formation of adolescents— tweens, teens, and twentysomethings—affirms Jesus' lordship over all the world and every phase of life. As Francis Schaeffer so aptly put it, spiritual formation is about becoming "fully human." What a great privilege and responsibility to participate in the holistic, multi-faceted work of God in forming a people for himself from among the emerging generations!

As we have seen, Scripture makes it clear that the adult community of faith is called to come alongside the emerging generation and cooperate in raising them in the Lord (Deut. 6). In doing so, adults who want to help facilitate the spiritual formation of young people would do well to keep an eye toward the key questions of the adolescent journey, seeking to answer them through word and deed, and in truth and life. They are the kind of adults who model a living faith that demonstrates and offers the hope for which the next generation longs. Since individuation is the quest of adolescence, then those concerned with adolescent spiritual formation will help youth to find their identity in Christ, a sense of belonging in the covenant community, and agency as individuals gifted and called to participate in God's kingdom work in the world.

Who Am I?

Adolescents are desperate to discover who they are. The world tells them they must forge their own existence and invent themselves. However, those who love the Lord and love youth will lovingly offer them hope, pointing out that God has created them and has made them to find themselves in him (Psa. 139). While the culture beckons them to find their identity in what they wear, who they know, or what they do, Jesus says, "You are mine" (Gal. 2:20–21). When parents fail and homes are broken, Jesus says, "You are mine" (John 14:18). When friends bail and loneliness and isolation set in, Jesus says, "You are not alone.... I am with you" (Matt. 28:20).

Questions for Reflection & Discussion

1. Describe early, middle, and late adolescence. How do you see young people trying to find the answer to this question at each stage?

2. How can your ministry push back the darkness by beckoning students to hear Jesus say, "You are mine?"

Where Do I Belong?

Issues of belonging and attachment are met in Christ and in his church. As the covenant people of God, we are to surround the next generation and lovingly enfold them into the community of faith. When families are broken, the church can become a surrogate family (Psa. 68:6). Those in the church need to work together to reach out to tweens, teens and twentysomethings and draw them into authentic, loving relationships with adults in the community. Even intact Christian families will seek to steward their children for the Lord—leading their children to discover their core community in the family of God, both theologically and practically (Eph. 4:1–16).

Questions for Reflection & Discussion

1. Identify one young person in your life. How do you see him or her looking for the answer to this question?

2. Where do the young people in your church most feel they belong in the community?

3. How might your ministry become more intentional at developing community?

Do I Matter?

Only in Christ will young people find a destiny that is captivating and compelling. The adult community of faith has the great responsibility and opportunity to model lives oriented around Christ's kingdom work in the world. They, in turn, have the duty and privilege of inviting adolescents and emerging adults to join them in the journey of faith—apprenticing and encouraging them in pursuit of God's work in the world.

Questions for Reflection & Discussion

1. List the answers to this question young people hear from the culture?

2. Can you recall a story of how your ministry helped a young person discover his or her gifts and calling? What can you learn from that experience?

Table 5. Questions of Adolescence and Spiritual Formation

Developmental Issue	Heart Question	Principle
Identity	"Who am I?"	Identity in Christ as beloved child of God
Belonging	"Where do I fit in?"	Community in the family of God, the Church
Autonomy	"Do I matter?"	Kingdom trajectory in life; eternal destiny

Trailblazing: New Directions in Spiritual Formation

The closing words of the Old Testament—and the opening words of the New—redound to this priority as integral to the Messiah's mission: "I will turn the hearts of the fathers to the children, and the hearts of the children to the fathers" (Mal. 4:6; Luke 1:17). What does it look like when the adult community of faith awakens to God's call, turning their hearts toward the young? They turn from abandonment to pursuit, from a now/instant mentality to an ongoing perspective, from isolation to community, from a culture of performance to grace, and from lives of boredom to the adventure of God's mission.

From Abandonment to Pursuit

Adults must recognize, become familiar with, and seek to enter the global youth culture. They must do this individually and personally, as well as corporately. It is incumbent upon every adult in the community to see themselves as responsible for reaching and raising our young. Nowhere should this be more evident than in the life of the church. Not everyone is called to "Youth Ministry," "University Ministry," or to work with twentysomethings as a vocation (nor is everyone called to parenthood), but everyone *is* called to pray for and serve the next generation. This happens as Christians open their homes and their hearts, and offer their resources and their prayers for the young in their community: As individuals pursue tweens, teens, and twentysomethings with a desire for a personal relationship; as the church demonstrates a commitment with intimate care and concern, seeking to be a community where those in the 10/30 Window are known, loved, and pursued, even when the pursuer is rejected. Individuals in the church must approach next generation ministry as cross-cultural missionaries. As would be done on a foreign mission field, adults will seek to enter the world of adolescents and to know them personally and intimately in order to have a gospel impact on their lives.

Doug and Sue Sinclair befriended their teenaged son's friends, Jim and Dave. Jim and Dave both came from broken and abusive homes, and had never been to church. In fact, because of trouble at home, both young men had spent significant periods living on the streets. The Sinclairs began inviting these guys into their home—having them over for dinner, helping them with their homework, and just spending time with them. The guys would often stay the night, and soon were being enfolded into the Sinclairs' Christian family. This included prayer time around the dinner table, where Doug and Sue would pray about what was going on in Jim and Dave's lives right along with the other family member's needs; family devotions where the Sinclairs would discuss the gospel and its impact in their lives and decisions, and would honestly grapple with Dave and Jim's questions about God and the Bible; and fun times, going to ball games and watching movies together. In fact, Doug and Sue would often show up to watch Jim and Dave's own sports games.

The Sinclairs began inviting the young men to church, giving a "heads-up" to some adults and leaders of the church in advance—soliciting their ready welcome and pursuit of these guys. They introduced Dave and Jim to the church's various youth ministry leaders and opportunities. In time, both Dave and Jim came to faith during one of the church's youth retreats. They continued to grow in faith through high school, becoming key leaders among their peers and serving in ministry to younger kids. Through Dave and Jim's college years and into their twenties (in spite of military deployments, and extended oversees missions service), and now into years of marriage and families of their own, the Sinclairs continue to maintain a close relationship with each of them (as have many in that local church). These guys—who were once homeless and abandoned and outside the church—are living testimonies to the power of God's pursuit of the next generation through his people.

Questions for Reflection & Discussion

1. What are some obstacles preventing adults from pursuing the young?

2. In what ways might the abandonment experienced in your own past shape your ministry today?

From Instant to Ongoing

It's important for us to adopt a long-term view and commitment to the journey when it comes to the spiritual formation of those in the 10/30 Window. No matter how sophisticated and independent adolescents seem, don't be fooled. Patience and steadfast perseverance are required, just as God is patient and steadfast with all believers. Disappointments may come, and setbacks may discourage, but it helps to remember that spiritual formation is rarely (if ever) neat, clean, and predictable. God himself cannot be controlled and bears an element of unpredictability. "He isn't safe, but he's good."[9]

The spiritual formation of young people takes a lot of trust. As adults we must trust in God the way they long for young people to trust him—with complete and reckless abandon. At times we will have to be an anchor in their lives, unshakable in the midst of the stormy seas of adolescence and emerging adulthood—and we'll need to make a long-term commitment to stay in touch with and walk beside a few over the greater course of their lives, certainly until they reach adulthood. At the same time, we recognize that God is the author of their story. Trust in him brings confidence and hope, and this moves us to prayer on each young person's behalf, looking to the One who began the good work in them to carry it on to completion (Phil. 1:6). We can trust God can use even the little bit that we have to offer (in terms of time and resources) to make a difference in a young person's life, knowing that the Lord sovereignly orchestrates the various times, seasons, and individuals he uses to play a part in each one's spiritual journey.[10]

I first met Ethan in Indonesia when he was 13 years old. His older siblings were struggling with self-injury, atheism and suicidal tendencies. He was quiet and withdrawn, and wrestling with same-sex attraction. While his parents were ministry leaders who loved the Lord, they were baffled by his behavior and unsure how to reach into his world. Since we were only together for a weeklong retreat, it would have been easy to say goodbye and never see each other again; but God forged a relationship that would continue for years to come. We've kept in touch—sometimes more frequently—and I continue to pray for Ethan. Through the years we've connected across the globe by email and Facebook, phone calls, and Skype. I've been able to meet with him and his parents in their home and on different occasions around the world. We've walked through his doubts about salvation, his withdrawal into the gaming world, his struggles with pornography, and others. There have been seasons of apparent growth in his life, followed by apparent setbacks. At times his parents were really afraid and defeated, wishing they could "fix" him immediately.

Many years have gone by. Ethan just recently sent me this message: "Hey Eric, I hope that all is well with you! Before I begin I would just like to thank you for all that you have done for me. After we spoke that one day on the phone my life has completely changed. I had finally understood the power and mind blowing love of grace. Amazing grace, how sweet the sound that saved a wretch like me. You showed me what it means and truly I am able to say with joy and confidence that my life is in Christ. I am now a slave to the Lord and have been ever since that day. I thank you once again."

Ethan's journey isn't over. There will be many seasons of struggle and seeming setbacks, as in all of our lives as fallen people living in a fallen world. Spiritual formation isn't instant or mechanical, and it's often messy. But God's Word (reflected in the testimony of his people down through the ages) assures us that growth in the believer is organic and inevitable over time. "And I am sure of this, that he who began a good work in you will bring it to completion on the day of Jesus Christ" (Phil. 1:6).

Questions for Reflection & Discussion

1. How have you seen God's faithfulness in an ongoing way throughout your life?

2. In what ways might adopting a long-view shape your church's approach to next-gen ministry?

From Isolation to Community

When it comes to the spiritual formation of young people, adults can't do it alone, but need to rely on each other. Mothers and fathers cannot raise their children in isolation, especially the vast numbers of single, working parents in our world today. Throughout redemptive history, God has called his covenant community to serve as such: a *community*. As Christians seek to make disciples of the next generation, they must commit themselves to the church, embedding themselves in the lives of other believers with whom they can partner and share in the call to MissionNext. The Body of Christ works together as each member shoulders each other's burdens and shares in each other's joys. Individual gifts and callings work in concert to offer support and service. In this context adolescents and emerging adults will find a home, a place of belonging and a source of identity.

I see my life as being like the Charlie Brown Christmas tree. If you've watched the Peanut's special, *A Charlie Brown Christmas*, you know what I'm talking about. Charlie Brown selects the smallest, most pathetic looking excuse for a Christmas tree. Under the weight of one ornament, it almost snaps and half the needles fall off. That's me. I'd like to picture myself as a tall and spreading oak tree that can carry the weight of the world. The reality is, I need a lot of help just to stand; all the more when it comes to reaching and raising the next generation in my own family and ministry. So the Charlie Brown tree—the sad little sapling that is my life—is dependent on a network of support surrounding it: the covenant community.

I am deeply grateful for other adults who love Jesus and love my kids: the Sunday school teacher who pulls me aside after church to tell me that my daughter shared about how my travel schedule was hurting her and challenged me to make a change; the parent volunteer who has become an adopted "aunt" to my girls—always present at their special occasions and taking each one out for a birthday date tradition; the youth minister that pursues each of my adolescent girls as individuals—providing each one a safe place to wrestle with their faith (and sharing in lament over their parents' brokenness); the members of the congregation who anonymously drop off clothes on our front porch, knowing we are raising four girls on a missionary budget.

A while back my wife bought me a real-life replica of the Charlie Brown tree (I'm not sure what she's trying to tell me...). And every year when I see it in contrast to the big beautiful Christmas tree—strong and adorned with ornaments—I am reminded of who I really am on my own, and my desperate need for the Christ of Christmas and the community of those who love and worship him.

Questions for Reflection & Discussion

1. In what ways does the culture contribute to isolation in young people's lives? In what ways does the church? How have you seen young people wounded by isolation?

2. Describe the healing power of community. Can you give an example from your ministry with young people? What can your ministry team learn from that experience?

From Performance to Grace

A recent news piece discussed the increase in unwed teen pregnancies. The journalist interviewed numbers of these young women, asking them what motivated them to keep their babies. What was the number-one reason they gave for keeping their children (and for many, why they got pregnant in the first place)? "I want somebody to love me unconditionally." Ouch. Christians may praise God they are not aborting their children, but must also see the tragic reversal of parent and child roles, and the recipe for perpetual cycles of family dysfunction. By the same token, believers must understand the longing in these young girls lives, even as they cringe at the results of the fall and the broken ways humans try to get what they long for apart from God. The Lord is a God of grace. He relates to his people not based on what they do, but who they are in his Son, Jesus. Jesus is the one he sees when he looks at us. What do believers see when they look at young people?

Believing parents and adults reflect God's grace when they see young people the way God sees them—accepted, redeemed, and a delight. When was the last time you paused to reflect on your attitude toward the adolescents and emerging adults in your life? And, just as importantly, to ask yourself the question: "How do they perceive I feel about them?" Take time to ponder the basis of your relationship with the young people in your life. Does it mirror the basis of our relationship with God? Or is it based on their performance?

As I grow in my appropriation of God's grace in my life, he enables me to extend that grace to the next generation—and I find myself longing to see young people come to experience life as a gift to be received, and God as a delighting father. Is the church standing in stark contrast to the message of the world, which screams at them to perform, to measure up, to fake it before failing? Or are believers instead creating a context of affirmation and acceptance, enjoyment and delight; of affection that can't be earned or lost, and is freely and lavishly given? Is the church a gospel-saturated community that invites the emerging generations to live for the Lord leaning wholly on his grace?

Questions for Reflection & Discussion

1. Do you think young people experience your church as a place of performance or grace? Why?

2. What can grace look like in discipline situations?

From Boredom to Adventure

In some cultures and communities, those among the 10/30 Window are increasingly resigned and defeated—growing up with little opportunity and low expectations. As national economies sink, more and more young people are growing up under a cloud of resignation and defeat. The cult of celebrity is the new religion of many in the emerging generation—clinging to the fantasy that they will be "discovered" and delivered from a life of mediocrity to a life of fame and wealth and significance. No wonder many tweens, teens, and twentysomethings spend more time in the computer gaming world—cultivating their virtual worlds and characters—than they do their real lives. When the James Cameron movie *Avatar* was released in December 2009, the news reported numbers of young people who were so captivated by the beauty and adventure of the film that they committed suicide over the despair they felt in the contrast with the reality of their own disappointing lives.

What kind of lives are believers living in front of the young people in their families, communities, and churches? What characterizes the life that the church is inviting them to join? Christians should long for youth to see life is not about achievement on one hand or escape on the other, but about purpose and utter abandon to God's great work in the world. Young people need to see their story caught up in Christ's story: smaller, but bigger—humble, yet infused with weight and glory in God's great drama of redemption. Only in light of redemptive history will those in the 10/30 Window find the grand meta-narrative lost in the global youth culture today.

Questions for Reflection & Discussion

1. What contributes to a sense of boredom and defeat among the rising generation? How does the church often bore young people with the gospel?

2. How has your ministry helped young people get caught-up in God's grand meta-narrative?

3. Gather some adolescents and emerging adults together with your ministry leaders and brainstorm ways you can expose young people to the adventure of faith.

There are Christians who are working with young people in India from the lowest caste—the children of lepers. Apart from the work of the church in reaching out to these students at an early age, providing a nurturing environment (including housing, meals, education, and spiritual formation), these youth would be raised Hindu and—relegated to the leper colony—inevitably contracting leprosy themselves. But God has used these missionaries as agents of grace to impact the lives of numbers of young people with the gospel. These children, who've been abandoned by society, are being pursued in Christ through loving adults.

The process is by no means instant; but, over the course of many years, cohort after cohort of these young people have emerged into adulthood as lifelong followers of Christ. From the far reaches of India and isolated by their caste, a community of faith has been forged where they experience fellowship and a network of support—not only locally, but on a global scale as they get connected to sponsors who pray for them and provide for their needs, reinforcing the reality of their new identity in God's global church—their true people. And rather than being judged by their deficiencies and trying to self-improve their karma, they are coming to know the gracious love of their Father in heaven. No longer trapped in a cycle of oppression and disillusionment as lepers of the lowest Hindu caste, they are discovering dignity and calling in the gospel as agents of God's kingdom mission in the world.

Trailblazing: New Directions in Spiritual Formation
Notes

1   Allister E. McGrath, *A Passion for Truth: The Intellectual Coherence of Evangelicalism* (Liescester, U.K.: Apolos, 1996), p. 63.

2   Sine, *Mustard Seed vs. McWorld*, p. 219.

3   Walt Mueller, *Youth Culture 101* (Grand Rapids, MI: Zondervan Publishing House, 2007), p. 35.

4   The Westminster Divines, "Concerning Sanctification," in *The Westminster Confession of Faith*.

5   Dallas Willard, *The Divine Conspiracy: Rediscovering Our Hidden Life in God* (New York, NY: HarperCollins Publishers, 1997), pp. 283–287.

6   *The Westminster Confession of Faith*.

7   *Ibid.*

8   Jerry Bridges, *Growing Your Faith* (Colorado Springs, CO: NavPress, 2004), pp. 49–59.

9   C.S. Lewis, *The Lion, the Witch and the Wardrobe* (New York, NY: HarperCollins, 1956).

10   See I Corinthians 3:6–9; And also Paul's ministry in Thessalonica (Acts 17 and I Thess. 1 and 2): While Paul may have only been with the Thessalonians for two weeks, God used that short season to produce much fruit. And Paul's affection is born of a deep relationship that was forged in a matter of weeks. God can do the same with us in our ministry with young people, whether we have the privilege of walking with them over many years, or a very short time.

PART III. THE ROAD GOES EVER ON AND ON

The Road goes ever on and on
Down from the door where it began.
Now far ahead the Road has gone,
And I must follow, if I can,
Pursuing it with eager feet,
Until it joins some larger way
Where many paths and errands meet.
And whither then? I cannot say.

The Road goes ever on and on
Out from the door where it began.
Now far ahead the Road has gone,
Let others follow it who can!
Let them a journey new begin,
But I at last with weary feet
Will turn towards the lighted inn,
My evening-rest and sleep to meet.

165

CHAPTER 9

This Old House: Is It Time to Remodel Your Ministry?

WHEN REBECCA AND I FIRST moved to St. Louis, we lived in a row house in the city. The close proximity of urban living made it easy to get to know most of our neighbors on the block. But we never got to know the couple who lived just a few doors down. Nobody knew them. In fact, they never answered the door, and never poked a nose outside. According to the landlord, the mysterious couple had rented the place for years, living in seclusion—never emerging, not even to take out the trash. One day we heard the couple had abandoned the house—just up and disappeared.

I've heard the renters had lived there for years in seclusion—never emerged, not even to take out the trash. Finally they abandoned the home; when the house's landlord opened it up, he was assaulted by a horrible smell. To his astonishment, he found the place filled with trash from floor to ceiling, even rotting the floor and filling the basement. The tenants had never once thrown anything away. They hoarded everything and lived in squalor. In the end, the landlord had to completely gut the house and rebuild it.

These tenants chose to ignore the garbage and stench and live with it as long as they could, rather than change—and in the end, they fled. The landlord was left to square up to what needed to be done. Ignoring the problem, or slapping a few coats of paint on it just wouldn't do. He needed to get rid of the junk and get down to the foundation.

We're guilty of the same in ministry when we continue doing what we've always done without ever reflecting theologically or thinking stra-

This Old House: Is It Time to Remodel Your Ministry?

tegically. As ministry leaders, we can fall into the trap of traditionalism by perpetuating outdated models of ministry without careful and critical evaluation of our practices and forms. Over time our next-gen ministries become a collection of old fads and once-popular programs, and may even begin to crowd-out and alienate the very young people we're trying to reach in the first place!

We must resist the myth of the perfect model; recognizing instead that our models and methods must always be checked and challenged by Scripture—and we must be willing to adjust—as we engage our changing context. By the same token, there is much that can be gleaned from various models of ministry, and it's important to identify and retain those underlying and enduring values and goals while finding new expressions and applications. For this reason, we need a *Meta-Model* to guide our approach in developing theologically grounded and contextually engaged (and therefore unique and often creative) models of ministry across time and around the world.

Too often the church has become more enamored with trappings and tradition than with theology; and more concerned with perpetuating its own vocabulary, methodology, and historic reference points than with the purpose behind them. Instead, the church must benefit from viewing itself as a house whose foundation remains secure, while the building is continually remodeled and repaired, restored and updated. Some next-gen ministry models are built on a thin theological foundation, though they may seem to have an effective, fresh approach. On the other hand, many churches (in the Reformed tradition for example), though they articulate a robust theological foundation, are often slow to re-examine or remodel their ministry practices.[1]

"Traditions" represent the handing down of theological reflection as it engages (or should engage) historical setting, which is always in transition. For this reason it is incumbent upon those who would lead the church in reaching the next generation to be about the business of remodeling; this consists of ongoing theological reflection, and results in new models of expression.[2]

Models are an extension of discipleship and an expression of practical theology. They are necessary and vital to the work of ministry. As those called to ministry among the 10/30 Window, we need models in order to guide our efforts. Such models stand between discipleship and scholarship, between the Word and the world, and provide a map for ministry that guides its trajectory, strategy, and methodology. Everyone functions within a model of some sort. For some it is done unconsciously or intuitively, for others it is more deliberate. Throughout this book we've emphasized how important it is to be intentional in developing models of next-gen ministry that are theologically grounded and contextually engaged.

The Mythical Model

Apart from God's grace, the natural human tendency is toward personal pride, ambition, control, success, and worldly effectiveness. This leads to a belief that one right model, executed the right way, will inevitably produce the desired results. People get famous, get published, and get wealthy promoting and perpetuating their "successful" models of ministry. The field of next-generation ministry is no exception. Anyone who attends one of the many conventions and conferences, examines ministry-related websites, or looks on the bookshelf of almost any pastor, missionary, or ministry leader will find a host of how-to books, materials, training guides, and seminars touting the latest models and methods.

Often the popularity of these models has more to do with slick marketing and the celebrity status of the spokesperson than it does with the actual effectiveness of the model. In truth, many of these approaches are not as new or innovative as they may claim to be: sometimes they are a mere revision or repackaging of previously accepted models of next-gen ministry. Those called as leaders in the field of next-generation ministry must be wary of the tendency to cling to and perpetuate ministry models that have become outdated or ineffective.

Perpetuating Models

There are several reasons why churches and individual ministry leaders tend to perpetuate existing models of ministry without regard to their theological foundation or contextual import. For some, it is the pursuit of comfort and manageability. For others, it's a commitment to their own

169

image and legacy. And for still others, it is more related to a simple lack of exposure to the myriad ways God can work.

Tradition

"This is the way we've always done it" is a refrain that often echoes throughout the ministry of the local church. Many denominations, organizations, churches, and individuals get caught in the trap of carrying on traditions rather than continually reflecting on the theologies or visions that birthed their original models. The pressure not to vary from the historical way of doing things can come from any and all directions: the leadership, elders, and/or congregation members. Many find security and comfort in maintaining the status quo.[3]

While there is certainly value in traditions and much to be celebrated in preserving heritage, the church needs to take care not to become so locked into traditional ways of ministering that new movements of the Spirit are ignored or dismissed.[4]

Personal Experience

I enjoy the privilege of meeting and talking with leaders in the field of next-gen ministry from all around the world. Many of these ministry leaders possess the rich experience of having been deeply affected by some form of youth ministry during their own adolescent years. The leader who invested time in them often serves as a role model in the way that they now carry out their own ministry to young people. For some, the model of ministry they grew up within becomes the model they adopt for leading and organizing their own approach to next-gen ministry. Nostalgia, loyalty, and even a desire to honor the ministry and/or minister who blessed their lives can lead to immortalizing a model of ministry without due theological reflection and contextual application.

Management Mentality

Amidst the demands and unpredictability of ministry, it becomes easy to see the ministry itself as the model, which is characterized by a repetition of the programs, patterns, and routines adopted over time. Inertia sets in when programs do not vary from year to year, making it difficult to resolve to spend energy and resources on renewal of the vision and work. This is especially true when the leader is seen as an expert in the model. Admitting it may no longer be as effective (and seeking to understand why) is hard to face.[5]

Legacy Building

Often the model of ministry becomes the source of significance and success for a minister or church and (often unintentionally) honoring God can be reduced to an insignificant part of the equation. Programs subtly take priority over people, and those involved must match their efforts to the program—rather than submitting the program to the needs of those it is seeking to serve. A model of ministry can become hard to let go of, if a sense of leaving a legacy is tied to it.

Jumping on the Bandwagon

When a model has proven "successful," others are quick to adopt it. Leaders are often lured by the promise of success in ministry without having to do the hard work of thinking theologically and developing their own contextually engaged model. The latest book, program, or method is embraced without question.

Being Innovative for Innovation's Sake

For many, the desire to be entrepreneurial and cutting edge drives them to try to be creative and innovative. Rather than being content with a single, focused model of ministry, the temptation is to cling to novelty for the sake of newness. Unfortunately, this is not often the result of deep theological reflection and conviction as much as a desire to be cutting-edge or original.

Lack of Exposure

Serving in one place or within one particular model of ministry for a long period of time—*without* being exposed to other contexts or approaches—can sometimes offer little impetus for challenge and change. Those in that situation are at risk of becoming myopic in their view of ministry and can sometimes fail to recognize blind spots they may have developed, let alone new horizons of ministry.

This Old House: Is It Time to Remodel Your Ministry?

These tendencies toward venerating a given model of ministry may flow from a number of reasons, including poor theology, pride, apathy, uncertainty, and ignorance. As humble followers of Jesus and servants in the church, our allegiance is to Christ and his calling—*not* to methods and models. This allegiance in turn compels us to discover and develop models of ministry as means of communicating the gospel, and never as a substitute for it. Allegiance to Christ must remain central, while that very allegiance requires that we adopt a posture of flexibility and humility in our approach to next-gen ministry.

Problems with Models

Churches and and their leadership need to be wary of perpetuating insufficient or poorly developed models of ministry. Some models may have inherent problems and pitfalls that must be confronted. Models are helpful tools, but it is important to acknowledge and address their limitations and liabilities.

Institutionalization

The evolution of an institution has been well documented. What begins as an idea is organized and eventually institutionalized. The often-unstated goal of an institution is to perpetuate itself. In the same way, proponents of a given model of next-gen ministry may institutionalize the model and subtly lose track of the original vision that the model was meant to realize.[6] This is in essence a form of idolatry.

Contextually Loaded

Once a model has been developed it is inherently contextual and therefore has a shelf-life. Models arise from, and in response to, the milieu in which they are formed. This limits the usefulness of the model outside the time and place in which it was developed. Though it may be effective in one context, a model is not always portable and is not always as effective in a different context.

Leadership-Dependent

Models of ministry are in some ways dependent on the vision, calling, gifts, resources, and personality of the leadership and community from which they arise. While a different context may share many similarities (e.g., suburban Houston and suburban San Diego), if the leadership and community are different in fundamental ways then the model may not translate well.

Reductionistic

All models are by nature reductionistic; that is, a model must be simplistic enough to be realized, and should only emphasize a few principles if it is to be useful. A model that is too comprehensive and exhaustive becomes cumbersome and offers little direction. On the other hand, once the model is created (following certain generalizations and emphases), it runs the risk of losing the flexibility necessary to meet exceptional circumstances.

Mining Models

While models of ministry to the emerging generation have their problems and pitfalls, their uses need to be mined, excavated, and explored. By examining and critiquing a model of ministry, we have the opportunity to gain insight as we continually do the work of refining and developing models of ministry to reach tweens, teens, and twentysomethings. For instance, examining an approach to ministry gives us a window into the theology driving the model, and the vision and values behind it. As a a result, careful critique can yield insight into history, blind spots and future trends—all important factors in developing and renewing the way we do ministry.

Theology

Theology finds expression in models of ministry. By examining and critiquing a model of ministry we can discern the working theology behind it and whether the church's theological distinctives are indeed being expressed through it. This is important, since the way we minister communicates our theology to those to whom we minister, and is often more instructive and influential than what we explicitly state. For example, some churches approach youth ministry from a theological commitment which elevates the role of the nuclear family while lowering the role of the church family in reaching and raising the next generation.

This Old House: Is It Time to Remodel Your Ministry?

Vision

Many churches and next-gen ministries have developed a statement of their mission and vision. Crafting a mission statement can be a very helpful process, and articulating a ministry vision is vital in championing a cause, rallying a team, and providing direction. Too often, however, mission statements and vision documents find themselves filed and rarely referred to after the lengthy process of drafting them. Vision paints a picture of the ultimate goal or reality that the ministry desires to attain— the cause that compels that ministry and its leaders. A mission or purpose statement succinctly articulates a ministry's contribution toward the cause. By evaluating a model of ministry, one can begin to uncover the true vision behind a given ministry model and discern whether the model indeed advances the stated vision and mission.

Values

By examining and critiquing a model of ministry, what it truly values will become evident. As with vision and mission, many ministries make an effort to think through and articulate their values—but this is no guarantee that their model flows from or reinforces those values. For instance, the ministry may claim to value the nuclear family, while the model effectively works at odds with this value: it may compete for young people's time with their families and subtly encourage parents to abdicate their role and relationship with their children to the ministry leaders.

History

Surveying the relatively recent history of ministry to adolescents and emerging adults as a movement proves valuable in helping church and ministry leaders understand the state of the field today. Likewise, it can be helpful to understand the historical context in which a particular model was birthed. By tracing the development of a given model of ministry, one can discern the reasons behind its various facets. If the model is adopted, it will be easier to remain true to its ethos by emphasizing the same principles on which it was founded. Then it can be revamped, renewed, and remodeled according to the current context.

Blind Spots

By engaging a variety of models, those called to reach the next generation have the opportunity to be sharpened and challenged in their approach to next-gen ministry. While it may be popular to strive toward creativity in our thinking, doing so can be unrealistic. All of us have our blind spots: personally, culturally, theologically, and in other ways. The same is true for our models of ministry. We frequently need an outside agent—a fresh perspective—to bring us new angles and insights into our lives and ministries. This rarely happens in a homogenous community. Having one dominant tradition, culture, or model of ministry may prevent us from looking at our ministries with fresh eyes. Exposure to other models of ministry to young people can reveal our blind spots, challenge our assumptions and methods, and stimulate new and effective approaches to ministry.

Future Trends

By surveying dominant and emerging models across the landscape of next-gen ministry, leaders can gain insight into future trends and new directions in the field. They can also better discern where the Holy Spirit may be leading their churches, recognize correctives that need to be made or issues addressed, and even note areas where the field of ministry to the 10/30 Window may be heading off course. Engaging emerging models and methods not only stimulates forward thinking, but also allows for both a contribution to the conversation and constructive critique.

A Meta-Model for Ministry Praxis

One single model of next-gen ministry would be insufficient to serve the church in all times and at all places. Instead we need a *meta-model* which will allow for the development of many different, highly contextualized models of ministry—emphasizing universal principles applied to unique settings. By focusing on the intersection of global realities and local particulars, this meta-model will encourage the church to take a *glocal* approach in reaching emerging generations: MissionNext. This book was written to help the church develop models of ministry that may be unique and diverse in structure and style; yet which will flow from, and are anchored by, biblical grounds and goals.

This Old House: Is It Time to Remodel Your Ministry?

This meta-model is one employed by Next (a global next-gen ministry), and has been developed through years of pastoral ministry among the 10/30 Window, together with extensive research (including doctoral study). Ongoing conversations and collaborations between Next teams and local church planters and indigenous church leaders have served to shape and sharpen this meta-model approach. It has been field-tested by practitioner experts from around the world.

Informing the Next Institute's teaching of practical theology courses, this approach has been taught through our many partnership sites in the USA, Mexico, South Korea, Japan, Hungary, and the U.K.; with new sites opening-up in India, several countries in Africa, and other parts of Europe, Asia, and Latin America. The aim is to see ministers equipped to lead the global church in engaging the emerging generation, armed with a framework that enables them to develop a faithful and fruitful model of ministry in the community where God has called them to serve.

The theological grounds and goals proposed in this book elicit both unity and diversity in the call to reach the nations and the next generation: unity and camaraderie in the shared corporate call to reach adolescents and their families with the gospel, and tremendous diversity in practices for living out that calling in each given locality.

The meta-model developed in this book forms a reflective loop—a dance of practical theology—continually forming and reforming our model of ministry as our grounds and goals engage our context. This helps us avoid pragmatics, polemics, and panic, and leads us to pursue healthy praxis. Reflective practice is ministry praxis. (Figure 9).

FROM GROUNDS   GO   MODEL   THROUGH CONTEXT   METHODS   TO GOALS

Figure 8. Meta-Model for Ministry Praxis

Questions for Reflection & Discussion

1. Why is it easy for churches to fall into the "trap of traditionalism"? What are some practical steps you can take to help your ministry avoid this trap?

2. Which natural human tendency do you find you struggle with most in ministry? Is it personal pride, ambition, control, success, worldly effectiveness? Some other? Identify a ministry ally who can walk with you in this struggle.

3. What are your church leaders' expectations for next-gen ministry? How do these expectations affect you?

4. Imagine you've been asked to consult with a new pastor/ministry leader to help them avoid merely perpetuating a ministry model. What questions would you ask? What advice would you give?

5. Run your ministry through the "Mining Models" filter (pp. 173–175), and asses its strengths and weaknesses. What can you celebrate? Where can you grow?

This Old House: Is It Time to Remodel Your Ministry?

Notes

1   Mark Driscoll, *The Radical Reformission: Reaching Out Without Selling Out* (Grand Rapids, MI: Zondervan Publishing House, 2004), p. 50.

2   Michael Frost and Alan Hirsch, *The Shaping of Things to Come: Innovation and Mission for the 21st-Century Church* (Peabody, MA: Hendrickson Publishers, 2003), pp. 6–9.

3   Mark Driscoll, *The Radical Reformission*, p. 50.

4   Chris Folmsbee, *A New Kind of Youth Ministry* (Grand Rapids, MI: Zondervan Publishing House, 2007), p. 20.

5   *Ibid.*, p. 29.

6   Richard R. Dunn and Mark H. Senter III, *Reaching a Generation for Christ* (n.p., 1997), p. 163.

CHAPTER 10

Starting Out... Again:
Re-Envisioning for MissionNext

THE GOSPEL IS RELEVANT FOR all peoples, at all times, and in all places. Those called to next-gen ministry need to extend the gospel in a relevant way. If the gospel is no longer deeply connected to the context, then as leaders we run the risk of truncating the gospel. The method, the medium, and the message are intimately entwined. The ancient Greeks saw the message—the truth or *logos*—as disconnected and ethereal, distinct and wholly "other." In his incarnation Jesus turned the Greek notion on its head: the *Logos* became flesh, personal, embodied, united to his creation, and known in and through this intimate encounter. This is the call of the church: to live out Christ's ongoing work in the world by infiltrating and engaging every aspect of life with the life and love of Jesus.

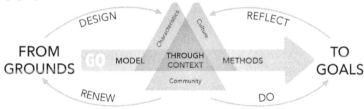

Figure 10. Meta-Model: Design... Do... Reflect... Renew...

Therefore, how we go about the work of ministry communicates as much about what we believe as what we explicitly state. This means being intentional and strategic in developing models of next-gen ministry that flow from, represent, and reinforce our theology. While biblical grounds and goals will never change, the way leaders accomplish their goals needs to be continually reshaped in order to reach a changing world.

This chapter concludes with a tool for the development and renewal of next-gen ministry models in local communities across contexts and around the world, based on the meta-model developed throughout the book. This meta-model for ministry praxis forms a reflective-loop, and guides us through four repeating dance steps, giving rhythm to the dance of MissionNext: **Design... Do... Reflect... Renew.**

Step 1: Design

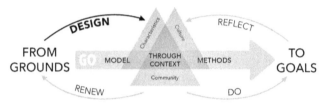

Figure 11. Meta-Model: Design

Let's begin by taking care to ensure that our assumptions and approach to next-gen ministry are grounded in God's redemptive work and his revealed will. This elicits an appropriation of God's heart for the young, and a love and passion for reaching the rising generation. Further, it informs an understanding of the biblical precedent for next-gen ministry in line with God's concern for young people throughout redemptive history. Finally, it promotes a commitment to enveloping ministry to tweens, teens, and twentysomethings into the overarching ministry of the church, his covenant community.

Church

We are meant to be his family on earth and his instrument for shepherding the next generation. The church is called to be the community in which rising generations discover and embrace their core identity as children of God, transferring their allegiance from their earthly parents to their heavenly Father, from their nuclear family to the family of God.

A healthy model will intentionally endeavor to help young people develop a biblical world and life view, and seek to communicate and instill biblical-theological teaching toward that end. In turn, the model must be strategically designed to assist youth and families in the task of integration; that is, their growth in personal and vital relationships with Jesus. Such a model of ministry should be designed to attend to and identify transformation in the lives of the community, recognizing the progressive adoption of the characteristics of Christ in its young people.

Next-gen ministry, as part of the overarching ministry of the church, will focus on leading young people to know God's love, grow in relationship with Christ and his people, and go as agents of grace in kingdom living. This happens as the adult community pursues and engages tweens, teens, and twentysomethings through the four purposes of the church: celebration, growth, love, and impact.

What Does This Look Like?

Designing a model that is...

Theologically Orthodox

Everything is theological. The key is to align theology with the foundational truths of the historic Christian faith derived from Scripture and affirmed by the universal church down through history and around the world. While all theologies are developed within a cultural context, leaders must avoid theological relativism. As they develop models of next-gen ministry, theological orthodoxy—standing within the historic biblical tradition—must be the commitment:

> An orthodoxy that confesses the deity of Jesus, the reality of salvation by grace through the death and resurrection of Christ, the necessity of conversion, and the authority of scripture, to name a few. Throughout history a broad array of Christian thinkers agree on these issues—Augustine, Aquinas, Luther, Calvin, Simons, and Wesley.[1]

One of the challenges with *assuming* the theological orthodoxy of a ministry is that it is difficult to judge until it is tested. Consider the predicaments of James and Martha:

James had been a youth worker for a number of years, and was considered to be pretty good at his job. He developed key relationships with students, planned great programs, and grew his groups to a large size. However, nothing prepared him for the night one of his key and most visible leaders confessed that she was a practicing lesbian—and had been so ever since she had started at the ministry. James had no idea what to do—while the leader's sexual orientation couldn't be justified by historic Christianity, removing her would be a public affair that would force hard theological positions to be taken. Students would leave; the programs she was in charge of would possibly fold. Wouldn't it be easier to simply ask her to continue to not tell anyone?

Martha loved caring for people, and felt that it was a key aspect of Jesus' ministry on earth. So when she was put in charge of her church's student ministry, she knew exactly what she wanted to do. Drawing from her Peace Corps days, Martha aggressively pushed her students to consider the poor and needy, and designed programs that allowed them to serve in many areas in their community. These programs were incredibly well-received, and soon the student ministry was growing by leaps and bounds. Martha was overjoyed, and thus ran the ministry in this way for a number of years—until she was stopped in her tracks when she visited one of the work sites where a small group was serving and overheard two of her students telling a friend they were serving with how much they were growing after learning about Buddhist meditation. Suddenly she realized that something might have been missing in her ministry model over the years...

Christ-Centered

Our understanding of God is inextricably tied to what he has done for us as believers in Christ. God's redemptive work is the central unifying theme of all of Scripture and all of life. Theologian Geerhardus Vos writes: "Revelation is inseparably linked to the activity of redemption... Revelation is the interpretation of redemption."[2] Jesus is Savior and Lord, the hero of the big story. Every model of next-gen ministry must be grounded in dependence on Christ and point to Christ in all things. Union with

Christ—believers in him and he in us—causes Christians to celebrate that everything flows from, through, and to him. He receives the glory in all things (Rom. 11:36). As leaders develop models of ministry, the desire must be to see young people find life in Christ, living with and for him. Michael Horton writes: "The Reformation brought freedom back to the Christian conscience by restoring the gospel from being us-centered to being God-centered, Christ-centered. We need that kind of shift again today."[3]

Some involved in next-gen ministry may incorporate Christ-centeredness through an educational-method approach. Chris is an ordained university campus pastor in his denomination, and preaches a 30-minute sermon weekly to the group of students that gather at his church for fellowship and discipleship. Regardless of his topic, Chris has a "Where's Jesus" moment in every sermon he preaches, complete with a special Powerpoint slide and corny hand gesture. While the moment gets laughs, it also provides a weekly opportunity for Chris to show how Jesus is central to the biblical story. This serves one of Chris' meta-goals as well—he not only teaches his students about Jesus, but he also teaches them to look for Jesus in every Bible passage they read and every sermon they hear.

Janet, on the other hand, is one of many youth workers who incorporates Christ-centeredness in the scope of her ministry. As a youth director in charge of planning the variety of Bible studies, sermon series, and small groups her church offers each semester, Janet makes sure that Jesus never becomes a blind spot in a student's life. She does this by tracking which events and studies her youth attend, making sure no demographic goes a year without spending quality time in the Gospels. Regardless of whether students "know" about Jesus, Janet makes them return again and again to the story of Jesus so that they can connect what they learn in 'practical' (topical) classes to the center of the biblical narrative.

Grace-Based

In a world where students are surrounded by voices reinforcing the message of self-reliance and performance, the gospel of God's grace in Christ is a radical message.[4] The ministry itself must be grounded in grace, in God's sovereign, saving work. His divinely initiated and sustained love for his own in Christ is not dependent on their efforts, and is given in spite of their sin. This is what must drive the engine of ministry and fuel the heart of every minister. God's grace compels us to reach the nations and the next generation, and propels us from a posture of rest by that very grace.[5]

What is difficult about 'grace-based ministry' is that it often never leaves the doctrinal table to be incorporated into the structure of the ministry itself. Corey was the type of pastor who was sure his ministry was all about grace—his students learned about it, showed it to others, he modeled brokenness and repentance to them, and taught it to their parents. So he was surprised when he interviewed a student who had recently gone off to college from their ministry, and had expressed struggles with Christianity as a result of her experiences in her youth group. This girl noted that her experience in youth group was no different than her experiences at her college-prep high school or her travelling club softball team: she was always on the run. "There was no grace in learning about grace!" she said. "We were expected to be at everything, to study hard, to work for the mission of the church, to grow into mature Christian believers that could resist the evils of college... But you never saw how tired we were, and we were too afraid of being judged to say anything."

Corey saw in that moment that his ministry actually reflected incredibly works-based principles. Further, he realized that those principles actually came from his own insecurities as a pastor—he felt like his church judged him on how 'mature' his students seemed when they graduated high school. He knew then he had some conversations to schedule.

Dependent on Prayer

Prayer is the ultimate act of dependence.[6] Communicating with the God whom we serve and crying out to him to fulfill his promises, to care for and carry his people, and to consummate his kingdom is the call to prayer.[7]

"In his heart a man plans his course, but the Lord determines his steps" (Prov. 16:9). Any attempt at the strategic design of a ministry model must be a prayerful undertaking, and involves looking and listening to the Lord, then responding to his leading. Ministry models that are not developed in a prayerful way—and which are not intentional about prioritizing prayer in the ministry—are in danger of failing in dependence on Christ. They will tend to move away from being based on grace, and drift toward dependence on human wisdom and effort.

In prayer, hearts are attuned to the Spirit's leading. In prayer, God is reaffirmed as the hero. In prayer, rest is received. Through prayer, we are invited to participate in God's work around the world. Every model of ministry among the 10/30 Window must be steeped in prayer. If models of next-gen ministry are steeped in prayer, young people will be encouraged to adopt the same practices.

"It just seems like wasted time," Brad moaned. "I know I'm supposed to do it, but there always seems to be something more important to do." While this might sound like the whining of a teenager, it was actually the desperate confession of a veteran university campus minister, tasked with teaching prayer to 100 staffers at a regional training conference. Brad then explained that he had made an unconscious value judgment—that time spent *with* a student was more important than time spent praying *for* that same student.

Those staffers ministered to Brad that day, and he sought the counsel, not of an 'expert' on prayer-based ministry, but of an 80-year old man in his church that simply always reminded him that he was being prayed for. This elderly giant of the faith showed Brad his prayer bench, noting that he spent two hours every morning there praying for the needs of the church. Brad balked, noting that such an exercise of even half that time would mean he had less time to minister to students. But then he remembered his value-judgment—time spent praying for students would be time ministering to them, just not necessarily on campus or the corner coffee shop.

Today, Brad says this practice has transformed him as a minister and his ministry as a whole. He is more connected to Jesus, as the commitment to prayer also helped him rediscover his own devotional life. He sees his students less as projects to work on, and more as individuals he deeply loves and is invested in. And, he has seen the value of prayer in the structure of his ministry change, because he now values it personally. Brad realizes now that prayer cannot be a ministry value until it is a value of the leadership of that ministry in their personal lives.

Starting Out... Again: Re-Envisioning for MissionNext

Flexible and Adaptable

If the model is grace-based and dependent on prayer, then it is already well on the way to becoming flexible and adaptable. This allows the ministry, and those called to minister, to remain pliable in the Master's hands. God is on the move and his kingdom is breaking through to hearts and lives in every corner of the globe and in each generation. While he never changes, the way he works in a given time and place can be unique and highly personal. For this reason, models of ministry must be designed with this in mind, and be ready to move or adapt as the Spirit leads and the context changes. Any model that is developed with an eye toward self-perpetuation or institutionalization is in danger of becoming irrelevant at best, and damaging at worst. Instead, models of ministry must be strategic about retaining flexibility and adapting to change.

Kara knew the moment Stacey walked into her small group of twentysomethings that things would be different forever. Stacey was a Muslim graduate student and an extrovert who liked to challenge Kara's every position, yet who also seemed captivated by the idea of the gospel and wanted to learn more. Based on how the first few Bible studies went, Kara saw that the group would never make it even halfway through the provided curriculum. One night, she called the rest of her small group to talk about using the small group to minister to Stacey instead. Her girls agreed, and each and every week they grew as they were challenged by Stacey's questions and gained the ability to explain their own faith.

Kara's situation is a perfect example of the flexibility necessary in a ministry setting. Consider the implications of what a lack of adaptability would have caused:

- If Kara was required by her superiors to finish the curriculum as published, Stacey's important questions may have never even have been addressed.
- Kara's small group may not have been capable of the mature love and commitment to Stacey that Kara asked of them. If not, an inability to move Stacey to a different group, or add students to the current group to aid in ministering to Stacey would be tragic.
- If Kara herself was not trained to be flexible and listen to the Holy Spirit's leading regarding Stacey, she might see Stacey as a threat to the continued growth of her current girls and might (at least

unconsciously) ignore or otherwise be inhospitable to Stacey.

Creates Space for the Work of the Spirit

God is the one who transforms hearts and lives. We are privileged to be used by him as tools in the spiritual formation of the emerging generations. But take care not to assume the role of the Holy Spirit in the lives of the adolescents and emerging adults served by your congregation. Nextgen models of ministry need to be intentional in moving youth along in their spiritual growth, but leaders must be careful not to be reductionistic or simplistic, or to assume too much responsibility. Remember to make room for the Holy Spirit to do his work his way—in, through, and around our ministry.[8]

The goal is not that young people participate in programs—nor is that the litmus test for their spirituality. The goal is that Christ be formed in them. Is the church creating models that allow adults to come alongside young people in such a way as to partner with the work of the Holy Spirit in their lives? To do so might mean avoiding over-programming or assuming too much in the role of leaders in their lives. Often, leaders feel that ministry is activity—doing things, running programs, organizing and implementing events, even purposely pursuing and managing relationships. While Christ calls ministry leaders to action, by the same token they must protect against so filling young people's lives with demands, programs, and structure that they miss the opportunity to hear and respond to the still, small voice of God—to be filled with the Spirit, to see the fruit of the Spirit emerge, and to experience the gifts of the Spirit exercised in them.

Mike was surprised to learn that the recent drop in his weekly small group program was due to 15 of his students meeting together at one of their houses, because they didn't feel that the curriculum he had chosen was speaking to them. After fighting the urge to become defensive or offended by the criticism, Mike asked to come visit the group. He spent most of the hour simply sitting in the kitchen, listening to the students in the next room seek the Lord together. Finally, he came in, almost with tears in his eyes. Rather than scolding them, he expressed how much they had encouraged him. He asked them questions about why the curriculum he had picked hadn't worked, and trusted this group to give him helpful feedback. He then promised two things: first, he would talk to the other small groups and perhaps incorporate their suggestions, including possibly picking a new curriculum. But many would stop after that and ask the students to return to "the system." Not Mike. He also asked if he could equip these students to keep on meeting by helping train the older students and give them ideas on leading small groups, buying snacks, and helping them pick topics to discuss. Eventually, Mike's small group program was changed to offer two choices—either a pre-determined track with chosen small group leaders, or an option where students would submit proposals for small groups (topic, leadership, format, location, purpose, etc.), and like a venture capitalist, Mike would equip chosen groups to live out what they had proposed.

Pursues/Produces Relationships of Intimacy and Authenticity with Christ and the Church

The goal of seeing those in the 10/30 Window find their identity in Christ and in community with his people is central to the mission of any model of next-generation ministry.[9] A strategy must be in place for intentionally developing relationships of intimacy and authenticity with Christ and the church: One where students are introduced to Christ and discipled in walking with him.[10] Where spiritual disciplines are taught and practiced. Where adults demonstrate intimacy with Christ by honestly (and yet prudently) sharing their struggles and stories with the rising generation. Where young people are engaged in open and safe relationships with each other and with caring, committed adults who love the Lord and have hearts for them. Where spiritual friendships are fostered and formed. An understanding of the church and each one's place in it needs to be taught from Scripture and experienced in practice. A healthy desire is that the next generation see themselves as the church of today, and not only as the church of tomorrow. Ministry to young people should include plans to fully integrate them into the body of Christ as interdependent adult members of the community of faith.

The beauty of Gloria's ministry was how well balanced it was. She had been raised in a church that had heavily invested in youth, but despite being active for years there, she had never met her pastor and had few relationships with adults who weren't youth leaders. This had led her to a church that actively pursued integrating young people into the myriad of ministries of the church, all the while fostering relationships with mentoring adults. Gloria thought she was in heaven, and served there for a number of years. However, something eventually bugged her—while the church served the young people who had been born there well, there were never any visitors. Further, while teens and twentysomethings at the church seemed mature in a number of ways, it was difficult to connect them with a passion to tell their friends about Jesus. Some didn't even have non-Christian friends at all—because they didn't relate to them. Out of this, Gloria realized adolescents and emerging adults need both peer-relationships and peer-oriented structures that promote loving community, and key relationships with the wider body of Christ. Gloria's next-gen ministry now serves as a bridge—young people come and invite their friends, learn about age-appropriate and relevant topics, and also plug into other church ministries that challenge them to expand their view of the body of Christ.

Opportunities for Youth to Explore/Live Out Calling and Gifts beyond the Local Church

Identity in Christ and community with his people leads to living in line with his kingdom trajectory.[11]

The goal of next-gen ministry is to intentionally provide opportunities for young people to explore and live out their calling and gifts beyond the local church. The church is the only institution that doesn't exist to meet its own needs. Good models of ministry must be designed to strategically help tweens, teens, and twentysomethings discover how God has uniquely gifted and called them, then empower them to use their gifts and follow God's call in their community and around the world.[12]

As a result, effective models of next-gen ministry must be intentional about meeting young people in their present circumstances and inviting them into the formative family of God—life in the community of faith. As a way of conceptualizing this, think through the stages of progression of spiritual formation in terms of outreach, entry, community, intimacy, and assimilation (Figure 12).

Outreach involves connecting with young people and families in their world outside the bounds of the visible, organized church. *Entry*

Starting Out... Again: Re-Envisioning for MissionNext

refers to creating opportunities through which tweens, teens, and twenty-somethings are introduced to the church. *Community* requires consistent participation in the local church. *Intimacy* is the process of developing close spiritual friendships with adults and peers based on mutual love for Christ and each other, marked by transparency and authenticity with a desire to see one another grow spiritually. *Assimilation* is achieved when each young person becomes a fully integrated, interdependent member of the body of Christ, living in line with Christ's kingdom trajectory.

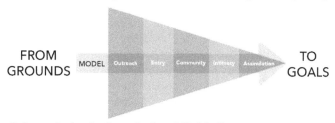

FROM
GROUNDS

MODEL Outreach Entry Community Intimacy Assimilation

TO
GOALS

Figure 12. Progression from Pre-Conversion through Discipleship

Many ministries will structure their various programs along this trajectory. Andy's ministry to adolescents, for instance, does feature 'attractional' activities familiar to (and often derided by) long-time practitioners of youth ministry, like concerts, fun trips, and an over-abundance of pizza. However, Andy's staff and students are well trained in noticing new students, befriending them, and trying to be a welcoming and safe face for Christianity as a whole. Contrary to the advice of many, Andy doesn't preach the gospel at all at these events—not even a short devotional. He doesn't want to give the appearance of the infamous 'bait and switch' technique. Without spamming these new students, Andy will allow the basic relationships between his staff and students and these newcomers to invite them to a Bible study, a small group, or perhaps a specific night of a sermon series that will be accessible to them. For students who respond, it is at this level that many make commitments to Christ, perhaps at a camp or retreat event. Andy then slowly incorporates these students into the church, discovering their gifts, inviting them on mission, and even calling some to be mentored and discipled in specific programs and relationships.

Step 2: Do

Figure 13. Meta-Model: Do

Once designed around biblical grounds and goals, we do ministry with context in mind. Thoughtful leaders continually survey the landscape of their given context in order to strategically implement their model of ministry. Key components that make-up the context for next-gen ministry include: psychosocial characteristics of adolescence (see chapter 5), cultural forces (see chapter 6), and the community of faith.

Adolescence is a period of unprecedented growth and development. If we would do the work of ministry among the 10/30 window, we should do our homework to build bridges for the gospel into their world. If our approach is going to be effective, it will consider the changes that are taking place in an adolescent's body and brain, will address issues of individuation, and seek to support the family.

Over 50 percent of the world's population is under the age of 30. As the church strives to carry out the Great Commission, it must be both geographic and generational in fulfilling its mission. A missional model of next-gen ministry will do the work to understand and address the cultural forces impacting the world of rising generations such as globalization, and systemic adult abandonment.

For any model of next-gen ministry to be done well, it must consider the community of faith: the church and its leadership. The covenant community is responsible for ministry to tweens. teens, and twentysomethings. The members and leadership of the local church, ministry/agency, and denomination must be engaged in order to marshal lives and resources to do the work of reaching the next generation.

What Does This Look Like?

Doing what you've designed with these things in mind…

191

Starting Out... Again: Re-Envisioning for MissionNext

Psychosocial Issues

Spiritual development ought not be separated from human development. Part of the church's redemptive work in the world is to build bridges for the gospel into each age and stage of development in the lives of adolescents and emerging adults. Models of next-gen ministry ought to consider the implications of lengthening adolescence, adolescent brain development, and the unique needs of each stage of adolescence (early, middle, late) if they are to effectively see young lives transformed with the gospel.

Issues of Individuation

Resolving the issues of individuation—including identity, autonomy, and a need to belong—is central to the quest of adolescence. An effective model of ministry will strive to help students answer questions such as: "Who am I?" "Where do I belong?" and "Do I matter?" Any healthy model will also implement a plan for connecting tweens, teens, and twentysomthings with adults, while equipping the adult community of faith to surround young people with the support they so desperately need.

Javier was a new pastoral intern given responsibility for the church's college ministry. For all outward signs the group was incredibly healthy—20 students who all knew their catechisms well, and who studied theology as deep as anything he had studied in seminary. To say he was intimidated was an understatement. Yet Javier quickly discovered that his students often struggled with other issues—knowing God's will for their lives, interacting with non-Christians, and forming their own opinions on local and global issues. Using a dialogue-based approach and weekly case studies, Javier formed small groups with the intent on challenging his students' worldviews in a safe and supportive environment where they could experience healthy doubt.

Support for the Family

Young people need to experience communication, closeness, and trust in their relationships with parents and caring adults. A good model of ministry will proactively encourage and coach such interactions. Rather than further reinforcing division between youth and their families, next-gen ministry can strive to be a reconciling and supportive force in the lives of the families under its care. An effective model will seek to develop ways to nurture the family and equip parents to love and lead their kids, while rallying the church to function as an extended family in reaching and raising the young.

This is where knowing your familial context is key. Susan made that mistake her first year. Young and excited, Susan rushed into her first ministry opportunity with gusto – pouring herself into a busy ministry model that emphasized relationships with students throughout the week. Yet by the end of her first summer, she was burned out and ready to quit. Susan had made the mistake of not talking with her students or parents prior to planning her first year. She didn't realize that because of the high-energy, high-extracurricular environment she was doing ministry in, every event she planned made the parents of her students fight to squeeze one more thing onto their calendar. Susan didn't make this easier, either – used to an organic ministry model, she struggled to communicate to parents who desperately needed details weeks in advance. Understanding family culture helped Susan to reevaluate her model in her second year.

Robert struggled with family culture as well–in the opposite direction. The rural environment God had called him to featured loving families that valued their time together. He faced a backlash over the numerous events he planned because parents wanted to spend time with their children, and felt he was taking their youth away from them. Facing a church that was seriously considering cancelling youth ministry as a whole, Robert changed his ministry model to build relationships with families, and spent many nights during the week playing board games, eating dinners, and talking with families about their struggles and joys.

Globalization

Adolescents everywhere are growing up in a globalizing world.[13] Today's young people are part of an emerging global youth culture unbounded by traditional cultural and national markers. As a result of worldwide technology, international media and markets, and an increasingly high mobility of the world's populations, those in the 10/30 Window are finding they have more in common with their peers across the globe than they do with the adults in their own local setting. With an explosion in the world's youth population, global youth are rapidly becoming the largest under-reached people group. The church and her mission agencies must strategize to reach this population.

Tristan sits at his home each evening, working on his computer designing beats for the hip-hop duo he is in with his best friend since grade-school. He looks up at the clock and realizes he is late for a get-together with friends at an underground club. He grabs his flat-billed hat and oversized jacket and heads out the door for a night of dancing and music. Brooklyn? Atlanta? No—Tristan is a high-school student in Istanbul, Turkey, who writes music in support of a Palestinian state. Yet because of globalization, despite his Islamic faith, Tristan shares more in common with students in Chicago than with his own parents. Youth leaders in both locations would do well to communicate with one another to strategize about how to reach emerging cultural people groups that are no longer bound by geography.

Engaging the Local Cultural Setting

Today's emerging generations are growing up in a culturally diverse and pluralistic society. Gone are so many of the old markers of convergence and congruence in the community. While diversity brings richness and beauty, pluralism can lead to a disintegration of foundational values, religious beliefs, and social structures.[14]

In this milieu, many young people are set adrift without an anchor. Societies and local settings are on different points along a continuum: some are still highly cohesive, maintaining traditions and relatively closed systems in which young people are somewhat insulated from the growing global youth culture; in other systems, local languages, customs, and values must be learned. The unique ethnic history, values, and practices of each setting must be considered together with the common global youth culture in developing a missional model of ministry within a given context.

Jason goofed during his first night on the job. He had imagined designing an engaging student ministry that would both draw students in and teach them about Jesus. However, nothing could prepare him for the blank stares he received when he first blared a popular Christian rap artist on loud speakers and then opened his sermon with an illustration from Saturday Night Live. Jason would come to realize that his context was actually very introverted and quiet—his kids were not 'sheltered' or 'backwards', like many ministry stereotypes would unfortunately label them, but enjoyed alternate cultural products such as classical music, television shows made by the BBC, and knitting DIY projects. Jason was able to shape his ministry around this culture, shifting to worship led by piano and violin, and sermons delivered in a circle of couches rather than on a stage. His students knitted countless blankets for local women's shelters, and began a tutoring ministry at a local elementary school. Ministry interns who come to visit Jason's ministry now often seem disappointed at it's lack of flash, but leave seeing a healthy ministry where students are growing and serving in a way that fits their local setting.

Addressing Abandonment

Systemic adult abandonment of the young has reached epidemic proportions around the world. Youth from every corner of the globe increasingly feel isolated, marginalized, and oppressed. While such neglect may be expressed differently in specific regions, the net result is the same: young people have been relationally orphaned by the older generation. This consequently creates a sense of distrust of adults, and adolescents and emerging adults often band together for survival and mutual support.

Systemic adult abandonment creates an interesting relational dynamic between youth and youth workers. Ashleigh feels misunderstood and overlooked by her teachers at school. Her father is too busy with work to care about the details of her life. Her mother is more concerned with Ashleigh's weight and appearance than she is about the hurts and struggles of her daughter. As a result, Ashleigh does her best to navigate her way through each day trying to leave as small a footprint as possible. By necessity she exists in the areas of her life that adults populate but she prospers in the space that she and her friends have created for themselves. Ashleigh shows up at youth group one Sunday night. Before she can adjust to this new relational environment, a youth leader comes up and loudly says "Ashleigh, I am so happy that you came tonight! How was your week?" In that moment, Ashleigh is forced to go through an internal struggle of trying to figure out if this is just another adult who doesn't really care or if this adult truly wants to know about her week. Life has taught her to guard herself around adults but the youth leader seems genuine in her concern. Ashleigh decides to take the risk and open the door to her life just a crack hoping the youth leader won't abandon her once the truth about her life comes out. Ashleigh sighs and says "not so good, my mom keeps criticizing me because of how much I weigh..." It is in moments like these that those of us who work with the next generation can either add to the systemic adult abandonment epidemic or we can for one teenager show that we do care and are willing to swim around with them in the messiness of their lives.

Engaging Postmodernism

Adolescents are growing up in a postmodern world marked by relativism, pragmatism, pluralism, materialism, hedonism, deconstruction, and a loss of a meta-narrative. Radical individualism flowing from and forging a sense of isolation and disconnection marks the world of today's youth culture. Even in traditionally collective societies, young people are finding ways to push at the boundaries, or are dropping out all together. Effective models of ministry to emerging generations will seek to be aware of and intentional about engaging the postmodern mind.

Alejandro's parents moved to southern California from Mexico in the mid-1990s. He was born a few years later, and although he has lived in SoCal his whole life he grew up in a multicultural context. He attends a school for the fine arts where he excels in the drama program. A number of his friends have begun to identify themselves as gay; others are experimenting with their place on the gender spectrum. As a result, Alejandro begins struggling with how he should respond as a believer. He values his friends and knows that he would never stop loving them because of sexuality or gender issues. However, the belief system that he has been told that he should have by his church and his parents doesn't leave a lot of room for debate concerning those issues.

Alejandro decides that he will bring up his questions the next time his small group meets for breakfast before school. Over breakfast, he starts talking about his confusion and asking difficult questions about sexuality and gender. The youth leader is quick to give answers about how wrong homosexuality is and why God makes us male and female. Alejandro decides in that moment that if this is how the church feels about his friends, he doesn't want any part of the church. As he stands up to leave for school, he says to his youth leader, "Why is society more accepting and loving than the church?"

Though the evangelical church is a late arrival (we were still calling it a fad in the late 90s) to the postmodern discussion, next-gen ministry folks are trying hard to catch up. If we will keep in mind that we need to create room for young people to ask questions—being willing to put our focus on the journey to the answers and not only on the answers themselves—then we may yet have an impact on the postmodern mind.

Considering Demographics

Acquiring knowledge of the makeup of the local population is crucial for gaining insight and developing a contextually relevant model of next-gen ministry. Such factors as socioeconomic, educational, geographic, and political/tribal structures and trends need to be researched and understood.

Considering demographics almost feels like a no-brainer when it comes to next-gen ministry. However, because a majority of the resources and training available for evangelical next-gen leaders is written from an anglo, middle class, suburban and North American context it can be easy to forget that the majority of the world's population are not those things.

As a high school student Steve was part of great youth ministry in his hometown of Marietta, GA (a suburb of Atlanta). They played fun games, put on awesome skits, sang the newest contemporary Christian worship songs and the talks were almost always relevant to his life at his private Christian school. He loved his youth group. Because of his youth ministry experience, when he was offered a two-year youth ministry internship at a local church on the edge of the Kibera slums in Nairobi, Kenya after he graduated from college, he jumped at the opportunity. Armed with his favorite games and songs, he plans his first youth group meeting in Nairobi.

Things started out well. Steve was working the room greeting and meeting as many young people as he could just like his youth pastor used to do. He then announced that they were going to play a few games and had everyone sit down. The first game was one where guy/girl pairs are blindfolded and have to feed each other with messy foods. This game didn't seem to connect with the crowd, so Steve cut it short and said they are going to dig for worms now. He pulled out several containers with pudding and gummy worms in them. Steve asked for volunteers who would come up and "dig" for worms with their faces in the pudding. To his dismay, no one volunteered. Thinking that it would help if he demonstrated, Steve buried his face in one of the containers of pudding and pulled out a worm with his mouth. Despite his best efforts to generate excitement, not only did no volunteers step forward but Steve was almost certain that many of the young people had a look of shock on their face. This game always worked with his old youth group. It was messy and funny—two of the main ingredients necessary for a good youth group game.

Steve couldn't figure out why the games didn't work out. It wasn't until he asked the pastor of the church that he found out, to his chagrin, that wasting food like that was not a good idea with an audience including a number of young people who would have had very little food to eat that day. Asking a student to do something that might ruin their clothes was an equally bad idea.

Without proper consideration of ministry context the impact of our efforts to reach the next generation is, at the very least, diminished. The only way to keep from making mistakes similar to Steve's is for those called to work with students to become themselves students—of ministry contexts. It may be difficult to figure out the various cultural nuances, but it will keep from you digging worms alone in front of the crowd.

Vision Is Clear

Every model of ministry must have a clear vision and seek to transfer that vision to those involved. It's important that the leadership share and embody the vision. Strategic implementation necessitates a clear picture or description of the ideal ministry purpose. This becomes the benchmark that serves as a guide and helps keep the ministry on target. It will also attract those who resonate to serve together in the ministry. All the elements of the model of ministry must align with the vision.

Two years into her first job as youth director, Libby was ready to quit. She was tired of parents complaining that they didn't know what was going on in the youth program. She was tired of volunteers who sometimes show up and sometimes not. She was tired of students who only came for the "fun" events. She was done.

During her next meeting with the pastor, Libby had made up her mind to resign. At her monthly meeting with her ministry mentor, Libby explains her reasons for resigning. After listening for a while, her mentor asks Libby to pretend they are on an elevator and that she has less than a minute to explain her vision for the youth program. Her mentor then starts the timer on her phone and tells Libby to start talking. Five minutes later Libby is still trying to explain the vision of the youth program.

At this point, her mentor says "Libby, you are burning out because the youth ministry has no vision. The parents are frustrated because they don't know what the vision is for the stuff the youth ministry does. The volunteers are non-committal because they don't understand where they fit in the vision. The students are only there for fun because they don't see the value in the other aspects of the youth program."

After a deeper discussion about creating a shared vision for the youth program, Libby's mentor encourages her to do two things (1) don't resign until after we meet one more time and (2) take the next month to create and refine a vision for the youth ministry. Six years later, Libby did resign —not because she was burned out, but because she was ready to complete her counseling degree.

The creation of a clear, concise, shared vision didn't take away all of Libby's youth ministry frustrations. It did, however, give her something to hold to when the frustrations came and something to rally parents, students and volunteers around. Doing the hard work necessary to develop a vision may not seem as productive as teaching the Word. Continually selling the vision may not excite you like doing relational ministry with youth. But for next-gen ministry practitioners it is imperative that a shared vision is developed. To paraphrase the famous line from Proverbs 29 about lack of vision: without vision the youth worker burns out and the youth program flounders.

Gifts, Skills, and Resources Are Developed and Utilized

Effective models of next-generation ministry seek to assist people in discovering their spiritual gifts, skills, and resources. This, in turn, will empower them to become involved in ministry, utilizing what God has given them for service to others and to Christ. The personalities and leadership styles of those called to ministry must be considered as well in developing a healthy model. Every model is somewhat dependent on—and dictated

Starting Out... Again: Re-Envisioning for MissionNext

by—God working through the gifts and personalities of those he's called into service. Diversity of age, stage, disposition, resources, skills, and talents should be celebrated and encouraged in the ministry. An effective model of ministry will also include intentional discipleship and training in the stewardship of gifts. In the end, the people and resources God provides shape an effective model of next-gen ministry.

Let me introduce you to four students from Church of the Redeemer's university ministry. First, there is Antonio. He is a graffiti artist. After hearing a talk about using our gifts for God, he asks the ministry director if he can paint a mural on the wall of the youth room. Then there is Claire; she has taught herself to play the ukulele, and asks if she can join the praise band. The third student is Devonte. He lives in the neighborhood and walks to the group meetings. He always arrives an hour early, right when the leaders are setting up. Finally, there is Alexis. She is a poet, and turns most of her struggles, fears, joys and successes into verse. She recently read one in her small group about the pain that causes young women to cut themselves. The poem is full of language that would make others uncomfortable. Her small group leader asks the ministry director if Alexis could read her poem to the youth group because it deeply impacted their small group.

What should the director do? The reason that creating an environment where young people can use their gifts is so important is that it is in those moments that the three questions of adolescence (1. Who am I? 2. Why am I here? 3. Do I matter?) are answered for the young person. That adults who work with students can play a role in helping them answer those questions is not only a great privilege but it is our great responsibility as well.

Passion and Calling Are Shared

An effective model is one that does ministry with a team of leaders who are called to next-gen ministry and who share a passion for reaching emerging generations. Every member of the team must share a sense of ownership for the ministry while making room for different roles, responsibilities, and levels of involvement. There also needs to be a sense of unity and harmony amongst the congregation and leadership.

"Love Jesus, and love teenagers—and you too can be a youth leader" used to be the recruiting pitch of many youth pastors. While those two things are important aspects of being an effective youth leader, they are far from the only ingredients that make a good one.

Jamie loves Jesus and loves teenagers, but travels so much for work that he can rarely come to youth group. Maria loves Jesus and teenagers, but she is 82 and is house bound. Billy and Sharon love Jesus and love teenagers, but they are concerned that their two daughters who are in the youth group won't want them helping out. Mr. Simpson loves both Jesus and teenagers and has taught high school Sunday school for 23 years; The problem is, Mr. Simpson simply isn't a good teacher and everyone is afraid to tell him.

As you can see, just having a shared calling to the next generation and shared passions for reaching the next generation aren't enough unless you have a variety of roles for different personalities, different skill sets and different schedules to fit in. The ministry that creatively defines the roles for leaders is one that is able to engage more adults in relationally investing in the next generation.

Jamie should be able to come to youth group when he can. He can share responsibilities with another youth leader. One small group of girls can adopt Maria as their youth group grandmother, visiting her regularly with a meal that they eat together. Over dinner they can seek Maria's advice about issues in their lives. Maria can become a great prayer warrior for the youth ministry. Billy and Sharon can start small, perhaps helping with food or opening their house for a small group to meet or helping drive to an event; that may help ease any anxiety their daughters feel about having mom and dad around. Mr. Simpson might be celebrated for his years of service, then invited to make room for new leaders to develop in the same role.

Constraints Are Considered

In implementing a model of next-gen ministry, attention is needed for organizational, institutional, and/or denominational constraints. Limitations should be recognized, organizational protocols followed, denominational standards upheld, and the church's culture considered. And in light of these, goals and expectations need to be realistic.

Katie always operated with an "it is easier to ask forgiveness than it is to ask permission" approach to college ministry. As a result, she often found herself in conflict with other church leaders. Oddly, she also ended up having to ask forgiveness quite a bit. The biggest issue with her approach is that the college ministry itself was often punished. Students were judged more harshly when they did something wrong in the church. When they did ask for permission to do certain things, the church leadership said "no" more often than they said "yes." In short, the trust relationship between the college ministry and the church was tenuous at best.

Every denomination, church, or Christian ministry will have certain limitations and constraints. While some of those might complicate your attempts at next generation ministry they need to be in consideration at all times. Take for instance, the church that wants their college students to go on a mission trip each summer, but won't allow the mission team to raise money within the church for fear that it will negatively impact tithing. That would indeed be a frustrating situation; however, it isn't an insurmountable obstacle. As with most obstacles in next-gen ministry, it is an opportunity for creative thinking to take over. The problem is, if you took Katie's "ask forgiveness" approach to this situation, the mission team would be hurt. In fact, in Katie's case, when she decided to try to challenge the rules and sneakily raise money within the congregation, the leadership of the church decided to cancel the trip.

Though frustrating to many folks who are called to next-gen ministry (we tend to like operating in wide open spaces) rules, limitations, and constraints are usually there for a reason. Our focus should be on operating within them, not trying to circumvent them.

Step 3: Reflect

Figure 14. Meta-Model: Reflect

Some will **design** their ministry model by thinking deeply about the theological grounds and goals that should form and focus a biblical approach to reaching emerging generations. Many **do** the work of next-gen ministry—and often implement their model with an eye toward contextual realities, but often not. Few, however, take time to **reflect** and evaluate their ministry model.

Taking time to take stock and evaluate one's approach is a mark of healthy next-gen ministry. As has been discussed in chapter 9, models have a tendency toward decreasing effectiveness over time; it is therefore incumbent upon the leadership to continually evaluate the model according to the grounds and goals, and contextual realities. This involves humble, honest, prayerful critique. It's important to ask incisive questions and wrestle together in community as we look to the Spirit to lead us in areas where we may need to renovate and reenvision our approach to reaching tweens, teens, and twentysomethings.

What Does This Look Like?

Evaluating your ministry model by…

Reflecting on Grounds

In evaluating the theological grounds on which the ministry model is based, one helpful question would be: "Is there a well-articulated theology of ministry?" The leadership should be able to support their philosophy of ministry both biblically and theologically. In many churches, the leadership may have drafted and/or adopted a written theology or philosophy of ministry. While this can be helpful, it is not necessary; in some cultures, orality (oral tradition) renders the capacity to have a written theology of ministry somewhat unnecessary. The key is to determine whether or not the ministry is committed to its stated theology of ministry, written or otherwise.

It is important to determine if there is a theological rationale behind each program element. For example, one model may be very intentional about making small groups a priority in their program; their theological rationale is based on the scriptural injunction to be engaged in community and living authentically with Christ and each other. Another ministry may refuse to employ small groups until they have the mature leadership necessary to guard and guide the students' hearts in wisdom and Christ-centered intimacy. These two different choices may both be the result of careful theological reflection.

Other questions that would help identify theological rationales are:

- How is Christ presented (e.g., curriculum, teaching; experientially, relationally)?
- Is he presented as merely a good teacher or good example?
- Is his divinity denied?
- Is perhaps only one aspect of his nature or work emphasized?
- Are our current worship practices reflecting our views on the place and method of worship, or are we simply reflecting the times?
- Where are our blind spots—what are the elements of our theology that are (even unconsciously) ignored in the structure, programming, and curricula or our ministry?

Reflecting on Goals

In evaluating a ministry model according to its goals, one might ask: "How does the model of ministry intentionally try to move students along in their relationship with Christ and his church?"

Many proponents of next-gen ministry are quite content to go through the motions in their programming as long as students continue to attend. Participation in programs or events becomes the default measure of spiritual growth. This raises the question, "Is participation an accurate indicator of a young person's walk with Christ or their commitment to his church?"

Another goals-oriented question might be: "Are adults mentoring and shepherding adolescents and emerging adults into the life of the broader church family?" For example, one church has a student-mentoring program in which youth are assigned an adult mentor or "assimilation guide," whose role is to care for them, disciple them, and help enfold them into the life of the church. Such a program would help the youth ministry meet its stated goals.

The model's commitment to a kingdom trajectory might be discerned by asking: "Are opportunities created for service and mission?" and "Are the young empowered and endorsed to live out their faith outside the organized church?" For example, some models do a good job of intentionally developing opportunities for young people to be involved in serving and exercising their gifts, but only in the context of the local church or ministry program. Such ministries might consider introducing their adolescents and emerging adults to a broader range of service possibilities.

All in all, this will require ministries to define 'success' more clearly. Though it is no often longer in vogue to actively pursue numbers as a ministry goal, one might ask what the 'critical mass' required is for sustaining current ministry structures. This exercise in avoiding extremes can also be asked of another long-neglected statistic, once the chief marker of ministry effectiveness: conversions. Are adolescents coming to Christ through the ministry?

Finally, as you reflect on these goals you must also consider what scenarios will challenge them. If you have a ministry built around catechizing those who come through your program, what do you do with a visiting non-Christian? A young person with mental disabilities? A twentysomething who will only be there for six months?

Reflecting on Psychosocial Characteristics

It is important to look at how the model attempts to address the psychosocial needs of adolescents. For example, early adolescents need a safe and secure environment, emotionally and physically. The leadership of the ministry might want to explore the meeting of that need through such questions as: "How does the weekly gathering accommodate that need?" and "Do the adults stand along the walls patrolling the perimeter or do they engage young people in a friendly and familiar way?"

One ministry chooses to gather early and middle adolescents together in order to achieve "critical mass" and limit the leaders' number of nights out. They are proud of the fact that the younger students are relatively quiet and well behaved during the youth group meeting; little do they know that these early adolescents are so intimidated by the older young people and so self-conscious that they are unable to feel safe or loved, let alone able to truly listen to any teaching or engage in genuine relationships.

Do the educational methods used reflect the age/stage of the adolescents present? One oft-debated characteristic is teaching-time: early-adolescent teachers may want to heed the 'one minute per year of age' attention-span rubric, while those who interact with middle adolescents may be able to engage them for much longer. Are these educational methods taking into account different learning styles? Those in the 'anti-game' camp may feel the need to reconsider, for instance, not for entertainment reasons but to engage kinesthetic learners and create muscle-memory connections for active learners.

Reflecting on Cultural Factors

It is important to discern whether or not a model considers globalization, engages the local cultural setting, addresses abandonment, engages postmodernism, and considers demographics.

For example, leaders might assess how technology, media, high mobility, and isolation impact the students. To a large degree, interactions between today's young people are through social media. This fact needs to be addressed—or even capitalized upon—by the ministry, not ignored. Some churches intentionally use social networks to connect with students, communicate announcements, gain insight into their lives, and share the gospel. Rather than ignore these media and the virtual community they create, these leaders utilize it—and also coach parents in the dangers and opportunities technology presents. In the same way, other ministries might intentionally choose to avoid such technologies, in an effort to emphasize physical presence and a sense of place for their students.

Systemic adult abandonment runs the spectrum from place to place. In Guatemala, too many young people are left by their parents to wander the streets and live off of the community trash dump. In Sudan, too many young boys are abducted, brainwashed, and forced to become child soldiers. In Cambodia, too many girls are sold into the sex slave trade. In crime-ridden urban centers, the gang culture recruits children desperate for a sense of family. In upwardly mobile western communities, parents—too busy pursuing their own selfish agenda—base their relationships with their children on their performance.

It is important to evaluate whether or not the unique needs of the local community are understood and addressed, and design the model with those needs in mind. For example, in suburban St. Louis, parents tend to overvalue achievement and academics. As a result of this pressure to perform, children are growing up with material comforts but little emotional support. Parents need to be challenged with this truth and equipped to change their orientation. On the other hand, in urban Manila many children live on the streets with no parental involvement and little opportunity for education. The church should stand in the gap for these children and may need to assist with housing and education.

The model and approach to ministry must be relevant to socioeconomic conditions. For example, a church in El Paso, Texas, may be led to develop a bilingual (English/Spanish) ministry. On the other hand, a twentysomething ministry in Tokyo may choose to speak English in its coffee house ministry because the demographic data reveal that the target population values learning and speaking conversational English.

Reflecting on the Community of Faith

It is important to discern whether a model has been developed in light of its unique leadership and community of faith. It must be evaluated for its clarity of vision; its development and utilization of people's gifts, skills, and resources; and whether its passion and calling are shared and constraints considered.

One ministry team attempts to accomplish this is by beginning the weekly leaders' meeting by reading through the vision statement and discussing its implications for their model of ministry. As a result, the leadership may be led to begin a new program—or change an existing one—in order to realign the ministry with the vision. In addition, they might spend some time praying through aspects of the vision as it relates to the ministry.

Another question for evaluation: "Is there diversity in personality, age, and gifts represented in the leadership?" For example, some youth ministry models rely on college students and emerging adults to lead the work with tweens and teens, ignoring the rich experience and wisdom that older leadership offers. On the other hand, some models rely almost entirely on parent volunteers, which means they miss the energy, creativity, insight, and fun that a younger leadership can contribute, let alone the opportunity to model intergenerational ministry and apprentice emerging leaders.

Another: "Does the church leadership and congregation support the next-gen ministry?" For instance, far too many models of ministry are developed and led by a single leader, without the involvement of others in the church. This can lead to a myopic vision, ministry burnout, and even moral failure. Such a "Lone Ranger" mentality in ministry must be confronted and replaced with a plurality of leadership. There is biblical precedent for mutuality in ministry. Shared leadership is, by its very nature, instructive as it models for young people the body life of the church. In addition, the advantages of a plurality of leaders include the multiplication of efforts, effectiveness, resources, and fun. Healthy models are led by healthy teams.

Also: "Are goals and expectations realistic?" and, "Is fiscal prudence demonstrated?" A church plant struggling to become self-supporting, for example, may find it premature to invest in developing an intern program and hiring multiple youth staff. As a result, they might consider a more decentralized, grassroots, and collaborative approach to reaching youth in their community.

Step 4. Renew... Repeat

Figure 15. Meta-Model: Renew

I don't know about you, but there are times where I would like to put ministry on cruise-control: get things up to speed, and just let the ministry run. But it's not that easy, is it? The reality is we are broken people living in a broken world. Ministry is messy and never easy. But God is redeeming the world and us. He is in the business of renewal, and he promises to do his renovating work in our lives personally and corporately. He is the head of his church, and the gates of hell will not prevail against her. We have great cause to hope as we lean into the Spirit's work of renewal in our lives and ministries.

What follows is a tool to help you and your church or organization's leadership pursue renewal in your approach to nex-gen ministry.

Reaching the Nations and the Next Generation

Based on the *MissionNext meta-model* and content of this book, the MissionNext Inventory has been designed to help develop and diagnose the health of your model and discern areas for renewal. Next uses this tool in consultation with pastors, missionaries, church leaders, and ministry directors engaging tweens, teens, and twentysomethings in communities around the world. Feel free to adopt this tool as it is (see appendix 1 for reproducible version), or to adapt it to suit you. In fact, some of those who have received the greatest benefit from this tool have been those who have revised and customized the inventory with their ministry team—using it as a template and spring-board to reframe, add or substitute their own categories and questions for reflection and renewal. Please share your customized version with us at contact@nextconnect.org.

Reaching the Nations and the Next Generation

A biblical theology of next-gen ministry should lead to unity of purpose and great charity in diversity amongst those engaged in reaching tweens, teens, and twentysomethings. There is much we can learn from one another.

There is much we can affirm and celebrate together, even as the Lord leads us in very different ways to reach adolescents and emerging adults with the gospel.[1] For as many different contexts and young people as there are, there should be as many different churches and ministries. With a focus on the kingdom of God and not our own little empires, we can demonstrate the unity Christ longs for in his disciples.[2] We can partner together, encourage one another, challenge and stimulate each other, and pray for one another.

Any spirit of competition, antagonism, territorialism, and arrogance needs to be replaced by the work of the Spirit of God.[3] May God use broken ministers and broken ministries to reach broken youth with the healing work of the gospel.[4] May egos and agendas be laid bare and laid down at Jesus' feet, as together we serve him and see him come alive in young people's lives.

Adolescents and emerging adults are crying out for someone to answer the questions of their hearts, to help them know who they are and that they belong. They need to know that theirs is a life of purpose and destiny. Without adults in their lives who love the Lord and love them,

Starting Out... Again: Re-Envisioning for MissionNext

youth are left lost and defenseless. As the church, we can rally together in reaching those in the 10/30 Window by surrounding and supporting them throughout the journey of adolescence. Only in a relationship with Christ and connected to his covenant community will young people find the life they long for. Only in reaching the nations and the next generation will we as the church live the life God has called us to.

Keep Dancing

Design. Do. Reflect. Renew... Repeat. So goes the dance of practical theology and the rhythm of MissionNext. And it goes on and on as the church endeavors to engage emerging generations with the gospel. What a joy to know that our Father has invited us to the dance and he will lead. Who would have thought that the journey of next-gen ministry would turn into a dance? But that's just like God, isn't it?!

Keep dancing.

Questions for Reflection & Discussion

1. Does your ministry have statements of vision, mission, goals, and values? If so, what process did you use to develop them? Who was involved? How do these help guide your ministry today?

2. If you were to take a survey of the parents in your church/ organization, what do imagine their grounds and goals for next-gen ministry would be? What do you think your response should be?

3. If you were to survey the young people in your church/organization, what might their desires and expectations for the ministry be? How might this inform your ministry?

4. "Design. Do. Reflect. Renew… Repeat. So goes the dance of practical theology and the rhythm of MissionNext" (p. 180). Which dance step does your ministry need to focus on at this time? What's one practical way you can start?

Starting Out... Again: Re-Envisioning for MissionNext

Notes

1   Alan F. Johnson and Robert E. Webber, *What Christians Believe: A Biblical and Historical Summary* (Grand Rapids, MI: Zondervan Publishing House, 1989), p. xii.

2   Vos, *Biblical Theology*, pp. 5–6.

3   Michael Horton, *Putting Amazing Back into Grace: Who Does What in Salvation?* (Grand Rapids, MI: Baker Books, 2000), p. 19.

4   Jerry Bridges, *Transforming Grace: Living Confidently in God's Unfailing Love* (Colorado Springs, CO: NavPress, 1991), p. 20.

5   *Ibid.*, p. 80.

6   Jerry Bridges, *The Discipline of Grace: God's Role and Our Role in the Pursuit of Holiness* (Colorado Springs, CO: NavPress, 1994), p. 137.

7   Dallas Willard, *The Spirit of the Disciplines:Understanding How God Changes Lives* (New York: Harper Collins Publishers, 1988), p. 184.

8   Mark Yaconelli, *Contemplative Youth Ministry: Practicing the Presence of Jesus* (Grand Rapids, MI: Zondervan Publishing House, 2006), pp. 72–73.

9   *Ibid.*, p. 141.

10 Bilezikian, *Community 101*, p. 62.

11 Clapp, *A Peculiar People*, p. 158.

12 Peters, *A Biblical Theology of Missions*, pp. 208–222.

13 Ian T. Douglas, "Globalization and the Local Church," in *The Local Church in a Global Era: Reflections for a New Century*, ed. Max Stackhouse, Tim Dearborn, and Scott Paeth (Grand Rapids, MI: Wm. B. Eerdmans Publishing Co., 2000), p. 202.

14 Paul Hiebert, *Anthropological Reflections on Missiological Issues* (Grand Rapids, MI: Baker Books, 1994), pp. 93–94.

Appendices

MissionNext Inventory
A Diagnostic Tool for Ministry Development & Renewal

The following inventory is offered here with full permissions for reproduction. It can also be downloaded for free from the book's website (www.mission-next.org) or from the Next website (www.nextconnect.org).

Church/Organization: _____

Location: _____

Date: _____

Ministry Leader(s): _____

Evaluator(s): _____

Grounds	Low 1 2 3 4 5	High

Grounds   Low   High
                1 2 3 4 5

A commitment to theological orthodoxy ☐ ☐ ☐ ☐ ☐
Is there a well-articulated theology of ministry?
Is there a theological rationale behind each program element?

Christ-centered ☐ ☐ ☐ ☐ ☐
How is Christ presented (e.g., teaching, experiential, relational)?

Grace-based ☐ ☐ ☐ ☐ ☐
Does the model breed a culture of grace or works (in the leadership, structure/style, measure of success, etc.)?

Dependent on prayer ☐ ☐ ☐ ☐ ☐
What role does prayer play in this model?
Is it woven into the structure?
Is it central?
Does leadership practice it?

Flexible and adaptable ☐ ☐ ☐ ☐ ☐
Has there been a history of change in the model?
Does the model have self-evaluation built into it?

Grounds

Low   High
1   2   3   4   5

Creates space for the fruit of the Spirit   ☐☐☐☐☐
    Is the priority the vision or the organization?
    Does the model try to micro-manage spiritual formation?
    Is the model too complex and demanding?
    Is there room for relationships to form and be fostered?
    Is there room for gifts to be explored and expressed?

Section Total: _____ **/30**

Goals

Low   High
1   2   3   4   5

Pursues intimate relationships with Christ and the ☐☐☐☐☐
church
    How does the model move students along in their faith?
    Are adolescents coming to faith in Christ?
    Are people encouraged to wrestle with questions openly?
    Do adults model lives of repentance?
    Are spiritual friendships formed?
    Are adults mentoring/shepherding into the life of the church?

Helps explore calling/gifts outside the local church   ☐☐☐☐☐
    Do adults model lives of radical abandon to God?
    Are students empowered and endorsed to live out their faith beyond the local church?
    Are opportunities created for service and mission?

Section Total: _____ **/10**

Psychosocial Characteristics

Low   High
1 2 3 4 5

Takes seriously psychosocial issues   ☐ ☐ ☐ ☐ ☐
> Was the model designed with psychosocial issues in mind?
> Is there an attempt to meet developmental needs of adolescents and emerging adults?
> How does the weekly gathering accommodate that need?

Addresses the issues of individuation   ☐ ☐ ☐ ☐ ☐
> How are the issues of identity, community, and trajectory identified and addressed?
> Are there training times where these issues are discussed?
> Is observation, reading, and research encouraged?
> How does the teaching answer the question, "Who am I?"

Supports the family   ☐ ☐ ☐ ☐ ☐
> How does the model support the family?
> What's the role of parents in the program?
> Is there space for families to be together?
> Are there strategies/programs for resourcing parents/families?

Section Total: _____ /15

Cultural Factors

Low   High
1 2 3 4 5

Considers globalization   ☐ ☐ ☐ ☐ ☐
> Does the model address issues of global youth culture?
> How are technology, media, mobility, and isolation engaged?
> Are parents informed of the dangers/opportunities this presents?

Cultural Factors

Engaged local cultural setting ☐ ☐ ☐ ☐ ☐
  Are the needs of the local community understood/addressed?
  Are parents challenged with the realities of local culture and equipped to change?
  Does the ministry provide for local needs?

Addresses abandonment ☐ ☐ ☐ ☐ ☐
  Is the adult community engaged in ministry in the 10/30 Window?
  What's the ratio of adults to young people?
  How old are the adults involved?
  Are parents involved?
  Are parents coached and challeneged in this regard?
  Are individual relationships between adolescents/adults fostered?
  Are young people included in the broader life of the church?
  Are one-on-one mentoring relationships being developed?

Engages postmodernism ☐ ☐ ☐ ☐ ☐
  Is postmodernism understood and engaged?
  Does the teaching address the postmodern mind?
  How is truth presented?
  Is the gospel presented in narrative or didactic form?
  Are young people encouraged to wrestle with questions?

Considers demographics ☐ ☐ ☐ ☐ ☐
  Was the model developed with understanding of the local community?
  Are approaches relevant to socio-economic conditions?

Cultural Factors	Low				High
	1	2	3	4	5

Section Total: _____ /25

Community of Faith	Low				High
	1	2	3	4	5

Vision is clear ☐☐☐☐☐
  Is there a clear and concise vision statement?
  Do the leadership know this vision?
  Is the vision statement regularly reviewed and consulted
  in developing, implementing, and evaluating the mod-
  el?
  Are calendar events mapped out with vision in mind?
  Are elements added, changed, or dropped to align the
  ministry with the vision?

Gifts, skills, and resources are developed and utilized ☐☐☐☐☐
  Are people discovering their spiritual gifts?
  Is ministry shared and given away?
  Are people challenged to give of their time and resourc-
  es?
  Do people feel they have a valued contribution to make?
  Are there regular/strategic training opportunities for
  leadership?
  Is there diversity represented in the leadership?

Passion and calling are shared ☐☐☐☐☐
  Is there a leadership team?
  Is shared ownership encouraged?
  Is there a sense of excitement and energy about the min-
  sitry?
  How do those involved describe the ministry?
  Is there harmony in how the leadership describes it?
  Are the church leadership and congregation on board?

Constraints are considered ☐☐☐☐☐
  Are limits recognized?
  Are organizational protocols followed?
  Are denominational standards upheld?
  Is the church culture considered?
  Are goals and expectations realistic?

Section Total: _____ /20

Grounds:	————	/30
Goals:	————	/10
Psychosocial Characteristics:	————	/15
Cultural Factors:	————	/25
Community of Faith:	————	/20
OVERALL SCORE:	————	/100

Missionnext Inventory: Case Study

THE BEST WAY TO UNDERSTAND how the MissionNext Inventory works is by taking the details of the ministry that you are involved in and plugging them into the inventory. Short of doing that, you can test drive the inventory by running a case study through it. The case study provided here is of a non-traditional, large, suburban-American church. It isn't meant to be exhaustive in detail so there will be some areas of the inventory that you may struggle to answer.

However, this case study is designed to help you see the benefit of the MissionNext Inventory. It will work best if you read through the entire case study before starting the inventory. Because the church in this case study, Hilltown Community Church, is in the middle of a ministry shift it may be beneficial for you to go through the inventory twice, once with the details of the old program and once with the new program. This will help you determine which of the two youth ministry models that you most agree with.

Case Study

"Hilltown Community Church"—a non-traditional, large, suburban -American church.

Ministry Context

The current Assistant Pastor of Youth Ministry has only been at HCC for five months. The previous Youth Director (non-ordained) was well liked and was able to grow the youth program numerically during his four and a half years from 65 students (combined junior and senior high) to over

MissionNext Inventory: Case Study

150 students (about a third don't attend HCC) during the weekly youth group meeting. He was not good at organization, administration or communication with parents. He tended to make big decisions unilaterally and at the last minute.

Furthermore, a group of vocal parents, several ruling elders and the senior pastor felt like the previous youth director placed too much emphasis on fun and games and not on "serious" Bible study. Consequently, when the search committee was formed they were tasked with finding someone who was administratively strong and serious about the Bible. The assistant pastor of youth ministry that was hired met those qualifications, but had never run a youth program. Having gone straight from college to seminary and straight from graduation to this position, he is just now realizing that he may be in over his head and needs help. The ruling elder over youth ministry suggested that he form a youth ministry leadership team to help him better lead the youth ministry. The team is comprised of the Ruling elder, several parents and a couple volunteers.

Congregational Makeup

HCC is a church of 1,000. The pastor is the founding pastor and has been there 28 years. The congregation is predominantly middle to upper-middle class and white. There is minimal socio-economic or racial diversity at HCC. The congregation places a high value on consistent, quality, safe programming for the children and youth of the church.

Worship

The worship style is contemporary blended with a praise band, worship singers, and a blend of popular CCM-style praise music, modern hymns, and a few of the "classic" hymns.

Philosophy of Ministry

The previous youth director named the youth ministry "HCC FUSION" with the tag line "Boring Doesn't Happen Here." His rationale was that, in order to impact students with the Gospel, you need to get students to come... no students, no transformed lives. On the website, philosophy of ministry for their youth ministry is "FUSION exists to provide a loving, fun and safe environment for students in sixth to twelfth grade to experience the beauty of the Gospel." From the design of the youth space to the games played to the videos shown during the Bible talk to the activities chosen to the new t-shirts produced for each of those activities even to the food that was served, every ministry decision was judged on whether students would perceive it as boring.

The assistant pastor of youth ministry believes that a new philosophy of ministry must be developed if the youth group is ever going to become more serious about the Bible. His belief is that all of these "non-boring" activities distract from true discipleship. Shortly after starting at HCC, he began to make changes to the youth group experience to help students focus more on the Word. One of the unintended results of his changes was a decrease in the number of students that come to youth group and youth group activities. In the five months that he has been there, average attendance at the weekly FUSION meeting(s) has dropped from just over 150 to an average of just under 100. Some of the parents who were dissatisfied with the previous youth director told him not worry because most of the students who have stopped coming don't attend HCC anyway.

Structure and Program

The Bible lesson time during the Sunday night program has changed to a 25–30 minute sermon. Game time has been reduced at FUSION and FUSION FRIDAYS are now to twice a month.

About three years ago, to help accommodate the growth in the youth program and to give more space for the teenagers to hang out, HCC built a new youth building that is across the parking lot from the main building. The former youth director spent months convincing the church leadership of the necessity of the new building. Oddly enough, the decision was made in favor of a youth building following a FUSION lock-in at the church where two chairs in the Wisdom Fellowship Group's (the 60-plus group) sitting parlor were broken during a game of sardines. The presentation of the new building plan during a congregational meeting included talking about the need for the youth to have their own space that they could take ownership of, the growth pattern of FUSION, the amount of new ministry that could be done, and mentioning that it would protect the church building from getting destroyed... followed by congregational laughter.

Just under a million dollars later (HCC still owes $200,000 on the building), the new youth building was completed. With a coffeehouse-inspired hang out area, the X-Box room, a stage area with great lighting, sound and video equipment, a gym, youth ministry office, and a state-of-the-art kitchen, the youth building was indeed something that HCC could be proud of. The unintended consequence for the youth director was the increased pressure to produce exciting programs and to fill the building with hundreds of students.

The youth program, when he left, included:

- Sunday Night FUSION (junior high from 4–6pm, senior high from 6–8pm, year round)—games, hang out, singing and 15 minute Bible talk.
- FUSION FRIDAYS (during the school year from 7–9pm for junior high students)—open game night.
- FUSION FIRST (every first Saturday during the school year)—special senior high events.
- Fall (or winter) and spring weekend retreats for junior and senior high.
- FUSION SERVES—special ministry project for senior high followed by a lock-in during the Fall.
- RADICAL FUSION outreach events—these include occasional open-mic nights for local bands, and serving a free upscale meal for students going to prom (this has been a big hit in the community)

The program changes during the summer.

For the last five summers, part of the FUSION SUMMER has included a mission trip to Jamaica for the senior high. The trip is a tradition in the youth group and is well-attended. In fact, the youth director invited both Christian and non-Christian students, believing that once the non-Christian students saw the Gospel in action, they would be more inclined to become followers of Christ. The trip is a week of working on a work project in the morning and hanging out on the beach, shopping, fishing and relaxing by the pool in the afternoon. They eat breakfast at the resort, lunch on the work site and dinner at the resort or at a local restaurant. Most nights include a debrief time about what the Lord has taught them before bed.

The youth director believed by combining this type of beach trip with work in the morning, he struck the perfect balance between fun and ministry. To the new assistant pastor of youth ministry this trip sounds like "vacation" missions. He believes that the students would grow more if they went to work with an inner-city mission work where students would work on a widow's house in the morning and early afternoon, lead evangelistic Bible Clubs for children in the evening, and have a worship service each day before they went out. He agrees that some "fun" activities need to be included, so they are going to block out one afternoon to go to a local amusement park and one night to eat at a restaurant. All other meals will be provided by the church they are working with. They will be sleeping in bunkhouses.

Index

Index

B

C

Index

G

H

I

J

Index

Netland, Harold 112, 125
Next-Generation Ministry 3, 5, 6, 13, 14, 15, 16, 17, 18, 25, 29, 39, 40, 48,
    54, 58, 59, 60, 63, 71, 81, 82, 95, 96, 97, 100, 110, 150, 166, 167,
    168, 170, 172, 173, 174, 179, 180, 181, 182, 183, 185, 188, 189,
    191, 192, 193, 197, 199, 200, 201, 202, 203, 204, 208, 215, 216

O

Owen, John 56

P

Pahl, Jon 7
Parachurch 2, 15, 54, 60, 98, 100
Peters, George 210
Peters, George W. 56
Peterson, Eugene 37
Philosophy of Ministry 71, 203, 212, 213
Pixar Animation 57
Pluralism 112, 125
Polemicism 15
Pornography 88, 156
Postman, Neil 21
Postmodernism 19, 27, 110, 112, 114, 117, 121, 196, 197, 223
Pragmatism 9, 11, 12, 13, 16, 21, 26, 112, 196
Praxis 24, 25, 27, 30, 31, 59, 175, 179
Prayer 9, 14, 15, 51, 66, 67, 93, 155, 156, 184, 185, 186, 201, 220

R

Rahn, Dave 7, 56
Rayburn, Jim 97, 103
Robbins, Duffy 146
Romanowski, Bill 107, 124
Rosenbaum, Janet Elise 21
Rousseau, Jean Jacques 83

Index

Index of Figures & Tables

Figures

237

Index of Figures & Tables

Bibliography / Works Cited

"A Brief History of the YMCA Movement," http://www.ymca.net/about_the_ymca/history_of_the_ymca.html; accessed February 20, 2007.

"Special Report: The World's Youngest Populations," *Euromonitor International.* 13 February 2012; retrieved 8 February 2013.

"History of Youth for Christ," 2003, http://www.yfci.org/yfci/history.php; accessed February 20, 2007.

Shift Happens. http://shifthappens.wikispaces.com.

The Westminster Confession of Faith and Catechisms. Brevard, NC: The Committee for Christian Education and Publications for the Presbyterian Church in America, 1983.

Anderson, Ray S., *The Shape of Practical Theology.* Downers Grove, IL: InterVarsity Press, 2001.

_____. *The Soul of Ministry.* Louisville, KY: Westminster John Knox Press, 1997.

Aristotle, *Nicomachean Ethics*, trans. Martin Ostwald. Indianapolis, IN: The Library of Liberal Arts and Bobbs-Merrill Educational Publishing, 1962.

Barlett, Hugh, "Truth," Chesterfield Presbyterian Church, http://www.chespres.org/resources/sermons.asp (accessed February 18, 2006). Notes from his sermon of the same title preached on January 22, 2006.

Berkhof, Louis, *Summary of Christian Doctrine.* Grand Rapids, MI: Wm. B. Eerdmans Publishing Co., 1998.

Bersamin, Melina, Samantha Walker, Elizabeth Waiters, Deborah Fisher, and Joel Grube, "Promising to Wait: Virginity pledges and adolescent

Bibliography / Works Cited

sexual behavior" in *The Journal of Adolescent Health* vol. 36 no. 5 May 2005, pp. 428–436.

Bilezikian, Gilbert, *Community 101: Reclaiming the Local Church as Community of Oneness.* Grand Rapids, MI: Zondervan Publishing House, 1997.

Boice, James Montgomery, *Foundations of the Christian Faith: A Comprehensive and Readable Theology.* Downers Grove, IL: InterVarsity Press, 1986.

Borgman, Dean, *When Kumbaya Is Not Enough: A Practical Theology for Youth Ministry,* 4th ed. Peabody, MA: Hendrickson Publishers, 2002.

Borthwick, Paul, "Cross-Cultural Outreach: A Missiological Perspective on Youth Ministry" in *Christian Education Journal* 3 (1999).

Bridges, Jerry, *The Discipline of Grace: God's Role and Our Role in the Pursuit of Holiness.* Colorado Springs, CO: NavPress, 1994.

———, *Growing Your Faith.* Colorado Springs, CO: NavPress, 2004.

———, *Transforming Grace: Living Confidently in God's Unfailing Love.* Colorado Springs, CO: NavPress, 1991.

Calvin, John, *Commentaries on the First Epistle of Peter,* trans. John Owen. Grand Rapids, MI: Baker Book House, 1979.

Chandler, Paul-Gordon, *God's Global Mosaic: What We Can Learn from Christians around the World.* Downer's Grove, IL: InterVarsity, 2000.

Clapp, Rodney, *A Peculiar People: The Church as Culture in a Post-Christian Society.* Downers Grove, IL: InterVarsity Press, 1996.

Clark, Chap, *Hurt 2.0: Inside the World of Today's Teenagers.* Grand Rapids, MI: Baker Academic, 2011.

———, "Strategic Issues in Youth and Family Ministry" (lecture, Fuller Theological Seminary, March 2005).

———, "Youth in an Age of Delayed Adulthood," *Youthworker* (November/December 2000).

———, YF721 Doctor of Youth and Family Ministry (lecture, Fuller Theological Seminary, February 22, 2005).

Clark, Chap, and Dee Clark, *Daughters and Dads*. Colorado Springs, CO: NavPress, 1998.

_____, *Disconnected: Parenting Teens in a MySpace World*. Grand Rapids, MI: Baker Books, 2007.

Collins, C. John, *Genesis 1–4*. Phillipsburg, NJ: P&R Books, 2005.

Crabb, Larry, *Inside Out*. Colorado Springs, CO: NavPress, 1988.

Currie, Elliott, *The Road to Whatever*. New York, NY: Metropolitan Books, 2004.

Damon, William, *The Youth Charter: How Communities Can Work Together to Raise Standards for All Our Children*. New York, NY: Free Press, 1997.

Dean, Kenda Creasy, Chap Clark, Dave Rahn, eds. *Starting Right: Thinking Theologically About Youth Ministry*. El Cajon, CA: Zondervan Publishing House and Youth Specialties Books, 2001.

Driscoll, Mark, *The Radical Reformission: Reaching Out Without Selling Out*. Grand Rapids, MI: Zondervan Publishing House, 2004.

Douglas, Ian T., "Globalization and the Local Church" in *The Local Church in a Global Era: Reflections for a New Century*, Max Stackhouse, Tim Dearborn, and Scott Paeth, eds. Grand Rapids, MI: Wm. B. Eerdmans Publishing Co., 2000.

Dunham, Craig, and Doug Serven, *TwentySomeone: Finding Yourself in a Decade of Transition*. Colorado Springs, CO: Waterbrook Press, 2003.

Dunn, Richard R., and Mark H. Senter III, *Reaching a Generation for Christ*. n.p., 1997.

Elkind, David, *All Grown Up and No Place To Go: Teenagers in Crisis*. Cambridge, MA: Perseus Books, 1998.

_____, *The Hurried Child: Growing Up Too Fast Too Soon, 3d ed*. Cambridge, MA: Da Capo Press, 2001.

_____, *Ties That Stress: The New Family Imbalance*. London: Harvard University Press, 1994.

Fields, Doug, "The Power of God," *Youthworker* 14, no. 6 (1998).

Bibliography / Works Cited

_____, *Purpose Driven Youth Ministry*. Grand Rapids, MI: Zondervan Publishing House, 1998.

Folmsbee, Chris, *A New Kind of Youth Ministry*. Grand Rapids, MI: Zondervan Publishing House, 2007.

Frost, Michael, and Alan Hirsch, *The Shaping of Things to Come: Innovation and Mission for the 21st-Century Church*. Peabody, MA: Hendrickson Publishers, 2003.

Gale, Fay, and Stephanie Fahey, "Youth In Transiton: The Challenges of Generational Change in Asia," in *The Association of Social Science Research Councils in Association with The Academy of the Social Sciences in Australia* (2005).

Goetz, David, *Death by Suburb*. New York, NY: Harper Collins, 2006.

Gonzales, Justo, *The Story of Christianity*. San Francisco, CA: Harper & Row, 1984.

Gonzales, Laurence, *Deep Survival: Who Lives, Who Dies, and Why*. New York, NY: W.W. Norton Co., 2004.

Grentz, Stanley J., *A Primer On Postmodernism*. Grand Rapids, MI: Wm. B. Eerdmans Publishing Co., 1996.

Gullota, Thomas P., Gerald R. Adams, and Carol A. Markstrom, *The Adolescent Experience, 4th ed.* San Diego, CA: Academic Press, 2000.

Hall, Edward T., *Beyond Culture, 2nd ed.* New York, NY: Doubleday, 1989.

Hall, Stanley G., *Youth: Its Education, Regimen, and Hygiene*. New York, NY: Appleton and Co., 1906.

Harter, S., et al., "The Complexity of the Self in Adolescence," in *Readings on Adolescence and Emerging Adulthood*. Upper Saddle River, NJ: Hall, Prentice, 2002.

Henry, Matthew, *Commentary on the Whole Bible, vol. 1, Genesis to Deuteronomy*. Peabody, MA: Hendrickson Publishers, 1998.

Hesselgrave, David J., "Contextualization of Theology" in *Evangelical Dictionary of Theology*, ed. Walter A. Elwell. Grand Rapids, MI: Baker Book House, 1984; pp. 271–272.

Hesselgrave, David J., and Edward Rommen, *Contextualization: Meanings,*

Methods, and Models, 2d ed. Grand Rapids, MI: Baker Book House, 2000.

Hersch, Patricia, *A Tribe Apart.* New York, NY: The Random House Publishing Group, 1999.

Hiebert, Paul G., *Anthropological Reflections on Missiological Issues.* Grand Rapids, MI: Baker Books, 1994.

_____, *Cultural Anthropology,* 2nd ed. Grand Rapids, MI: Baker Book House, 1995.

Hine, Thomas, *The Rise and Fall of the American Teenager: A New History of the American Adolescent Experience.* New York, NY: Harper Collins, 1999.

Horton, Michael, *Putting Amazing Back into Grace: Who Does What in Salvation?* Grand Rapids, MI: Baker Books, 2000.

Hunt, Susan, *Heirs of the Covenant: Leaving a Legacy of Faith for the Next Generation.* Wheaton, IL: Crossway Books, 1998.

Ingoldsby, Bron B. and Suzanna Smith, eds., *Families in Multicultural Perspective.* New York, NY: Guilford Press, 1995.

Johnson, Alan F., and Robert E. Webber, *What Christians Believe: A Biblical and Historical Summary.* Grand Rapids, MI: Zondervan Publishing House, 1989.

Kelly, Gerard, *Retrofuture.* Downer's Grove, IL: InterVarsity Press, 1999.

Kimmel, Tim, *Grace Based Parenting.* Nashville, TN: W. Publishing Group, 2004.

Kindlon, Dan, and Michael Thompson, *Raising Cain: Protecting the Emotional Life of Boys.* New York, NY: Ballantine, 2000.

Levine, Madeline, *The Price of Privilege.* New York, NY: Harper Collins, 2006.

Lewis, C.S., *The Lion, the Witch and the Wardrobe.* New York, NY: HarperCollins, 1956.

_____, *The Weight of Glory.* New York, NY: Touchstone, 1996.

Luthar, S.S., and S.J. Latendresse, "Children of the Affluent: Challenges to

Bibliography / Works Cited

Well-Being" in *Current Directions in Psychological Science* 14 (2005): pp. 49–53.

Mahedy, William, and Janet Bernardi, *A Generation Alone*. Downer's Grove, IL: InterVarsity Press, 1994.

Manning, Brennan, *Abba's Child, rev. ed.* Colorado Springs, CO: NavPress, 2002.

McGrath, Allister E., *A Passion for Truth: The Intellectual Coherence of Evangelicalism*. Liescester, U.K.: Apolos, 1996.

Miller, Donald, *To Own a Dragon: Reflections on Growing Up Without a Father*. Colorado Springs, CO: NavPress, 2006.

Mueller, Walt, *Engaging the Soul of Youth Culture: Bridging Teen Worldviews and Christian Truth*. Downers Grove, IL: InterVarsity Press, 2006.

_____, *Youth Culture 101*. Grand Rapids, MI: Zondervan Publishing House, 2007.

Netland, Harold, *Dissonant Voices: Religious Pluralism and the Question of Truth*. Vancouver, B.C.: Regent College Publishing, 1997.

_____, *Encountering Religious Pluralism: The Challenge of Christian Faith and Mission*. Downer's Grove, IL: InterVarsity Press, 2001.

Pahl, Jon, *Youth Ministry in Modern America: 1930 to the Present*. Peabody, MA: Hendrickson Publishers, 2000.

Peters, George W., *A Biblical Theology of Missions*. Chicago, IL: Moody Press, 1972.

Peterson, Eugene, *The Message*. Colorado Springs, CO: NavPress 2002.

Peterson, Roland, *Globalization: Social Theory and Global Culture*. New York, NY: SAGE Publications, 1992.

Postman, Neil, *Amusing Ourselves to Death: Public Discourse in the Age of Show business,* 2nd. ed. New York: Penguin Books, 2005.

Rayburn, Jim III, *Dance Children, Dance*. n.p.: Tyndale House, 1984.

Robbins, Duffy, *This Way to Youth Ministry: An Introduction to the Adventure*. El Cajon, CA: Zondervan Publishing House and Youth Specialties Books , 2004.

Romanowski, Bill, *Eyes Wide Open*. Grand Rapids, MI: Brazos, 2001.

Rosenbaum, Janet Elise, "Patient Teenagers? A Comparison of the Sexual Behavior of Virginity Pledgers and Matched Non-pledgers" in *Pedatrics* vol. 123 no. 1 January 1, 2009: pp. e110–e120.

Saintonge, Serge, Pier Angelo Achille, and Lise Lachance, "The Influence of Big Brothers on the Separation-Individuation of Adolescents from Single-Parent Families" in *Adolescence* 33, no. 130 (Summer 1998): p. 2.

Sayers, Dorothy, *Letters to A Diminished Church*. Nashville, TN: W Publishing Group, 2004.

Senter, Mark III, *The Coming Revolution in Youth Ministry: And its Radical Impact on the Church*. Wheaton, IL: Victor Books, 1992.

_____, ed., *Four Views of Youth Ministry and the Church*. El Cajon, CA: Zondervan Publishing House and Youth Specialties Books, 2001.

_____, *When God Shows Up: A History of Protestant Youth Ministry in America*. Grand Rapids, MI: Baker Academic, 2010.

Schaeffer, Francis A., *How Should We Then Live? The Rise and Decline of Western Thought and Culture, 50th anniversary ed*. Wheaton, IL: Crossway Books, 2005.

_____, *True Spirituality*. Wheaton, IL: Tyndale House Publishers, 1971.

Sine, Tom, *Mustard Seed vs.McWorld: Reinventing Life and Faith for the Future*. Grand Rapids, MI: Baker Books, 1999.

Smith, Christian, and Melinda Lundquist Denton, *Soul Searching: The Religious and Spiritual Lives of American Teenagers*. New York, NY: Oxford University Press, 2005.

_____, and Patricia Snell, *Souls in Transition: The Religious and Spiritual Lives of Emerging Adults*. New York, NY: Oxford Univeristy Press, 2009.

Stevenson, Burton E., ed., *The Home Book of Quotations, Classical and Modern*, 10th ed. New York, NY: Greenwich House, 1984.

Stott, John R.W., "Your Mind Matters," *Youthworker Journal* XXII, no. 2 (November/December 2005.

Bibliography / Works Cited

Strommen, Merton, Karen E. Jones, and Dave Rahn, "A Recent Invention: The Profession of Youth Ministry," in *Youth Ministry that Transforms*, 1st ed. El Cajon, CA: Youth Specialties Books and Zondervan Publishing House for Youth Specialties Academic, 2001.

Tolkien, J.R.R., *The Hobbit* (London: George Allen and Unwin Ltd., 1937)

_____, *Lord of the Rings*. London: Harper Collins UK, 2004.

Vos, Geerhardus, *Biblical Theology: Old and New Testaments*. Grand Rapids, MI: Wm. B. Eerdmans Publishing Co., 1948.

Walsh, David, *Why Do They Act That Way? A Survival Guide to the Adolescent Brain for You and Your Teen*. New York, NY: Free Press, 2004.

Waltke, Bruce, *Genesis*. Grand Rapids, MI: Zondervan, 2001.

Ward, Pete, *God at the Mall: Youth Ministry that Meets Kids Where They're At*. Peabody, MA: Hendrickson, 1999.

Waters, Malcolm, *Globalization*. London: Routledge, 1995.

Weichold, Karina, Rainer K. Silbereisen, and Eva Schmitt-Rodermund, "Studying Links Between the Timing of Puberty and Psychological Individuation." *Paper presented at the biennial meeting of the Society for Research on Adolescence* (March 30–April 2, 2000).

Wells, David F., *The Courage to Be Protestant: Truth-lovers, Marketers, and Emergents in the Postmodern World*. Grand Rapids, MI: Eerdmams, 2008.

Whitehead, John W. , *Grasping for the Wind: The Search for Meaning in the Twentieth Century*. Grand Rapids, MI: Zondervan Publishing House, 2001.

Willard, Dallas, *The Divine Conspiracy: Rediscovering Our Hidden Life in God*. New York, NY: HarperCollins Publishers, 1997.

_____, *Renovation of the Heart*. Colorado Springs, CO: NavPress, 2002.

_____, *The Spirit of the Disciplines:Understanding How God Changes Lives*. New York, NY: Harper Collins Publishers, 1988.

Winter, Richard, *Still Bored In A Culture of Entertainment*. Downers Grove, IL: InterVarsity Press, 2002.

Wright, Christopher J.H., *The Mission of God: Unlocking the Bible's Grand Narrative*. Downers Grove, IL: IVP Academic, 2006.

Yaconelli, Mark, *Contemplative Youth Ministry: Practicing the Presence of Jesus*. Grand Rapids, MI: Zondervan Publishing House, 2006.

Acknowledgements

"You write a book 50 times," said an author I met at a conference in Amsterdam. He wasn't kidding.

This book has gone through several revisions thanks to the contributions of many who've helped along the way.

My wife, Rebecca, has endured me talking about this project (while not actually working on it) for many years. Her wise insights, willingness to read draft after draft, and development of the concepts for the diagrams have all been invaluable contributions. I never would have finished the book without her steady encouragement.

My children, Abby, Meghan, Natalie, and Emma have cheered me on and kept me humble. Writing a book about reaching the next generation while raising four adolescent daughters has at times felt like an exercise in hypocrisy. I've been blessed by the grace my girls have shown me.

I'm indebted to my father, Dr. Sam Larsen, who has shaped my missiology and biblical theology throughout a lifetime of his influence, example, and teaching. And mom, you're the best! Thanks for putting-up with your "brat-boy" all these years!

Ed Eubanks and the Doulos Resources team for their missional partnership and mutual commitment to this project, And Dr. Robert Peterson for his publishing advice and for connecting me to Doulos. I am deeply grateful for their patience and guidance for this first time author. This book would not have happened without them.

Stephen Yates and Danny Mitchell generously contributed their expertise in research, revisions, and case studies.

Andrew Dickson and Jenny Smith skillfully and beautifully reimagined and redesigned the diagrams.

Sharon Baca, Tasha Chapman, and Brooks and Riva Cain contributed their expertise in crafting the questions for reflection and discussion.

John Cavallaro, for embodying Jesus' passion for the next generation—inspiring and sharpening my approach to MissionNext for over

Bibliography / Works Cited

two decades as my dear brother in life and ministry. You it, b-funk!

My pastor, Dr. Hugh Barlett, with whom I served for 10 years on the pastoral team of Chesterfield Presbyterian Church. I am thankful for his influence and the freedom to experiment in the laboratory of our local church.

Team Next and our Advisory Board, prayed and cheered me across the finish line.

The many professors, missionaries, pastors, and ministry leaders serving around the world whom I am blessed to call colleagues and friends who took time to read, field test, offer input, and endorse my work.

You, the reader, for picking up a copy of this book in your pursuit of God's call to reach the nations and the next generation with the good news of Jesus. May he use you in the advance of his kingdom and the praise of his glory.

About the Author

Dr. Eric Larsen is a PCA pastor and missionary with Mission to the World, and has worked with adolescents and emerging adults for more than 20 years. Eric founded Next in 2007—an international ministry serving the global church in reaching the next generation. He holds degrees from Covenant Theological Seminary and Fuller Theological Seminary, where he earned a doctorate in Youth, Family and Culture. Eric leads a growing global team-of-teams serving on four continents reaching young people, training global church leaders, and sustaining mission kids and families. But the role Eric most enjoys is as husband to his beautiful wife, Rebecca, and as father to their four precious girls, Abby, Meghan, Natalie, and Emma.

About Next

Next was founded in 2007 by MTW missionaries, Eric and Rebecca Larsen, working among the world's largest under-reached people group: the 10/30 Window (10–30 year olds). Today Next has become a growing "glocal" team-of-teams based across Europe, Latin America, Asia-Pacific, and the USA. Our mission is to serve the global church in reaching the next generation. We pursue our mission in three strategic ways:

- Sending men and women around the world to reach and disciple adolescents and emerging adults.
- Training church planters, missionaries, ministry leaders and local churches seeking to reach the young people in their own communities.
- Sustaining Third Culture Kids and families through resources, training, care and counseling.

Find out more at nextconnect.org OR mtw.org.

About Doulos Resources

Our goal is to provide resources to support the church and kingdom, and to build up and encourage the pastors and leaders within the church. Our resources follow the model of Ephesians 4:12—"to prepare God's people for works of service, so that the body of Christ may be built up." We produce books, curricula, and other media resources; conduct research to advance our goals; and offer advice, counsel, and consultation. We are Reformed and Presbyterian, but not exclusively so; while we do not lay aside our theological convictions, we believe our resources may be useful across a broader theological and ecclesiastical spectrum.

Our goal with *MissionNext*, as with all of our resources, is to offer well-edited, high-quality, and useful materials at an affordable price that makes our resources accessible to congregations and members of the church.

If you are interested in ordering additional copies of *MissionNext*, or to order other materials that Doulos Resources offers, please visit our website: www. doulosresources.org. If you are ordering in quantity for a church or other ministry, contact us to inquire about a discount for quantity orders.

Doulos Resources Contact Information:
Telephone: (901) 201-4612
Internet:
website: www.doulosresources.org
e-mail: info@doulosresources.org

At Doulos Resources, we've found that we often appreciate owning both print and digital editions of the books we read; perhaps you have found this as well.

In our gratitude to you for purchasing a print version of this book, we are pleased to offer you free copies of the digital editions of *Mission-Next*. To obtain one or more of these, simply visit our eStore (estore.doulosresources.org) and enter the following discount code during checkout:

MissionDigital

If you purchased a digital edition, you may use the same discount code to receive a discount deducting the full price of your digital edition off of the purchase price for a print edition.

Thank you for your support!